LIFE AND LABOUR OF THE PEOPLE OF INDIA

LIFE AND LABOUR OF THE PEOPLE OF INDIA

ABDULLAH YUSUF-ALI
M. A., LL.M. (CANTAB.), I.C.S., BARRISTER-AT-LAW

GYAN

Published by

Gyan Publishing House
5, Ansari Road
Daryaganj, New Delhi-110002
Phone: 011-47034999, 9811692060
E-mail: books@gyanbooks.com

Distribution Network
gyanbooks.com
India, USA, Canada, UK, Australia, France

ISBN: 978-81-212-8616-9 (PB)
First Published, 1907

2nd Impression 2023

Printed at: Gyan Press, Delhi.

LIFE AND LABOUR OF THE PEOPLE OF INDIA
Author: Abdullah Yusuf-Ali

LIFE AND LABOUR OF THE PEOPLE OF INDIA

Frontispiece.]

SHARIFA BEGAM, DAUGHTER OF ABBAS TYABJI, ESQ.

"Music, too, has been cultivated—not only on the hackneyed piano, but on the Bin, an ancient musical instrument of India." [p. 285].

LIFE AND LABOUR OF THE PEOPLE OF INDIA

BY ABDULLAH YUSUF-ALI

M.A., LL.M. (CANTAB.), I.C.S., BARRISTER-AT-LAW

WITH ILLUSTRATIONS FROM DRAWINGS AND PHOTOGRAPHS BY NATIVE ARTISTS, AND A DESIGN ON THE COVER AFTER AN ORNAMENT IN THE ROYAL PALACE AT DELHI

"For wel I wot that ye han her-biforn
Of making ropen, and lad awey the corn;
And I come after, glening here and there,
And am full glad if I may finde an ere
Of any goodly word that ye han left."

—CHAUCER,

LONDON
JOHN MURRAY, ALBEMARLE STREET, W.
1907

TO

SIR GEORGE BIRDWOOD,

M.D.EDIN., K.C.I.E., C.S.I., LL.D.,

WHO TO HIS SPECIAL INSIGHT OF
THE INNER CONSCIOUSNESS OF THE EAST,
ADDS AN EVER-HELPFUL SYMPATHY
WITH THE ARTISTIC AND LITERARY LIFE
OF THE IMMEMORIAL PEOPLE OF INDIA,

THIS LITTLE BOOK
IS DEDICATED,

AS AN AFFECTIONATE APPRECIATION
OF THE MANY KINDNESSES AND COURTESIES
RECEIVED FROM HIM

BY THE AUTHOR.

PREFACE

An account of the genesis of this book may help to explain some of its peculiarities.

The nucleus of the volume was formed by certain lectures which the writer delivered at the Passmore Edwards Institute and elsewhere. During the autumn and winter of 1905-6 India occupied a good deal of the attention of the British public, on account of the memorable tour of their Royal Highnesses, the Prince and Princess of Wales, in that country. The writer happened to be on furlough in England, and was frequently requested to speak on Indian questions. At the Passmore Edwards Institute he undertook a series of six lectures. They began in the small lecture-room, but week after week the audience increased, until the warder had to give us the largest hall for the purpose. This showed that the subject attracted considerable attention, and that the Metropolis of the Empire was by no means as indifferent to Indian questions as is sometimes assumed.

The writer had the good fortune to have in his audience or in the Chair some of the most distinguished men and women of letters, as well as some well-known authorities on Indian matters. They were pleased not only to approve of the method of presentment, but even to suggest that the matter was of sufficient importance to be presented to a wider public than that to which it had hitherto been submitted. The papers were, therefore, subjected to a thorough revision, and with some additions are now laid before the reading public.

Some new ground is covered in these pages, but the main interest to English readers will lie in the fresh point of view from which all questions are approached. To an Indian, looking at things from within, they must necessarily wear a somewhat different aspect from that in which they appear to the numerous administrators, judges, business men, and travellers, English and foreign, who visit India or make it their home. At the same time an endeavour has been made to avoid all controversial topics. A comprehensive picture of the life of the people of India and an estimate of their social tendencies need not include any matter which cannot be accepted by men of all shades of opinion.

Mrs Humphry Ward presiding at one of the lectures, was kind enough to mention three qualifications in the present writer for dealing with Indian life. In the first place, being born and bred in India, he is of the people. In the second place, his association with the Government of the country enables him to view life also from the administrative point of view—viz.: as a whole, and with special reference to social organisation and cohesion. In the third place, a Cambridge education and a lengthened study of European life and methods should enable him to present facts in a form which may appeal to European readers and be not unacceptable to that large body of University men in India whose minds are still seeking an adjustment between Western ideals and Eastern traditions. If a fourth qualification may be added, it is the possession of an open mind and the consciousness that in private and public life the influences that go furthest are not those that are most talked about, but that, in any case, there can be no finality in the discussion of social problems.

Some of these papers in their original form have already appeared in the *Indian Magazine*, the *Hindustan Review*, and the *Imperial and Asiatic Quarterly Review*. The paper on Economic Problems was printed in the journal *Anglo-Oriental Commerce*, while that on Public Health has seen the light in the journal of the Royal Institute of Public Health. Those on the Leisured Classes, Woman's Life, and Social Tendencies have not been published before.

The list of private friends to whom my thanks are due for much assistance and encouragement is long, and only a few names can be mentioned. Sir George Birdwood may be styled "the onlie begetter" of this volume. Mr T. W. Arnold has given much valuable time in reading over the proofs, and his suggestions have been most helpful. Mr C. A. Latif, Mr S. Athim, Mr Narottam Morarji Goculdas, and Mr Abbas Tyebji have helped me to obtain the excellent illustrations from India. The design on the cover is taken from the Hall of Justice in the Royal Palace at Delhi, but instead of the date inscription I have ventured to put in a couplet from Hafiz, transcribed specially for this book by Miss Fyzee, the distinguished young Indian lady whose versatile accomplishments are so highly prized by her friends. The couplet from Hafiz is specially appropriate on the eve of my departure from England, and may be paraphrased:—

> "Though we are far from the carpet
> Whereon ye sit with your nearest,
> Yet our spirit is not far;
> For do we not serve your king,
> And do we not remember you
> Ever in our praises?"

A. YUSUF-ALI.

ST ALBANS,
30*th January* 1907.

CONTENTS

ILLUSTRATIONS

"I lived with visions for my company,
Instead of men and women, years ago,
And found them gentle mates, nor thought to know
A sweeter music than they played to me.
But soon their trailing purple was not free
Of this world's dust,—their lutes did silent grow,
And I myself grew faint and blind below
Their vanishing eyes."

—Mrs BROWNING,
Sonnets from the Portuguese, xxvi.

I

TOWN LIFE

"Here's
A crowd to make a nation!—best begin
By making each a Man, till all be peers
Of Earth's true patriots, and pure martyrs in
Knowing and daring."

—E. B. Browning, *Casa Guidi Windows*, I. xix.

"Don't mix yourselves in others' strife,
But gather in the proffered fruit—
That is a practical pursuit
That does not call for blood and knife;
That asks no sacrifice of life,
And gives you its good things to boot."

—Ibsen, *Brand.*

TOWN LIFE

In describing town life in India there are two main difficulties. First, every town or city has its own characteristics and peculiarities, which mark it out from the other towns in quite a distinctive way. Secondly, there is no unity of life in the towns. A town in India is merely a geographical expression, without corporate life. There is no centre in which the activities of the different parts of the population can be focussed. There is no common measure of social conduct. There is no combining force or personality to which the different strata of society look up as in some way setting a standard. The village in India, on the other hand, is a distinct unit, a centre of life, and in some measure a common bond of action.

The reason of these differences is that the conception of a village as an entity is of very great antiquity, whereas the conception of a town is comparatively modern. I do not assert that town life or city life was unknown in the earlier history of India, but towns in those days were centres of a Court, with a king at its head. The

Court was often peripatetic. It moved about from place to place as the exigencies of political life required. The Emperor Aurangzeb, who reigned fifty years, was more than thirty years absent from his capital. During the last twenty-five years of his reign he never saw Delhi, and was scarcely more than once or twice within a thousand miles of it. He was constantly moving about on military expeditions in the Deccan. The Italian traveller, Gemelli Carreri, visited Aurangzeb's Court at Galgala in March 1695, and describes it as a huge camp more than thirty miles in circuit, and containing over 1,500,000 souls.[1] There were 250 bazars or markets, every nobleman having a special one of his own. The shops, the offices, the dwellings of the noblemen, and the royal apartments themselves—hung with silks and cloth of gold—were all tents, more or less splendidly equipped. Thus the life and soul of Delhi was wandering about, like a disembodied spirit, in the Deccan. Anything like a stable town with a corporate life, the centre of commerce or industry, with a mayor, or chief functionary, who did not depend for his appointment on the favours of the central Court, was absolutely unknown. Anything like the association of the inhabitants of one town with another in common commercial, industrial, social or political objects, such as we find in mediæval Europe, was entirely undreamt of. The village was the creation of

[1] Churchill's *Voyages*, 1704, vol. iv. p. 233.

Aryan gods; the town was the child of Greek civilisation; while the modern State is the town grown adult, with increased powers and activities. In India, though we have some huge cities, the life in them had not, until quite recently, developed beyond the village stage. Indeed, if social aims be taken as the test of advancement, the town was in many respects behind the village. The village I mean was an adult village, the like of which perhaps has existed nowhere else in recent times.

As the different towns have their own peculiarities, I will select a particular town in order to describe it. That town will be Lucknow, the capital of Oudh. When it is spoken of as the capital of Oudh, the word must be understood in a limited sense. Oudh is not now a country or a province separately administered. It forms a part of what are known as the United Provinces of Agra and Oudh, with a common capital at Allahabad. The Lieutenant-Governor of the United Provinces makes a point of spending a few weeks of the cold weather in Lucknow in order to keep alive Oudh traditions, but although he keeps up a separate Government House in Lucknow, his visit there must be considered in the nature of a prolonged stay in camp. There is undoubtedly a certain amount of social life centred in Lucknow on account of the Barons of Oudh having a common meeting-ground in the Kaisar Bagh. In this respect

Lucknow differs from most other towns in India. Neither Bombay, nor Madras, nor Lahore, nor Allahabad, is a centre of social life in the widest sense of the term. Calcutta is to a considerable extent becoming the centre of Bengali life. Hence the loud outcry raised against the partition of Bengal. But Lucknow is *par excellence* the centre of the higher life of Oudh, although this must be understood only in a social and not in a political, industrial, or intellectual sense. In literature, though Sarshar and Sharar are still living, the exclusive côterie which claimed to lay down the laws of taste and elegance in modern Urdu has passed away, never to be revived again.

Lucknow is the largest city in the United Provinces, having a population of 264,000 by the census of 1901. It is not an expansive city like Agra, Delhi, or Calcutta, the population having decreased by 3·2 per cent. since 1891 and 7·2 per cent. since 1872. Historically it is not an old city like Delhi, nor has it the commercial importance of Cawnpore, but it has nevertheless a romantic interest, which entitles it to rank as the premier city in the hearts and affections of the people of Upper India.

The name of the city is derived from the name of a mythical personage, Lakshman, the brother of Rama, the hero of the celebrated epic *Ramayana*. The name got corrupted into Lakhan in popular speech, and hence the city of Lakhan became Lakhnau, or as it is spelt in

English, Lucknow. It was quite a small place until the latter half of the eighteenth century. Its importance dates from the time when the Oudh dynasty transferred their capital hither from Fyzabad. The dynasty was founded by a Persian adventurer, who found favour at the Moghal Court at Delhi, and made himself master of a large number of provinces, including Rohilkhand, Oudh, and nearly the whole of the eastern part of the present United Provinces. He and his successors were great warriors and men of strong character. The third in succession from the founder was defeated at the battle of Buxar in 1764, and held his territories subsequent to that defeat by favour of the new and growing power of the East India Company. This was part of the settlement which Clive made in his famous journey to the Upper Provinces in 1765. Asaf-ud-daula first made Lucknow the capital of his kingdom in 1775. He was a great builder. He built bridges, mosques, bazaars, squares, streets, palaces, and other public edifices. His predecessors had built nothing but forts and walls. He was able to consolidate his power in peace and embellish his capital with various works of architecture. His buildings are free from tawdry ornaments such as are found in buildings erected by some of his successors. The most flimsy and unsightly buildings in Lucknow are those erected in the reign of Wajid Ali Shah, between 1840 and 1850. It is said that Wajid

Ali Shah called for designs based on European architecture. What he got was the bastard style of architecture seen in such places as the pavilions in Rosherville and Vauxhall Gardens, at a date when those styles had become the laughing-stock of the satirists of Western Europe. The result is that most of the buildings erected in the middle of the nineteenth century are nearly crumbling to pieces, while the more solid and chaste architecture of the earlier Oudh rulers still exists and goes some way to redeem Lucknow from the charge of vulgarity, which has justly been brought against its architectural pretensions.

If we take our stand on one of the four bridges that cross the Gumti river we shall see practically all the most important buildings of the city. The minarets of the Cathedral Mosque, standing out gracefully against the beautiful blue sky, lend that tone of delicacy to the outline wanting in the huge mass of the Imambara and the Rumi Darwaza. These three buildings form a picturesque group. A little further to the left may be seen the massive structure of the Residency, immortalised in the history of the Mutiny. It contains the tomb of Sir Henry Lawrence, bearing the simple epitaph composed by the hero himself:

> "Here lies Henry Lawrence, who tried to do his duty."

A little further to the left again will be seen the domes of two mausolea, and behind them is the Kaisar Bagh, which so well illustrates the debased style of European Architecture (so-called). Here will be seen the Saracenic arch blended with Gothic pilasters, the oriental dome surmounting pillars with Corinthian capitals. The whole place is covered with a pale orange colour, which seems to have been the imperial purple of the kings of Oudh. On the gates are the designs of two fishes, characteristic of the arms of the royal family of Oudh.

In another part of the city is the Martinière College, which was built by General Claude Martin, who was a favourite architect of Asaf-ud-daula. The General is buried in a vault in the College, and an interesting story is attached to his tomb. The General in his lifetime drew up a design for the building himself. Having shown it to the king of Oudh, the king immediately expressed a desire to purchase it for a million pounds sterling. Before the bargain could be completed, the General died. But he left ample funds to build and endow the College, with instructions that his body should be buried in the building, as that was the only plan by which he could ensure the land from confiscation by future kings. Whatever the failings of the kings of Oudh, they scrupulously respected burial-places, and to-day the Martinière College stands as a noble monument of its charitable founder. The College supports a hundred and twenty European boys of military parents, and there are similar institutions for boys and girls, established by the same founder, in Calcutta. An interesting parallel has been drawn by a competent authority between this school and its founder and the oldest of English public schools, Winchester College, and its founder, the generous and practical bishop-architect, William of Wykeham. Claude Martin was a most versatile man. Originally the son of a silk manufacturer at Lyons, he fought in India for the French East India Company, and was subsequently in the service of the English Company. In later life he was one of the grandees of the Lucknow Court. His accomplishments included those of a soldier, architect, watchmaker, and gunsmith.[1] He built up a vast fortune, which he left by will to charities in Lucknow, Calcutta, Chandernagore, and Lyons.[2]

Before we pass on to the native city, let us notice the Chhatar Manzil, or the palace of umbrellas, so called because golden umbrellas surmount the tops of several parts of the building. It was once a royal palace, but it is now used as

[1] A contemporary letter printed with the "Siyar-ul-Mutaakhkhirín," the Indian "Mémoires de Sully," published in Calcutta, 1789 (vol. i. p. 14, note 3), describes him thus: "As an architect (and he is everything) he has built himself at Lucknow a strong, elegant house, that has neither beams nor cupola, and is so contrived that a single man might defend it against multitudes."

[2] Mr Buckland's "Dictionary of Indian Biography" contains a notice, all too brief, of this remarkable man. Mr Buckland, following Mr Keene (except as to dates), calls him a deserter from the French; but Mr S. C. Hill, in his "Life of Claud Martin" (Calcutta, 1901), disposes of this charge (pp. 8-14, 155-6). Mr Hill also discredits the story of Martin's motive in directing his body to be buried in the vault (pp. 85-6). The building was called "Constantia" from Martin's motto: "Labore et Constantia." Its art treasures are worth a visit.

a club-house, the Chhatar Manzil Club being one of the finest European clubs in India. Government House, with its fine grounds, and the spacious parks, with their flower-beds and statuary, will no doubt attract the visitor's attention. The statuary is not by Phidias or Thorwaldsen, and lurks in corners as if it were ashamed of being seen where it is.

If you go to the native city you will not find any important or striking buildings. The only place worth seeing is the Chauk or market square, comparable to the famous Chandni Chauk or "moonlight street" of Delhi. Here a large number of people assemble every day for the purpose of buying and selling, as well as for seeing and being seen. It is an open space, the four sides of which are occupied by well-built shops. These belong to the superior merchants, who, dressed in loose oriental robes, sit on carpets of harmonious colours, more like princes in a show than business men who felt that time was money. The *hukka* is before them, and a slow sort of conversation is being carried on in undertones by two or three confidential companions, who are innocent of any intentions to patronise the shop. Woe betide the brisk customer who seeks rudely to disturb their somnolent repose, even with the pardonable intention of leaving a few of his rupees at the shop. For it is the unwritten law of the Chauk that you should approach the lords and masters of its merchandise with benign salutations and veiled apologies for your intrusion. These delivered, you will hear in reply many amiable compliments, with perhaps an apt quotation from a Persian poet about wealth being a humble handmaid ever dogging your auspicious footsteps. When you arrive at this stage, there is an opening for gently broaching your matter of business, a sort of suggestion that though both parties are personally above the claims of filthy lucre, the "handmaid dogging your auspicious footsteps" requires a little concession. But even so you must approach the matter delicately, and not show yourself too eager to obey the behest of your business instinct. Time may be convertible into money in a new sense: the less time you spend at the shop, the more you pay for it. To drive an equal bargain, take up casually a piece of *chikan* embroidery, lying in a corner of the shop as if by accident. It may be the finest sample of its kind you have seen, but you don't say so. You lament the decline in the art of *chikan* embroidery: of course you add politely, your remarks do not apply to your interlocutor's stock. This opens the campaign. He agrees with your opinion in general, but points out how his wares are the finest in the market, having been made by the only artisan of the old school living. You assent with ostentatious civility; but do not omit to give the knowing smile which says that you have heard the story before. The *onus* of naming the price is thrown on you. In your blandest manner you plead inexperience. He understands you perfectly. As you are not a greenhorn, he names a price only twice as high as that which he would be glad to take. You talk generalities, and pretend you do not wish to purchase it at all. He takes your cue, and expatiates upon the history of the article and the varying fortunes of its makers. After a variety of tactics, carried on with perfect good-humour—nay, with a show of superabundant politeness—the bargain is clinched at considerably less than the cost price as declared by the merchant. You part with mutual respect and many touching salutations. You have secured a bargain, but he too has made a deal. In the Chauk you will require no commentary to enable you to understand: "*Malum est! malum est!*" *inquit emptor; sed quum abierit tum gloriabitur!*

So much for the permanent shops in the Chauk—mostly art-ware and jewellery of a superior description. But turn to the open space in the centre, and you will find brisk business of a noisier and more vulgar description. There are pedlars and bead-makers, with tinsel jewellery made in Delhi or more probably in Birmingham. There are the bangle-sellers, "round whom the women folk do ever congregate." There are the sellers of sweets, each with a tray poised on a cane stool, whose contents are tersely announced as "*pera, barfi, mithai!*" There are fruit-sellers and vegetable-sellers; the humble cobbler with his unfashionable shoes and the still humbler grass-cutter with his load of grass which he has cut—or rather dug up from the roadside, or from ditch or bank, with a primitive hoe. All these humble votaries of commerce ply their busy trade with a great deal of brisk animation, and not without an amount of haggling over their farthing bargains, which keeps up the reputation of trade as sharpening the wits of man. They have no shops or stalls to sit on, but all squat on the ground, paying a market toll withal to the Municipality every time they come. Notice the lighting arrangements at night. Most of the dealers have none. But the fortunate few, such as the itinerant sweet-sellers, have flaring smoky lamps of kerosine oil, with leaky reservoirs of tin that never dreamt of the proximity of a glass chimney. Let us hope that the odours of the kerosine oil do not thrust themselves too shamelessly into the (presumably) appetising sweets offered by the confectioner—for this same "*pera, barfi, mithai*" is a whole day's dinner to some poor stranger who has not either the pots or the place where he can cook his meals according to caste rules.

If Joseph Addison were to return to life as a Lucknow citizen, what a wealth of copy he would find in a study of the cries and noises, the shouting and gesticulations, the unctuous tones of persuasion, and the biting gibes of sarcasm and anger, which he would hear in the Chauk!

Here is a man who has cut and brought a head-load of the milky pipal leaves, which he meant to sell as fodder for goats—abusing in a towering rage the unknown owner of a goat which has watched its opportunity and eaten half the old man's luscious stock-in-trade. Here is a vegetable-seller who is giving a piece of her mind to another who has undersold her, "with her wretched rotten stuff, which even baby donkeys would have too much discrimination to accept!" Move a little further, and you will find a *churan*-seller: he sells condiments and mixtures of digestive spices—sad commentary either on the quality of Lucknow cooks or the quantity which their patrons have time to eat but not stomach to digest. These little mixtures are carried in paper packets lying in two shallow baskets hanging from a pole slung over the man's shoulder. This man is an artist in patter-song; he would stand up to your fastest singing artist from the most up-to-date music-hall. Fast come his words like pattering rain. In rollicking snatches of doggerel verse does he run over the virtues of half his *churans* before he once takes breath. But the excitement is greatest when two *churan*-sellers meet and try to talk each other down. The retailers of the most dainty little verses, however, are the toy-sellers. The toys may be made of mud or clay, or paper and bamboo twigs; the more expensive (yet not above a pedlar's purse) are made of brass which is facetiously described as "glittering gold." How can I give an idea of the doggerel verse, the pathos, the wit, the thrust, and the homely simplicity, which the hidden poets who talk through these men bring to their task? Let me attempt a feeble imitation, doggerel and all, in a paraphrase:—

> "If some dear little children you possess,
> Whose lisp is to your ears a sweet caress,
> Then take this cow with the golden sheen;
> *(to be pronounced with a lisp)*
> If you refuse, you are—a parent mean."[1]

There are thus two kinds of bazars, two streams of commercial life, mingling side by side in this piece of ground called the Chauk. The Chauk is the true forum—the place of public resort—of Indian cities. In the olden days,

[1] Was Shakespeare a native of Lucknow? Were it not that the glories of Lucknow as a capital date from a time more than a century and a half after Shakespeare, I would offer this suggestion to the Baconians, and to those who find the facts of Shakespeare's ordinary life unsatisfactory. Is not Autolycus a typical Lakhnavi? And does not his song as a pedlar breathe the spirit of the Chauk?—

> "Lawn, as white as driven snow;
> Cyprus, black as e'er was crow;
> Gloves, as sweet as damask roses;
> Masks for faces, and for noses;
> Bugle bracelet, necklace amber,
> Perfume for a lady's chamber:
> Golden coifs, and stomachers,
> For my lads to give their dears;
> Pins, and poking-sticks of steel,
> What maids lack from head to heel:
> Come, buy of me, come; come buy, come buy;
> Buy, lads, or else your lassies cry; Come, buy."
>
> —*Winter's Tale*, IV. iii.

After a Photo.] *By* K. Beg.

A GREENGROCER'S STALL.

"The unctuous tones of persuasion, and the biting gibes of sarcasm and anger"—p. 14.

To face p. 14.]

when there was no police, if a man wanted to ventilate a grievance, he went to the Chauk. If we can imagine the elders of the city dispensing patriarchal justice, they would no doubt do it at the Chauk. The word "chauk" is frequently translated "market place," but there are six other words for "market" or "street" which connote different ideas. As the ideas underlying them illustrate some phases of town life, I will proceed to explain them. "Bazar" is the most general term for market. It is a Persian word introduced by the Muhammadans, and is also used figuratively, as in "bazar garm hai"—"The market is brisk." Having been introduced by non-Hindus, the word is also associated with foreign trade, *e.g.* the Kandahari Bazar and the Chini Bazar, in Lucknow, which were at one time the centres of the Afghan and the China trade respectively. The word "ganj" is generally confined to a grain market. It is derived from a Sanskrit word which means a mine, storehouse, or granary. As the lion's share of the trade of India is taken by grain and raw produce, it is not surprising that it occurs in so many place-names, either the names of streets or quarters in big cities, or the names of new centres of the grain trade which have grown into towns. Generally the name or title of the founder is prefixed to the word. Thus you will find in different parts of Lucknow, Hazratganj, Nawabganj, Wazirganj, Husainganj, the more recent Victoriaganj (called after the late Empress of India), and the cumbrously-named Drig-Bijaiganj (called after a popular ancestor of the Maharaja of Balrampur). "Mandi" is the word usually associated with the market for bulky articles of low value, such as vegetables, timber, grass, etc. Thus there is the famous Sabzi Mandi (vegetable market) of Delhi, and several other mandis, such as the Lakarmandi (timber and fuel market) and the Ghasimandi (grass market), in Lucknow. "Katra," as the name of a bazar, originally denoted the quarter or suburb where the humble artisans lived, manufactured their wares, and sold them. There would usually be only one katra in a town, but if a modern city has been formed by the amalgamation of several little towns, there may be more than one katra. Then the artisans who plied different trades and tended to form caste-guilds, gravitated into distinct and local groups, giving rise to streets or quarters named after the guilds. Such a quarter would be called a "tola," if it arose before Muhammadan words became fashionable, and "mohalla," if it arose during the supremacy of Muhammadan ideas. Thus we have in Lucknow, north of the river, Chamar-tola (or the cobblers' quarter), Thatheri-tola (or the quarter of workers in copper), and Murai-tola[1] (or the

[1] The nearest equivalent to "Tola" that I can think of in the English language is the word "Row." The "Rows" of Yarmouth are famous; those of Chester are *sui generis*. Doubtless "Bedford Row"

quarter of the vegetable growers). This scheme of names will furnish the key to the ancient distribution of the working population of a city or the gradual building up of a town, and will incidentally explain many place-names. It must not be supposed that the scheme of distribution remains unaltered through the centuries. The population of Indian towns is a particularly shifting population in contrast to the rural population, which is so attached to its ancestral acres. But the historical meaning that lies buried in names is significant of many of the features of the social system.

One of the most characteristic fancy industries of Lucknow is that of clay modelling. The workers are so clever that they can make a clay figure (face, draperies, and all) while you wait. They have been known to ask a person to sit in a chair while their partner engages him in pleasant talk, and before their customer has quite made up his or her mind what to buy, the clever artist has modelled an exact image, or series of

in London retains a relic of early phraseology; so does "Rampart Row" in Bombay. But the most interesting glimpse in this connection is afforded by Daniel Defoe in his "Tour through the Whole Island of Great Britain." Describing Stourbridge Fair at Cambridge, he tells us how the "Duddery" was a great square—a sort of chauk—in the centre, formed of the largest booths, where wholesale business was transacted. Then there were streets or "Rows" running in all directions, which were the scenes of different trades such as "Goldsmiths, Toymen, Turners, Milliners . . . in a word, all Trades that can be found in London." A passage like this vividly brings home eighteenth-century England to an Oriental. Perhaps, after all, West *was* East, and East is West.

images, to represent the customer in various attitudes and with different expressions of face. This will be shown in the rough, and if it does not please (which rarely happens), the artist is most voluble in telling you how the finished product will represent you exactly as you are (that is, exactly as you think you are), this being only a rough attempt to aid his memory in finishing his task. The subtle word of flattery in season, when the will is wavering, is so well understood and practised that these artists in clay command a large business, and used to earn good profits. Recently, however, they have fallen upon evil times, and with the decline in their business has followed a decline in their art. But some say that the decline in their art has led to a fall in prices. True it is that the modellers in clay do not receive as much patronage as they used to do, and the finest exponents of the art are now rare.

If you go to the interior of one of these workmen's houses you will find no more than one room occupied by the whole family. A large number of them, about two-thirds of the whole population, live in mud-built houses, but the better class of them can afford to rent a house built of bricks and plaster. The lighting and ventilation are left to chance. In the one room they can command, they put about three beds. They are not exactly French or Arabian bedsteads, but four posts joined by four pieces of

wood, and covered with string usually made of cocoanut fibre. A bed like that, called a *char-pai*, would cost about sixpence or eightpence, which, however, represents a day's work to the men. On the bed nothing more than a cheap blanket is placed, which in the cold weather serves the double purpose of sheet and coverlet. One of these beds is used for sleeping on. The others would be used as chairs or tables, in case there are no children in the family. There are no pictures in the room, no chairs nor tables. The walls are not covered with paper, and, of course, there are no hangings. There is usually no carpet or floor-cloth, but occasionally a cheap cotton print or a mat is spread on the floor, and when people are not sitting on the four-post beds, they sit on the ground on these floor coverings. One corner of the room serves as a kitchen, where four or five cooking utensils are stacked, and two or three brass vessels serve as vessels for drinking-water. In the hot weather porous earthenware vessels are filled with water, and the evaporation that takes place helps to cool the water almost to an icy temperature.

Let us go to a somewhat better-class house than this, say the house of a clerk employed in a Government office. His income would be about two or three pounds a month. Out of that he pays a rent of about five or six shillings, unless he has pretensions to a better style of living, in which case he would, perhaps, pay ten shillings for rent. He has, in most cases, at least two rooms to live in, one used by the women, and the other by the men. The children would usually be in the women's apartment. The cooking and all the domestic service would also be performed there, the men's apartment being usually reserved for the men's interests or for business purposes. In such a house they generally have some sort of a floor-cloth, but the walls of the rooms are not papered. In the men's apartments there may be a picture or two. Usually the pictures deal with subjects of Hindu mythology, if the owner happens to be a Hindu, or representations of sacred buildings, if the owner happens to be a Muhammadan. Sometimes cheap theatrical prints or Roman Catholic devotional pictures, or the two in juxtaposition, are hung up, without the owner realising the incongruous ideas they would suggest to any one who knew their meaning.

If you go to a still higher stratum in society you would come to the still larger and more open house called a bungalow. Lucknow is, in a sense, pre-eminently the city of bungalows. All the better-class Indians affect a bungalow in Lucknow, while in other cities or Indian stations, the bungalow is usually the habitation of Europeans only. The ground is called a "compound." Round the compounds are scattered out-houses for the servants, stables, and coach-houses. There is often a large garden with some flowers, but

the garden is chiefly remarkable for its fruit trees. The bungalow itself has a verandah, and any number of rooms from six to ten, all on the ground floor, but the plinth is raised a few feet from the ground. The style of living is of a mixed character, like all institutions in modern India. One room is perhaps fitted up in the European style, and would serve as a drawing-room in which to receive visitors accustomed to the Western mode of life. Another is fitted up in the Oriental style, with rich carpets on the floors, expensive hangings on the walls, and several ornamental *hukkas* and spittoons in different parts of the room. These are the only kind of houses which have separate kitchens. The sanitary arrangements, too, are of a better order, although it must not be supposed that the clean spick and span arrangements of an English home and the clock-work routine of an English household are to be obtained in the free, lackadaisical life of India.

The amusements of the city are not many, but an Eastern crowd generally manages to find amusement in most things in life. The bazar is a free lounging place or club, where you may meet your fellows and exchange any ideas you may have and any compliments you may think fit to bestow. The place of newspapers is supplied to the man in the street by bazar gossip. There are no billiard saloons, but at any shop you are allowed to play skittles with your neighbour's character. In Lucknow there are two or three theatres on Western lines, or rather theatres which attempt to mount pieces on Western lines. The dresses, however, are generally the same for similar characters, in whatever play they appear; thus the King wears the same crown and dress whether he appears as King Lear or as King Harishchandra, or as the god Indar in *Indar Sabha*. The female parts are acted by boys and the scenery is of the simplest description. The old style of plays, which may in some respects be called the national style, is that in which there are no set pieces, but only sketches of life, grave and gay, patriotic, satirical, or frivolous. There are a set of professional men, called Bhánds or Naqqáls, who hold grants of land given by the old Indian dynasties for their subsistence. They used to perform at Court and sometimes for the benefit of the public on occasions of public festivals without any fees. Many of those old families still exist and give performances, but not in a regular theatre where the spectators pay for entry. When a rich man wants to celebrate a wedding or a birthday, or the name-day of a child, or other auspicious event in his family, he generally has one of these men, or a troupe of them, to come to perform at night. The spectators would be his guests. The hosts pay for the entertainment from about £1 to £10 for the whole troupe for the evening. It would

not be the only entertainment. Other items on the programme include dances performed by professional dancing girls. The Indians consider it beneath their dignity to dance themselves. The performances of the professionals are often of a tedious character, and generally go on all night. The guests are not only those invited by special request, but anybody who chooses to drop in. The dancing girls also sing. The songs are like music-hall songs in character, and the dances are so adjusted that they are appropriate to the songs. The motions are slow and dignified, but dreamy and sensuous. The arms and fingers, the twisting of the wrists and ankles, the languorous manipulation of the head and the supple turnings of the waist and body, all contribute to the general effect. The music is in a minor key, a low, sad, dreamy monotone, played by a man with a *sárangi*, whose eyes and head show him to be a true artist living in a dream-land of his own, of which this world with all its fleeting show is a mere faint expression. The time is accentuated by a man with a hand-drum, whose nimble fingers strike against the vellum with energy and ease, while he closes his eyes and feels that he is the true master of the dancing measure. If the song happens to be a Hindi plaint, in which the lonely Radha pines because Krishna, the lord of her heart and the soul of her body, cometh not, there is nothing surprising in the spell it casts over an audience who understand both the words, the scenes, and the setting in which they are presented, and feel transported into a world where the artist and the audience, the motion and the music, fade into the depths of the Unattainable.

Other amusements indulged in are wrestling, cock-fighting, quail-fighting, kite-flying, and card-playing. The cards played with are different from the ordinary pack of 52 oblong cards used in Europe. They are round in shape and are called Ganjifa. The pack consists of 96 cards, consisting of eight different colours or suits. They are usually played by three persons. The ordinary four-suit pack of 52 cards is, however, coming into vogue, though there are no brilliant exponents of the game of bridge or whist among the people of India. Chess, on the other hand, is a great favourite among the better classes.

The art of kite-flying, as practised in Lucknow, is of a very superior order. The strings are covered with a composition containing ground mica, which makes it as hard as steel wire. The object of the kite-flier is to get his opponent's kite-string so entangled in his own in the higher regions of the air that with a judicious sawing motion of the hand he can cut that string. When he succeeds in cutting it, the opponent's kite gets detached and flies off whither the wind leads it. When it is nearly on the point of falling on the ground, a crowd of boys and men who are connoisseurs in the art of kite-flying run after it in order to try to capture the kite, which is supposed to be fair booty for whoever lays his hand on it first. Some of these kites are expensive affairs, and in the colours and decorations with which they are adorned are perfect little works of art. There are those with long tails that trail in the air. Such a kite is called a comet. There are other kites which are flown at night, to which is attached a small candle. Such a kite would be a star kite, but the star kite hobby is only confined to a superior class of connoisseurs, who can afford the time and money to indulge in their taste, and who have also the brains to devise novelties in the kite line.

The art of wrestling is the only one among the manly games practised in Lucknow. I will not here consider cricket, football, or tennis, which are exotic games confined to the school or college boys. Formerly sword-play, fencing, single sticks and other games of that description, were in great vogue, and a school of fencing existed in Lucknow, which claimed to expound the art in a way peculiarly original. In the opinion of its votaries it was superior to the art as practised in Delhi; but latterly the Arms Act, which has disarmed the civil population, has also resulted in the practical extinction of the art of sword-play. The only occasions when single sticks are used are unfortunately when human heads are broken. Some of these schools of arms train pupils for showing their skill in the *Moharram* celebrations, but even here there has been a sad decline both in number and in the quality of the art.

The mention of the *Moharram* celebrations recalls the fact that Lucknow is a stronghold of the Shiah sect in India, and therefore these celebrations are attended with peculiar splendour and solemnity. When the Lucknow Court existed, these celebrations were specially patronised by royalty. The Imambara and the Shah Najaf are buildings specially built to commemorate the event with which the *Moharram* celebrations are connected. Originally a sad and solemn festival, it gives the crowds, both Shiah and Sunni, both Hindu and Muhammadan, the opportunity of working up that spirit which, if not kept within bounds, would result in fanatical outbreaks. It is a peculiar religious frenzy, which is concerned more with the emotional expression of a crowd than with religion in its higher aspects. It sometimes takes the form of a show or sheer buffoonery, which is peculiarly revolting to those who understand the true significance of the solemn festival. The religious teachers always preach against it, but, nevertheless, it has established itself as a national institution in India, and the lower classes, irrespective of caste or religion, are entirely devoted to it. In Persia it takes the form of mystery plays or miracle plays. In India it confines its expression, as far as the crowds are concerned, to the making of paper images of the tombs of the martyrs. The framework of these tombs is of sticks or bamboos, but they are completely covered over with paper in a variety of colours and designs. Sometimes they are adorned with such artistic taste that a single one of these tombs costs as much as a thousand rupees. They are led in procession through the town and finally carried to a river or stream, where they are floated in the water. The paper is destroyed, but the framework is preserved for the next year's celebrations. The nobles vie with one another in having *Tazias* of their own. The different Akháras (schools of arms) have each a *Tazia* of its own. Sometimes a whole street subscribes to have a special *Tazia.* Sometimes a trade guild or a society combine to have a *Tazia* of their own. In all these cases the competition consists in making a *Tazia* of superior artistic finish to any of the others or to any of those of the previous year. In some respects the festival has the same aspect in the social life of the people as the Battle of the Flowers in a continental town, or the Lord Mayor's Show in London, but the occasion in the one case is that of civic mirth, and in the other it is buffoonery super-imposed upon a fanatic zeal in the commemoration of an event which is sad beyond expression in the history of Islam.

Having described the external appearance of the city, the interior of the houses, and the amusements of the people, let us review briefly the social and moral ideas which ferment this huge mass of humanity. One of the great factors in the social life of the people, which is specially prominent in the cities, but somewhat thrown into the background in the villages, is the division of the people into water-tight compartments. One section of the people scarcely knows the history, traditions, ideas, and aims of another section, and there are so many sections in the whole mass that the Indian city from a social point of view may be fitly described as a conglomerate of fortuitous forces, working blindly and often in opposite directions, for want of a guiding hand and a master mind, which would enable them to work in harmony and efficiency. Take the religious idea alone. Some people doubt whether there is any religion in the Indian cities. A form of religion there is undoubtedly, or rather a bewildering multiplicity of forms of religion, but they do not constitute a social or a moral force. A rich banker who feeds a hundred Brahmans and gives away large sums of money in charity, but does not hesitate to keep a double set of accounts, one fraudulent (for other people's use) and another real (for his own use), cannot be said to have any religious idea fructifying in his life. A devout Muhammadan who builds a new mosque, and if there is a dispute as to its site will not hesitate to forge a deed which would establish his title to the possession of the land, cannot claim to be working on a religious basis.

"Pious" people who allow their numerous and beautiful places of worship of ancient times to crumble to dust, and build new ones in order to perpetuate their own name, cannot be said to worship any god except that of self-glory. A family in which the sons are against their fathers, and the mothers of the sons are, without any social stigma, the heavy oppressors of their daughters-in-law, cannot be described as showing a real picture of home life or domestic affection. There may exist a vast diversity of religious forms and yet a real unity of ethical, social, or national ideas, as in the United States of America. But where the forms are dead and make no pretence to mould the growing ideas, where the sap of human experience which gave life to a system has run dry, the forms, rituals, and social observances will have no connection with the true inner life of the people. The priests are generally an ignorant body of men, whose knowledge is confined to a set of dead formularies. They have no possible position or vantage-ground from which they can impress their ideals, even if they had any, on their congregations. They have no access to any machinery for the spiritual elevation of humanity. I do not assert that there are no individual lives of purity, devotion, and self-sacrifice in the cities. But where these virtues exist, their lustre is dimmed by gloom and despair as regards the world in general. Where is the self-confident power which will ride on the gathering wave of hope, and batter the rocks of inertia, superstition, and a coarse and selfish greed?

As to the density of population, the problem raised by it is so vast and so appalling that it will have to be handled sooner or later by all social reformers. Hitherto, social reform in India has taken account only of individual or family life. As applied to mankind in the mass, and especially to those soulless agglomerations of seething humanity which we call cities, it is a gospel yet to be preached. Even the statistics dealing with the herding of the masses in cities have scarcely been brought into sufficient prominence. There are not many publicists who have devoted any special attention to the overcrowding which takes place in large towns. This evil is especially prominent in the new and growing towns as opposed to the old and decaying cities. Such towns as have increased with the growth of commerce and industry—for example, Cawnpore and Calcutta—are striking illustrations of this. The population of Cawnpore as a city has grown 61 per cent. since 1872. The growth of Calcutta has also been rapid. But concurrently with this growth no sufficient attention has been paid to the problems suggested by the density of population or the difficulty of housing the people in decent and comfortable homes.

Let us take a few figures. The density of population in Lucknow is 12,278 per square mile.

In Cawnpore it is 37,538; in Bombay it is 35,273; in Calcutta it is 42,390; and in London it is 37,000 per square mile. This comparison would only be useful when we recollect that in a city like London there are a vast number of houses with more than three storeys, while houses with a single floor are almost unknown. In a city like Calcutta, the majority of the houses, fully three-fifths, are mud-built hovels, and therefore the vast majority of the population live, if we may so call it, in a single layer, whereas the majority of the population in London live in triple or quadruple layers, one above the other. Assuming it to be a triple layer, which I think is very far below the mark, a true comparison between the Calcutta and the London populations would be shown thus: If the Calcutta population were housed in triple layers, the people occupying the same living space as they do now, there would be a density of nearly 127,000 per square mile against a density of 37,000 to the square mile in London. According to the Census Report, fully one-eighth of the population live in rooms shared with at least three persons, and one-half share a room with at least one other person. Only three per cent. have one or more rooms to themselves. Let me quote from the latest Census Report:—

"The minimum supply of air space allowed in barracks and common lodging-houses in England is 300 cubic feet per head, but special enquiries, made by Mr Blackwood, in some typical congested areas in Calcutta, show that the space generally ranges from between 200 and 300 cubic feet. In some instances it is greater, but it is also often less, and in two exceptional cases it was only 109 and 129 cubic feet respectively. The local conditions in England differ greatly from those in India; and in this country, owing to the style of buildings and to the fact that the doors and windows are more often kept open, the same amount of air space is not necessary. But even so it is clear that in areas such as those referred to the people are terribly overcrowded."

The conditions in Bombay have been carefully studied by Dr Bhalchandra Krishna and the Honourable Vithaldas Damodar Thakersey. Dr Bhalchandra Krishna has described them in a paper which he read before the Bombay Sanitary Association in 1904. The figures he gives are sufficiently startling. Out of every 10,000 residents in Bombay, as many as 2,492 live in rooms, each occupied by six to nine persons; 1,174 in rooms occupied by ten to nineteen persons, and 288 in rooms occupied by twenty persons and more. According to the same authority, the decade ending in 1899 saw a decreasing birth-rate, reduced to 18·86 per mille. and an increasing death-rate raised as high as 43·85 per mille. His words are not too strong when he says: "In such houses—the breeders of germs and bacilli, the centres of disease and poverty, vice and crime—have people of all kinds—the diseased, the dissolute, the drunken, the improvident—been indiscriminately herded and tightly packed in vast hordes to dwell in close association with each other."

This overcrowding leads to many evils, moral and physical. It is an appreciable factor in the terrible infant mortality in towns, though by no means its only cause. It has provided a most favourable set of conditions for the plague, which, since its outbreak (or discovery) in Bombay in 1896, has gone on increasing and spreading, until it has now almost penetrated all the provinces of India. In the year ending on the 30th September 1905, it claimed a million and a quarter of victims. As far as we can judge at present, plague appears to have come to stay. While its etiology baffles the scientific investigator, its presence has afforded a strong argument to the sanitary reformer in favour of a forward policy, and after many misunderstandings has in some measure opened the eyes of the people. Bombay the Beautiful has its City Improvement Trust, a body created and controlled by the Government, and independent of the Municipal Corporation. The Trust has cleared out large insanitary areas, and made an attempt to encourage the spread of the population in the suburbs. It has also in hand a scheme for model dwellings for the mill operatives, but the difficulty in giving it a large scope is that to cover the bare interest on the capital sunk, it would be necessary to demand a rent almost prohibitive to the mill hand. Nor have its building operations been invariably attended with success. One of the newest buildings erected by the Trust collapsed almost as soon as it was completed, involving the loss of some human lives. In Calcutta, a big scheme of Improvement is also under contemplation, though on somewhat different lines. As the project stands now, a sum of five millions and a half is to be spent on improvements. Congested districts are to be relieved, and open spaces provided. The expenses are to be met by loans, which are to be paid off in sixty years. Meanwhile special taxation to the amount of £70,000 a year will probably be necessary. But the question of cheap means of communication for workmen, which is bound up with the question of improved housing for the people at a distance from their work, has not, as far as I am aware, been much advanced either in Bombay or Calcutta. In the United Provinces large grants have been made by the Government to Municipalities, towns, and rural areas to carry out simple measures of sanitation; and I have no doubt similar steps have been taken in other provinces. Thus plague has undoubtedly stimulated sanitary activity in the authorities. But no success can be achieved or maintained until Indian publicists take up these questions in a practical spirit and infuse into the people themselves a strong impulse towards co-operative effort.

The intellectual status of the people can be

gauged from the sort of reading in which they indulge. But here again we find a discouraging picture. Scarcely one man in ten can read or write, and there is scarcely one woman in 144 who can do so. As to those who can read or write with facility, the numbers are far smaller, and in fact may be said to be confined to the following classes: (1) The men of the old learning; (2) The clerks and officials of Government or railway offices, or mercantile houses; (3) The lawyers. As to the men of the old learning, they live in the past. Their dreams are centred in those nooks and corners of history to which the light of modernity has never penetrated. Their ideals have never adjusted themselves to the demands of modern life. They have not been steeled to resist temptations and vices that have risen from the new conditions of modern India. From them, therefore, no progress can be expected. From them no writings can ever emanate which will carry the seeds of advancement to a higher life in this modern world. Though worthy of all respect, they cannot be trusted as leaders or teachers in the bustle of a life which is entirely alien to the life in which they live and move and have their being. As to the second class—the clerks—the conditions of modern India are such that they tend to set a premium on a soapy, supple sycophancy (as Mrs Brookfield would say), that thinks more of the advantage of the moment than of an artistic ideal or of an elevated purpose in life. The ordinary clerk after a day of sedentary work has neither the time nor the inclination nor the opportunities to read any works of the imagination, or any biographies or stories, which would lay before him the ideals of strong character or fruitful endeavour. The third class—the lawyers—have never been famed in any age or country for those tender flowers of human sympathy which bring sunshine into the secluded vale of human life. They stand for strength, accuracy, smartness, business prompitude, and stern unbending justice, but not for poetry, or the softer humanities. There remains a fourth class—the student class—from which much might be hoped for, only in proportion to the extent to which they do not, when they grow up, merge, pure and simple, into the three classes above-mentioned.

We have seen that city life in India is the adjustment of old habits to new forces, the putting of new wine into old bottles. There are decaying cities like Lucknow and growing cities like Cawnpore; old cities like Delhi and new cities like Calcutta; beautiful cities like Bombay and sombre cities like Allahabad. In none of them yet has the city life, or city government, come into line with the ideals and aspirations of the people. Their social life is wanting in unity. The civic virtues are yet dormant; civic enterprise yet lacks that strong moral incentive, which makes the needs of the many the opportunity for the devotion of the few. Civic renown is not yet the coveted laurel for which men live and die. But surely the time must come when the energies of the citizens will be crystallised into all the civic and social virtues which go towards the building up of a modern State, and make it a worthy product of evolution from the ancient city state of the Greeks, or the still more ancient village of the Aryans.

II

VILLAGE LIFE

"So, with good life
And observation strange, my meaner ministers
Their several kinds have done."

—SHAKESPEARE, *Tempest*, iii. 3.

"Love had he found in huts where poor men lie;
His daily teachers had been woods and rills,
The silence that is in the starry sky,
The sleep that is among the lonely hills."

—WORDSWORTH.

VILLAGE LIFE

In order to obtain an idea of village life, let us take a look round at a typical village. The one we shall choose is situated in the district of Sahāranpur. This is the westernmost district of the United Provinces, and lies on the border of the Punjab province.

The Village is generally taken to include the village habitations and the area of agricultural land attached to the village site. In our village there are about 600 acres of land. The soil is not uniform throughout, some being light loam, and some sandy; some is covered with light brushwood, and is so poor in quality that it would not pay to cultivate it. This is usually reserved for grazing. The meadows and pastures of England, covered with daisies and buttercups, and concealing within the folds of lazy streams the yellow gleam of the marsh marigold or the snowy fragrance of the meadow-sweet, are unknown in India. The stretches of black cotton soil, beloved of the ryot who grows cotton or grain, but a terror to the horse and its rider, are a feature of the landscape south of the Jamna, but are scarcely found in the tract we are examining.

There are two small streams, which empty into a small river hard by. There are four ponds in the whole area: three are situated in the outlying land, and are used principally for irrigation purposes during those short intervals in the rainy season when the rain holds off, and the crops would suffer without water. During a famine, when there is no rain at all, these ponds would be empty and useless; they are not fed by any springs, but depend on the rainfall for their water-supply. During short intervals of drought, however, the agriculturists make little channels out of them, and lift the water on to the fields on a higher level. The apparatus used is of the simplest description. Some matting is so manipulated that two or three thicknesses combined are able to hold quantities of water for the few seconds it takes to lift them up one or two feet. These are held by means of ropes, one on each side, by two men, who, with a swinging motion downwards, take the water as into a scoop, and then with a swinging motion upwards discharge it into a channel a little higher than the level of the pond. If the fields to be irrigated are five or six feet above the water level, this simple arrangement is repeated at short intervals three or four times, and is then quite sufficient for irrigating them on a small scale. In order to prevent any disputes about the times at which different agriculturists may want to irrigate their fields, a fixed rotation is agreed upon, and is well understood by the parties concerned. I am speaking now of a village that is not irrigated from a canal, or of portions of a village area to which canal water cannot be brought up.

Besides these ponds in the outlying area, there is a pond quite close to the village, which we may call the village pond, and to which the cattle are usually taken to be watered. The watering operation is usually performed at the close of the day, when "the lowing herd winds slowly o'er the lea." The cattle then come home from their pasture grounds, raising clouds of dust on the way to such an extent that evening time is known in village phraseology as "dust time." Before the animals are brought into the byres, they drink their fill at the village pond, and wait for the stragglers of the herd, which may, through accident or inexperience, have been left behind. After they have been watered they are taken to little sheds in the village, or sometimes left in fallow fields. They are frequently accommodated in the houses themselves, where men and cattle congregate and sleep in the most amicable and primitive manner. In the hot weather the cattle are often left in the open air, as it is both healthy and pleasant for them. The shade of a tree is all that is necessary to protect them from the heavy dews of a May night, when sometimes whole herds are left in the village streets. Any one walking through the village at night would have to make his way through labyrinths of oxen, cows, buffaloes, calves, ponies, and sometimes the heavy village carts with tireless wooden wheels.

Before entering the village site let us examine the fields. It is the month of March, and the fields are ripe with waving corn. The crops consist mostly of wheat, barley, oil-seeds, and potatoes, the fields being all unenclosed. The place of hedges is taken by small earthen ridges that serve to mark off one field from another. Each field consists on a average of an area scarcely larger than the fifth of an acre, and in some places often smaller. The rice beds are sometimes fifteen to an acre, but rice is an autumn crop. The roads are few and far between. Indeed, so great is the pressure on the soil that the agriculturists prefer to drive their corn-laden carts through their neighbours' fields which happen to lie fallow for the time being. There are a few foot-paths: even they follow the lines of the mud ridges which serve as the boundaries of the fields. If you could take a bird's-eye view of the whole of the cultivated area, you would find little patches of square or rectangular fields, some with crops, some lying fallow, and others ploughed and levelled for the sugar-cane crop of the next season.

It will be noticed that there are very few trees in the village. Those which do exist cluster together in well-defined groves. The largest tree area is that within or surrounding the village site. Among the fields here and there are two or three groves of mango trees. There are isolated trees of the kind that yield timber, such as the tún, the shísham, or the ním. The mango tree itself yields timber, but it is principally grown for the sake of its fruit, and on that account is very valuable. Usually, if there is an isolated tree, its shade is detrimental to the crops in the immediate vicinity, and therefore agriculturists always try to plant clumps or clusters in those parts of the village which are not very fertile for ordinary crops. The shade trees, such as the far-famed banyan or the pípal, are generally in or around the village site. They often mark the shrine of a tribal or a local god, and sometimes harbour snakes in their hollow trunks. As the snake, however, is considered sacred, and is sometimes looked upon as the guardian genius of the village, the villagers entertain no fear on that account. They sometimes feed them with milk, and therefore the snakes themselves rarely molest the human beings around them. In the branches of these spreading trees there is a large quantity of bird life. Pigeons, doves, mainas, green pigeons, sparrows, crows, and owls find a habitation there; while the pretty striped squirrel that skips with such wonderful agility from branch to branch, and playfully descends to the ground to snatch, it may be, a piece of bread from a village urchin, serves to diversify and render lively the ordinarily sober and lazy animal life around.

Herds of antelope—the famous black buck of India—roam wild from village to village. They are so tame to the villager that they will allow him to approach within ten yards of them; but with sportsmen they enter into the spirit of sport, and "play the game." Lucky would be the sportsman who can get within rifle-shot of three fine heads of a morning. In spite of their long, straight, spiral horns, which attain a length of 18 to 28 inches, they can make their way through dense sugar-cane fields with ease. The villager looks upon them as harmless friends, except when they approach too near the village site, and begin to nibble at the young green shoots of valuable crops in the immediate vicinity of habitations. Here the land is freely and specially manured, and the crops are more valuable; but as soon as the villagers have driven off the black buck, there comes a troop of monkeys who begin to help themselves to the more advanced corn. These cannot be quite driven away. On the approach of men they climb up into the branches of the trees, but descend again immediately the danger is past.

We are now approaching the village habitations. They are situated on a slightly-raised piece of ground, because the village site has been there for centuries, and the *débris* which has been accumulating has made quite a little mound. If we were only to dig into the ground we should find relics left by the ancestors of the present villagers in the form of pots, copper and silver coins, women's bangles, and pieces of earthenware vessels. But as our business at present is not that of archæologists, but of people interested in the life of the villagers, we will enter and pay a visit to some of their representative men.

Who is this man in a blue coat and red turban, carrying a long bamboo stick with brass knobs at both ends? The bamboo is about seven feet long, and its brass ends are sufficiently massive to account for a couple of enemies in a close hand-to-hand fight. Its owner carries his head high, and seems to look upon his stick as an emblem of divinity. He is merely the village watchman—called in the vernacular the *Chaukidár*—whose pay does not exceed six or seven shillings per month, besides such customary doles of grain as he may get at harvest. But he stands to the villagers as the representative of a strong central government. He is armed with the authority of the law to arrest offenders in certain classes of offences. As he is not a lawyer, he sometimes even arrests for offences in respect of which he has no legal power; but, as there are no lawyers in the village, his action is scarcely likely to be disputed locally, and if he treats his fellow-villagers with no more than the amount of severity which is necessary to keep up his "dignity," no one would ever venture to criticise his actions. If he adds to his accomplishments the gift of a rough and ready wit which is not too far above the villagers, and yet impresses them—say the wit of a Dogberry or a Verges—he is looked up to with the respect which an official hierarchy would pay to a governor. The terror he inspires has been well described by an Anglo-Indian poet in the following lines:—

> "The wisdom crammed in a long Report,
> Or a neatly writ G.R.,[1]
> Is less than a lie in a Sudder Court,
> Or the fear of the Chaukidár."

He not only performs the duties of a village police officer, but is also the registrar of births and deaths. He is quite illiterate, but he keeps a book which is given him by Government, in which are entered any births or deaths that occur in the village. He gets the entries made by others, such as the village accountant or the schoolmaster. This is not a disadvantage from his point of view. When the books are checked, if they are found correct and up to date, the credit is of course his, for being a smart chaukidár. But if any errors or omissions are found, he can say, nothing daunted: "Oh! it's that fellow X. Y. I thought he was accurate in his writing, but I shall have to speak to him. How could I judge of his merits, I, a poor illiterate chaukidár?"

[1] Government Resolution.

When he goes to the police station the head constable at the station copies out the entries into a proper register; but the whole basis of executive administration in India is the humble chaukidár. He generally belongs to the lower classes, sometimes to the classes which have been professional thieves or criminals. The high caste men object to duties which might bring them into contact with the criminal classes. A Brahman would be seriously put out if he were a chaukidár and had to arrest a criminal sweeper. Besides, the principle "Set a thief to catch a thief" applies to the village chaukidár just as much as to the instruments of which Scotland Yard occasionally makes use here in tracing important crimes.

With all his status and dignity he is sometimes a smart man, too, or can be if he likes. A magistrate once had a case of some difficulty. The evidence for the prosecution and the defence was fairly evenly balanced. It was asserted on behalf of the prisoner that it was impossible for him to have been concerned in the crime and arrested by the chaukidár in the manner in which the chaukidár stated he had arrested him, because the prisoner was a strong man, fleet of foot, whereas the chaukidár seemed to be a heavy, slow sort of man. On this the chaukidár put up his stick in court, like a schoolboy putting up his hand, who wishes to say something to the teacher. When the magistrate turned to him he said: "Your worship, try the relative powers of speed of myself and the prisoner, and you will see for yourself whether I cannot catch him." The idea struck the magistrate as irresistibly funny, and he adjourned the court to the village green, where he set the prisoner free and directed the chaukidár to run and arrest him. The chaukidár was as good as his word, for he caught the man in two furlongs. He therefore not only received the magistrate's thanks for solving a difficult question, but obtained a reward of two months' pay. The chaukidár wore his dignity to impress the people—he now showed his smartness to impress the magistrate!

The next man we shall interview will be the village accountant. He is in some respects a representative of the Government; but he is armed with no power of the law, and therefore is looked upon as less of a dignitary than the chaukidár. He is an educated man, and in dealing with large and intricate sums is quite as expert as a banker's clerk. The Government's chief source of revenue is the land-tax, which is assessed, in the ledgers at headquarters, on units, called maháls, which roughly corresponded, when the arrangements were made, to single villages; but as the landlords in a village are numerous, the shares being subdivided to a thousandth or two-thousandth part of a rupee unit, the collection of the Government revenue from individual landlords would be a matter of extreme difficulty were it not for the village accountant.

But this is only one side of his work. His records not only comprise the data upon which the Government revenue is apportioned, but also the intricate rights of the villagers among one another. For example, the landlords who do not cultivate the land themselves, but let it out to tenants, would be hard put to it to calculate the rent due to them were it not for the village accountant. The tenantry among themselves would never know how much land precisely they held, and what rent would be due to the landlords, were it not for the village accountant. Again, the landlords themselves are a petty class, and cultivate some fields as owners and others as tenants to other landlords, equally petty with themselves. The result is that the same men would be from one point of view the landlords, and from another the tenants. Sometimes they get quite mixed up as to which land they hold and in what capacity, and what rent they should pay and to whom. And it is here that the village accountant comes in to solve the difficulties.

Again, the village, as a whole, has certain common expenses. In the days when the village was a living organism, with the directing force within itself, the common expenses were numerous. If its balance-sheet was ever committed to paper in those days, and could now be unearthed, it would doubtless be found to be rankly socialistic. In the modern village, with its disintegrated life, its absentee "co-sharers" and its banker landlords, to whom landed property is an investment and nothing else, the common expenses tend to be more and more restricted. Whenever disputes are taken into Court about the calculation or division of profits, all items of "Village Expenses" are usually resisted, except the amounts actually assessed by Government as its own revenue. But tradition dies hard in an Indian village, as indeed in all villages. The local villagers, therefore, try their utmost, when the record of customs is being framed, to get clauses inserted about the expenses of entertaining and the like, in which absentees take no interest. The entertainments, whose expenses are shared by the village as a whole, may be charitable, or politic, or they may be amusements, pure and simple. In the absence of a Poor Law, the old village communities used to make it a point of honour to entertain strangers — the needy and afflicted who came within their gates. On this principle, Brahmans and beggars are still fed, and are charged to the common funds. Then the petty Government officials who come to the village have to be made much of and put at their ease, as their reports, favourable or unfavourable, would influence the material destinies of the village. It is politic to humour them, but the humouring is not always of a nature to be beyond the law of corruption. And here the accountant's tact and knowledge of the world come in. Sums spent on many a well-fed kanungo have gone down in the accounts as the "feeding of Brahmans." But the most curious form of village expenses occurs where gipsies and acrobats are entertained for amusement, or wandering bards in Rajput villages for the maintenance and occasional "touching-up" of pedigrees. Such charges can only be recognised in courts of law, if they depend upon customs expressly recorded in the village papers, whose custodian, the village accountant, has therefore a fruitful field for the exercise of his ingenuity in favour of one party or another. All such expenses are pooled together on one side, and the income from the rent-roll, market-dues, fisheries, or other rights (if any) is also pooled together on the other side of the account. A balance of profit and loss is then struck by the accountant, who has to divide it into minute fractional shares corresponding to the conflicting rights and interests of the different co-sharers.

The village accountant, therefore, is not a purely Government official, nor is his work entirely for the benefit of Government. He is as much the representative of the landed classes as of the Government. Indeed, as he is usually the only literate man in the village (every village having a village accountant either resident or visiting it at short intervals, while of the schoolmasters there is scarcely one to every fifteen[1]

[1] See the last *Quinquennial Review of Education*: the statement refers to the United Provinces.

villages), his assistance is of the greatest value to the people, who have to write or receive letters from their friends or relatives abroad (which in village parlance means outside the village), or to those who have documents to execute, or cases to be filed in court. To all such the village accountant is indispensable. He knows his own value, for, besides the pay of about 15s. a month (or less) which he receives, he generally gets a large number of gifts from the people whom he has served. He sometimes manages to extract still larger sums in ways that will not bear the strictest investigation, so that his true income would be about five or six times that which is shown nominally as his pay. He may belong to any of the castes, but he is usually a Brahman or a Kayasth, which is the writer caste throughout Upper India.

Let us now make the acquaintance of the Lambardár. His name would evoke a smile from those who knew its meaning. It is made up of two words—*Lambar*, the English "number," and *dár*, which is the Persian equivalent of "holder" or "possessor." Our Lambardár is therefore a man who possesses a number. Formerly, when the revenue system was remodelled by the British Government, they appointed for each village a man who was to be responsible for the whole of the land-tax, and who was allowed to collect the different shares from the hundreds of co-sharers in his

From a Photo.] [*By* Mr S. Athim.

LAMBARDÁR'S HOUSE.

"The Lambardár's house has some outside apartments which serve as a meeting-place for the village public"—p. 57.

To face p. 57.]

own way. Each of such men, who might from another point of view be called village headmen, was given a number in the Government registers; hence the funny-sounding name of Lambardár. He represents the more comfortable classes in the village, and, of course, belongs to the land-owning class. He is generally the most considerable land-owner, which, however, may mean nothing more than that he owns five or ten acres. He sometimes has a house built of masonry and covered with lime-wash, perhaps the only house of that character in the village. The rest of the houses are mere mud-huts, more or less compactly built together. The Lambardár's house, however, has some outside apartments, which serve as a meeting-place for the village public. If the village is large enough to have a school, but not large enough for a Government building for a school, the boys collect in the Lambardár's public apartments. They are also the place for the receipt of customs. When the time for collecting the land-tax comes round, the village accountant sits on one side with his volume of accounts and pen and ink; the Lambardár sits on the other side; and his messengers, who are usually his agricultural tenants, run from place to place to bring up the defaulters to plank down their money so that the Lambardár may pay the Government demand in due season. If the Lambardár is a friend of the poor and a protector of the needy and the fatherless, as he sometimes is, his public apartments are also besieged with suppliants in various forms, who come to pour their tales of woe into his sympathetic ears. Parish gossips are also free to come and go whenever they like and exchange the news of an evening. The Lambardár generally keeps half a dozen smoking pipes and hukkas in order that his guests might smoke while the conversation is flagging, and pretend the indifference associated with smoking when the conversation is at its most interesting stage. Any fakírs, or religious ascetics, passing through the village, are also sure of finding a ready hospitality in the Lambardár's public apartments.

Besides these he has his private house. Let us, with his permission, enter it, as it in a measure represents the houses of the whole village, although on a grander scale than the average. The general plan is that of a courtyard, surrounded by buildings on all the four sides. The front side is that in which the public apartments are; the three other sides contain the private apartments. The courtyard is quite open to the rays of the sun by day, and of the moon or stars by night; and these luminaries truly represent to the simple villagers as much actuality as any of the things they see in their daily life. Round the courtyard on three sides are grouped together a number of what might be called inner-rooms. Some of them are used as store-rooms, some of them as stables for the cattle, and occasionally for the bullock cart in which the Lambardár drives when he goes long distances. He rarely indulges in the luxury of a pony for himself, perhaps because he is fat and comfortable, but he keeps an undersized pony for mounting the village accountant if he happens to go to the headquarters of the district, or for the entertainment of guests of distinction, whom it might be his good fortune to receive in the village. These apartments are not closed rooms like those in an English house. Sometimes they are merely a long shed with a roof and no doors, the apartments communicating with one another. The side nearest the door, but facing the courtyard (though contiguous to the public apartments, which look on to the street), is occupied by apartments for the male members of the Lambardár's family. Here they sit and sometimes smoke; here they often sleep at night.

The side opposite to what we may call the public side is closed with doors, and shut in in every direction by walls. That is the side where the female apartments are. Perhaps they form a separate quadrangle. It must not be supposed that the women are all entirely shut in, as is the custom in towns. The village women go out into the streets of the village with as much liberty as they choose to exercise; but their lives naturally require a little more privacy than the lives of the men, who almost entirely live in public. The inner apartments are also those in which the Lambardár's valuables are stored. Here his clothes are kept, and, in fact, everything is preserved which requires doors to protect it, and cannot be put into the open apartments where any one can come and go freely. The furniture is of the simplest description. There are any number of beds of the kind described in speaking of town life, which are used for sitting and sleeping on, for putting clothes or babies on; in fact, for all purposes for which a cot, a table, a chair, a desk, a sofa, or a shelf would ordinarily be used in this country. Besides these there are some floor-cloths, and the usual cooking pots, the brass drinking pots, and a large number of earthen vessels; only everything is on a more liberal scale in the village than in the town. In villages there is not the same competition as in towns. There is not the feeling of hungry generations treading you down. There is peace and quiet. There is comfort and confidence, and not a commercial spirit of calculation. Many of the things are made locally. The Lambardár pays nothing in cash for his earthenware pots, but he keeps the potter in his pay, and the potter makes what is necessary for him. In fact, this relation may be said to hold as regards the whole village collectively in its dealings with the artisans.

The grain is stored in pits dug in the courtyard, which are covered up after they are full. The grain is taken out of each pit as required, and if the Lambardár happens to be the trustee for the co-sharers of the village, he would naturally have a large number of these pits. Some of them contain as many as ten or fifteen tons of grain, and the whole supply would often be sufficient for several years—that is to say, if the Lambardár and the whole village are not entirely in debt, as often happens. The only cash which the Lambardár has is generally kept for the purposes of paying the tax or of paying his debts. Otherwise his wealth consists in the cattle, the grain, or the ornaments which his wife and children wear. He has no bankers to keep his accounts or take charge of his savings. Any savings he may make he invests in ornaments of silver or gold. It is in the last resort that these ornaments would be sold, and that distressing calamity happens in famine years.

Let us now turn to the village Banya—a man who is often the subject of fierce diatribes, and described as a blood-sucker and a tyrant. He is the village financier and shopkeeper. His shop is generally a small mud-built shed, containing forty or fifty baskets, all put in tiers and rows, containing grains of the various kinds which are grown in the village; salt, pepper, and other spices; and the usual village groceries. He acts as the intermediary through whom the Lambardár sells his grain for town markets whenever the Lambardár wishes to raise money on gathered crops. He also advances seed to the poorer agriculturists. These live from hand to mouth, and they have not the wherewithal to wait for the harvest, but must be fed, while the crops are growing, by the village Banya. It is true the Banya makes a good thing out of it, charging interest as high as cent. per cent. ; but the people to whom he lends money are so abjectly poor that he often has not only to forego the repayment of his loan for the time being, but even to feed his debtors into the bargain, in order to keep alive the hope of being paid at some future time. The Banya is scarcely literate in the sense in which the village accountant is literate; but, of course, in the matter of accounts, he is a perfect prodigy. If you want to get an object lesson in mental arithmetic, go to the Banya. He keeps elaborate books, showing what he owes to the different people, and what they owe to him. He sometimes grows rich, and passes into the land-owning classes. Then he may give up his shop, and, if he is appointed Lambardár, sets up as a village magnate himself; but there is this difference between the Banya land-owner and the land-holder of the agricultural classes—that the Banya, being a sharp man of business, knows how and where to invest his capital, and if he is at all an intelligent man, he never starves the land of capital. As capitalist and financier his assistance in the smooth running of the wheels of agricultural economy is most valuable, and if he is occasionally prone to cheat, it is not that he is worse than his fellow-villagers, but that he has more opportunities, and makes full use of them.

It is the fashion nowadays to denounce the Banya, but the denunciation is a little overdone. In the absence of co-operative or village banks, the Banya, as a money-lender, is an absolute economic necessity, apart from his position as shopkeeper and trader. He finances the crops, and there is no other agency to do so on a large scale. Grain for foreign export is often financed by the large export houses in the presidency towns, but the internal trade cannot yet spare the Banya. The experiment of people's banks is being tried on a small scale, but it can only be successful when the ideas underlying the movement have taken firm hold of the people's minds. The Government Takávi system has not been hitherto as popular with the villagers as could have been wished, because of certain drawbacks, which have been recently considered by the Government of India. Government has issued orders for revising the system and working it efficiently, but some defects are inherent in the system, and in any case Government cannot possibly provide the vast amount of capital that would be required to finance the agriculture of the whole country.

The village artisans comprise the blacksmith, the carpenter, the goldsmith, the potter, the weaver, the washerman, and the sweeper. The oilman has almost been squeezed out of existence by the cheap and nasty mineral oil known as Kerosine, which comes from Baku,

Burma, or America. The artisans are all of separate castes, and the members of each caste are as proud of their rank and calling as if they practised some exclusive art. In many cases they are not paid for their work in hard cash: they get some land rent free for their support, which the women and children cultivate, and they always get their customary dues at harvest time. The blacksmith makes the hoes, the plough-shares, the iron utensils which may be necessary in cooking, and other things of that kind, and supplies them to the people who want them, without any money or only nominal payments passing immediately between them. The potter supplies the pots and the sweeper performs his duties in the same way, being recompensed by gifts from the better class of persons, and mutual services from their fellow-artisans, such as the carpenter, the blacksmith, and the weaver.

No account of village life would be complete without a description of the Fakír. He lives in a little hut or cave (if there is a cave) away from the village, so as to be free, and far from the madding crowd's ignoble strife. What he does there nobody knows. He is a mysterious being, who appears with only a loin cloth round his waist, apparently quite indifferent to the praise or blame of the world. He rarely enters into conversation about the ordinary affairs of mankind, and the gifts he receives in charity are those which his disciples and admirers beg for the honour of presenting to him, rather than doles extracted by a beggar from an unwillingly charitable public. The people look upon him with superstitious veneration, not because they know there is anything in his life, but because in person and habit he represents that ascetic ideal which renounces the world and lives an inner life of self-mortification. He carries a rosary of beads, and he often goes along the streets shouting "Rám, Rám," if he is a follower of that particular incarnation of God as worshipped by the Hindus. He has no religious ideals in the sense of a striving for the elevation of other men's lives; but he is possessed with the idea which finds a mere illusion in the whole world and in all humanity, and the only reality in the name of Rám. This simple monomania is revered by the people in proportion as they cannot translate it into their own lives. Though apparently indifferent to all that passes around him, the Fakír is a great observer of men and manners, and is often able to reconcile disputes and extricate people from difficult situations on account of his apparently isolated position. Sometimes he takes a vow of religious silence for seven years, and keeps it. Sometimes he undertakes to walk to all the sacred shrines of India, which may include a journey from Badrináth, near the glacier valleys of the Himalayas, to the sea-washed shores of Western Dwarka, or the torrid heat of Rameshwaram in the extreme south. He would thus cover a distance of thousands of miles on foot, with nothing but his rosary with him, not even the traditional staff of the weary wanderer. His life is a mystery to outsiders. His survival in the twentieth century is to superficial observers of Indian life a greater mystery still. The fact is that he represents a strain of that morbid love of self-mortification and self-abasement which, when healthy and turned into a useful sphere, gives us the greatest saints and heroes of history. If there is any one class in India more than another to which the famous lines of Matthew Arnold are peculiarly appropriate, it is to that rare individual, the true Fakír (as distinguished from the false Fakírs who figure in jugglery tales and the annals of crime):—

> "The East bowed low before the blast,
> In silent deep disdain;
> She let the Legions thunder past,
> Then plunged in thought again."

As the social life of the men centres round the Lambardár's reception-room, so the social life of the women centres round the village well, to which they go to draw water. The graceful figure of the village maiden, with two or three pots of different sizes—the smallest on the top—poised on her head, going to the river to fetch water, has been so familiarised in Daniell's pictures that it is scarcely necessary to describe it in words, but the social chatter which takes place at the well claims a little of our attention. In the first place, it must be realised that the water-supply of a village which is some distance from a stream or river (a description that would apply to a vast number of villages) is not derived from any water-works, but from deep holes dug in the ground to a depth of 15 to 30 feet, according to the spring level. The vertical hole thus made in the soil is lined with masonry. When the masonry tube is well sunk in, a ceremony is performed which is analogous to that of the going of a bride to the husband's house. The well is supposed to be a living being, and she is married to the god of the locality. No one is allowed to drink water out of it until the installation has taken place in due form. It is attended with some picturesque ceremonies, and forms quite an event in village history.

The exterior of the well is built up in the form of a round platform with an opening into the well in the centre. On this platform are fixed two or three poles, or a framework with a pulley and ropes, to help people to draw water. The mouth of the well is sometimes covered with a wooden grating to prevent accidents, as men and women have been known to lose their balance and fall into the water. The favourite mode of suicide, by the way—when an Indian woman finds herself unhappy in her married life on account of differences, not with her husband, but with her mother-in-law—is by jumping down a well.

The usual gossip of the women, morning and evening, is around the village well. It is the ladies' club, as exclusive as the aristocratic clubs of London. The higher castes have wells of their own, to which no lower class people are allowed to go to draw water. The conversation which usually takes place among the elder women when they are present is about the enormities or failings of the younger women who are their daughters-in-law. If they are absent or when they are gone, then comes the turn of the young wives to compare notes about their respective mothers-in-law and sisters-in-law, not often to the advantage of these relatives of the husband. Thus you will see the village well looms very large in the social history of the Indian women; but it would require a whole volume to enlarge upon the romance of the well. It will be remembered that even so in England, in the age of chivalry and romance, a great many legends gathered round wells. These still linger round the holy wells in Cornwall and Ireland. Southey wrote a famous ballad on the well of St Keyne, and the scene of one of Sir Walter Scott's novels is laid in the midst of the motley society that come to "take the cure" at St Ronan's well.

The men also come to the well, but the morning and evening hours are sacred to the women. These hours are usually avoided by the men out of respect to the fair sex. The most

After a Photo.] [*By* Mr S. Athim.

THE VILLAGE WELL.

"The village well looms very large in the social history of Indian women"—p. 68.

To face p. 68.]

perfect decorum and even privacy is observed in these matters in the village. Though the village women go about freely, there is never any molestation of them, and the men, in their own rough and ready way, show a chivalrous spirit that is not noticed by those who only look at life from a superficial point of view. All crimes, social or legal, against women in a village, are committed by strangers, but they are not many. Of course, the lot of the Indian woman requires improvement in many ways; but so does that of the Indian man, and, taking them altogether, we ought to be very cautious in judging either sex. Their lives are as happy as possible under the circumstances. The social evils of the joint family system are responsible for much friction between mothers-in-law and daughters-in-law, and for many attempted suicides on the part of the latter; but that is a large question, and need not detain us here.

It may be asked: If the men do not come to the well to draw water, and if they have their own meeting-places in the village, why should they come to the well at all? The answer is that the water which the women draw is mostly for drinking and cooking purposes. The bathing is all done at the well. Ablutions form a great feature in Oriental life. Every Hindu of the better classes is supposed to bathe before every meal, and he does not bathe at home, but comes to the well, divests himself of all his clothes except his loin cloth, and pours water over his head and shoulders. This is all done quite publicly in the open air. It is generally done on the platform round the mouth of the well, and sometimes the dirty water finds its way in. One of the problems of public sanitation in the administration of the villages is to make the platforms in such a way that the dirty water cannot possibly find its way in, but must all flow out. The best way is to have separate bathing platforms round about the well. But, even so, the water that flows out is apt to stagnate round the well, percolating through the soil, and eventually affecting the purity of the water in the well. There is no systematic drainage of the village streets, and all sanitary reforms in the villages have first to deal with this particular evil.

Speaking of sanitation, I must utter a word of protest against the idea which prevails that the Indian crowd is dirty in its habits. The other day, when it was announced that as a protest against the partition of Bengal, large crowds of Bengalis bathed in the River Hughli, it was said to me by a facetious English friend: "A very good thing, too, if it made them wash for once in their lives." This is based on a misapprehension. You cannot apply the opprobrious term of the "great unwashed" to the Indian proletariat. On the contrary, bathing is almost overdone. In person, the Indian is as clean as any one in the world. His immediate surroundings, also, he tries to keep as clean as possible. But ideas of co-operative sanitation—that is to say, sanitation as applied in concert to a large mass of people or to a large area, such as a village or a town—are not sufficiently understood. Cleanliness becomes so much a matter of religion and ceremonial, that it is apt to be forgotten that there are other sanitary demands in life than merely keeping the person and the house clean. There is much in the proverbial philosophy of the people, which urges the protection of wells from pollution, but the methods recommended are those of excluding certain kinds of people, and not those of an earnest co-operation of all for the common good. Sanitation is one of the most useful departments of activity to which Government energy can be directed.

Village life in India is far more familiar to the thousands of Englishmen who go out to administer the country than town life. There is no mystery about it. Every one lives in the open; every one talks in the open; every one sleeps in the open. The only thing about which there is any mystery or any privacy is the eating of food, but even that is due more to ideas of cleanliness and of caste than anything else. The idea about the "mystery of the East," about there being huge cavernous depths of feelings and thoughts over which the English ideas merely float like foam, is fostered by many admirable novels, but certainly does not grow on an intimate acquaintance with village life. Every civil official in the cold weather goes round camping through his district, and the opportunities he gets of intercourse with the villagers tends to produce a feeling of mutual sympathy and understanding, which is one of the most valuable features of Indian administration.

There are people who hate the mere sight of an Indian town, but take them to the simple life of the villagers, and the first glimpse will convert them. If they camp out in the orthodox Indian fashion, with a canvas tent merely to give them shelter when necessary, while passing their whole time as far as possible in the open air, they will get into touch with the whisperings of Nature, which are the first teachings of art and poetry. They will then get into sympathy with the homely villager, who uses his hut or house merely as a shelter, but not as a home, whose roof is, in fact, the vaulted blue above, and whose carpet is the spacious plains below. If they wander a little among the cattle or the wild animals, the children or the birds, they will see the intimate ties that exist between man and Nature in these mud-built villages, and perhaps understand, better than pages of the most beautiful poetry can explain, the reason why villagers object to a peacock being shot in the interests of sport, or to a diseased animal in his last stages being given his quietus in the interests of that more subtle humanity which is beyond their grasp. If they think life under the circumstances is humdrum and wanting in the exhilaration which every aspiring life has a right to expect, let them lose their way by night and find it again by the kindly help of the shining stars above or the flickering lights of the camp fires, which, penetrating through a crisp and clear atmosphere, bring a homelier but no less beautiful message to the heart that understands. The simple habits of quiet, unostentatious hospitality in times of plenty, and of infinite patience in times of suffering or in a time of famine, the tender domestic affections among these people, the feeling that each person has his own place and mission in life, from the sweeper to the Lambardár, evoke a feeling of restful sympathy which is especially welcome to the emigrants from a life of hurry, of luxury, of clubs, of amusements, of bridge, and of general heartlessness, which seems to make up the sum of existence in more advanced countries. The description of the Chaldean shepherds in Wordsworth's *Excursion* applies with peculiar force to the Indian agriculturist:—

> "Chaldean shepherds, ranging trackless fields,
> Beneath the concave of unclouded skies,
> Spread like a sea in boundless solitude."

As about sixty-five per cent. of the whole Indian population live on agriculture, and a much larger proportion live in the villages, it will be readily understood that village life forms a most important factor in the social economy of the country. The old-world spirit of aloofness which some people ascribe to the Indian village exists only in the imagination of those who generalise from imperfect knowledge. It is true that the home-loving ryot would agree with the lines:—

> "Blest is the man whose wish and care
> A few paternal acres bound;
> Content to breathe his native air
> In his own ground."

But that spirit does not prevent the easy and dignified reception of strangers. It, indeed, promotes the social code in accordance with which distinguished men from other villages are invited and welcomed, and a pleasant intercourse goes on between the different villages. In fact, if there is any social life in India, it is in the villages and not in the towns. Again, in villages which have retained their solidarity, public opinion is not only stronger than in towns, but is healthier and saner, as being built on the hard actualities of life. Unfortunately, it is too restricted in its scope; and having no organised and recognised means of public expression, it lacks the opportunity of being heard. The weakening of the authority of the Lambardár or headman is unfortunate. All measures for rehabilitating his position will be welcomed by those who have understood the many disintegrating factors that operate in village life. The trend of recent land revenue legislation has been to improve his worldly position by a statutory recognition of his remuneration for the collection of land revenue. The permission to wear a sword, in exemption from the Arms Act, adds to the dignity of his status. All these appear to be little matters to outsiders, but they are most important for the well-ordered government of a village.

The structure of rural society has generally rested on authority, while towns of healthy growth have generally identified themselves with new ideas and a spirit of restless independence. A happy balance between these two tendencies is necessary for the well-being of society, and this balance is in danger of being upset by an invasion of disruptive ideas. It must not be supposed that Indian villages are impervious to modern tendencies, or that the siren voice of the towns will always call to them in vain. The question to which all who are interested in the welfare of the country have to address themselves is of a different nature. Will the twentieth century spirit completely destroy village institutions, or will they, under the stress of modern conditions, evolve themselves to some form different from its historic type, but not alien to the habits and ideals of the people?

Destruction is impossible. The village has stood many a shock in history from the most ancient times, and to-day, in spite of its conservatism, it shows itself as freely open to conviction on questions of material and moral advantages as can be expected from people who think slowly and act deliberately. Some years ago it was the fashion to look upon the simple methods of village agriculture as stupid. It was said that the plough simply made a scratch in the soil, and for scientific agriculture deeper ploughing would be necessary. But scientific experiments have proved what such men as Dr Voelcker have contended all along: that the methods pursued in the Indian village are the best, most economical, and most efficient under the conditions under which the Indian ryot has to work. The object in India is not so much to drain the soil of unnecessary moisture, as to retain such moisture as there is in the ground; and for this reason shallow ploughing is far more reasonable than deep ploughing, although, of course, local circumstances may qualify this proposition. On the other hand, the old sugar-cane press, which was universally used in the Indian villages, has practically been supplanted by the new iron press. This complete revolution has taken place within ten or fifteen years. The reason was that economically the new press was sound. It gave more juice; it worked more expeditiously; and, in the long run, the cost of the production of sugar was reduced by its use. There was absolutely no difficulty in the way of the "stupid Ryots" adopting it wholesale.

This shows that their supposed conservatism and opposition to change are myths as much as their supposed exclusiveness.

It was supposed at one time that the Indian village system was an archaic system, and that it showed in its primitive structure a stage of human development which the Indo-European nations had left far behind. This was pointed out as an argument that the Indian village had remained absolutely unchanged from the most distant antiquity. This was the idea under which Sir Henry Maine worked. But later researches by Baden-Powell have proved that this was a mistake. The Indian village is no more the survival of some absolutely archaic form than is the present day manor of English law the evidence of an unchanged archaism in English rural life. Its historical affinity with the German "Mark" is probably a myth, fostered by an imperfect knowledge of both systems. The fact is that there is a type of village that existed in India, even before the Aryan invasion. When the Aryans came, they adopted the agricultural economy of the country, making such changes as were necessary for their altered circumstances. Their tribal organisation in a conquered country was devoted to the cultivation of the martial spirit which had established them. Their intellectual energies were absorbed by poetry, philosophy, and speculation. Agriculture they left to the subject races. But it underwent a change with the change in the times. We can prove that village life in the time of the brilliant Sanskrit writers who are called the nine gems of the Court of Ujjain, was very different from village life in later Hindu times. When the Muhammadans came on the scene there was further change or development in sympathy with the new political conditions established. With the establishment of the British Government further changes have taken place, and new forms and problems have arisen in village life which have led to further advances. We can trace the continuous growth of modern from ancient forms, and within the last few years there has been a complete remodelling of many of the old village customs and institutions, which have got stereotyped in the imagination of persons who have made the "unchanging East" their fetish. Only, these changes have taken place gradually, and have been in the direction of a continuous adaptation to new conditions.

Throughout the political history of India the central power never interfered—and even now it interferes little—with village life. And therefore there are not found in village history those striking revolutions in thoughts, methods, ideas, and institutions, which we meet with in the history of town life. But progress there undoubtedly has been. There can be no doubt that the village of 1800 is as obsolete now in India as the feudal system is in England. The fact that many of the older forms still influence village ideas, legal administration, and even legislation, shows nothing more than the fact that traces of feudalism survive in the land law of England, and have constantly to be eliminated to bring the modern English village into touch with the larger life which pulsates through the nation. This process of elimination is going on in the Indian village too, consciously or unconsciously, and in different forms. Let us hope that the *pax Britannica*, while it has broken village solidarity, will open up ideas of unity and co-operation on an enlarged scale. Let us hope that the frank understanding between the people and the governing classes which undoubtedly exists in the villages, will, in the fulness of time, lead to a better understanding of the people as a whole, welded into a form of polity in which they will understand, influence, and elevate public life.

III

THE LEISURED CLASSES

"Studious he sate, with all his books around,
Sinking from thought to thought, a vast profound—
Plunged for his sense, but found no bottom there,
Then writ, and floundered on in mere despair."

—POPE : *Dunciad.*

"'Tis not enough to mount and ride,
No saddle, bridle, whip, nor spur;
To take the chance of time and tide,
And follow fame without demur.

I want some reason with my rhyme,
A fateful purpose when I ride;
I want to tame the steeds of Time,
To harness and command the tide.

I want a whip whose braided lash
Can echo like the crack of doom;
I want an iron mace to smash
The world and give the peoples room."

—JOHN DAVIDSON.

F

THE LEISURED CLASSES

WHO is the man of leisure? It is the man who is free to lay out his time as he likes. He may, like the King of Yvetôt, rise late and go to bed with the sun, and sleep too soundly to dream of glory. Or he may be subject to "that last infirmity of noble minds, to scorn delight and live laborious days." He may be a man always in a hurry, with his "social" distractions—fashionable calls, parties, receptions, cards, and dinners. Or he may be the steady, sober man of action—with concentrated purpose and unjaded energies—who never inveighs against Time because Time is his best friend. If only he has the freedom to act, can choose his own method, and bide his own opportunity, he may be counted as a man of leisure. Coming to a lower plane, he may be a man fulfilling the destinies of his class and following the dictates of the customary code around him. So long as his whole time is not given over to the pursuit of the elementary means of livelihood, he is a man of leisure.

All these are individual temperaments. But every organised community consists of certain classes who have more leisure than others for the cultivation of these temperaments. The toiling masses have usually no leisure at all. If they have any, it is only in the more advanced communities. The highest aim of philosophic socialism is to secure a more equitable distribution of leisure rather than of wealth. But taking things as they are, it is upon the use made of their leisure by the leisured classes that the noblest impulses of a nation depend. It will therefore be useful to examine some of the features of the life of the leisured classes in India. The individuals comprising them are very few in number, but their influence on the social structure, whether for good or for evil, is incalculable.

The first class I am going to speak about is that of the territorial magnates, the ruling princes, the Rajas, Maharajas, and Nawabs. They form an aristocracy quite different from the aristocracy of any other country. Their patents of nobility have different sources, one from the other. Their castes, tribes, and social spheres are different. They are not all governed by the same customs, nor are they the products of the same conditions; and the history behind them is different in each case. But they are all united, in modern India, by the common bond of political sympathy. They are all staunch and loyal feudatories of the British Crown. The flag unites them; the empire that guarantees to them their territory and their titles, brings them into relations one with another. The personality of the Sovereign furnishes them with that human element of loyalty which is the best of all political sentiments, better than a sense of security, or an expectation of favours to come.

The type varies from that of a petty chieftain whose rule is as of yesterday to that of the Rajput Rana of Udaipur, who claims descent from the Sun and has never bowed the knee to the conqueror in all the chequered history of mediæval India. The Rana belongs to the noblest of the Rajput clans, and in one sense may be considered the head of the whole of the Rajput confederacy. His territory is in the sandy deserts of Rajputana, but firmer than the rock which lies beneath that sand is the devotion of his kinsmen and his people. No softness will you find under the shadow of his royal umbrella. His people are hardy and rugged, but true as steel. If we may judge from their past history, and from the songs of the bards that delight them most, they will be ready, match-lock in hand, to face gunpowder and quick-firers for the honour of their clan. Warriors and chieftains are all animated with the most lively spirit of chivalry and daring, which does credit to their ruling House. Civil government in such conditions is mostly a matter of personal rule. The place of law is taken by loyalty and a corporate conscience. There is very little red tape. There are no social strata. The ruling prince himself is only the first among equals in his relations to the noblemen of his court. Each of these noblemen again forms a social or feudal centre, in which he himself occupies a similar position to those immediately below him that his ruling prince occupies to those like himself and his class. The dignity of a prince is fully secured on all ceremonial occasions, but in private life every one has free access to the palace.

Noble birth, or, indeed, membership of the clan (for they hold to the American maxim "We are all noble") gives the title to a man to be heard, and he is freely heard in all the counsels of the State. As representing the British Government, the Resident or Political Agent finds his work the easiest among such people. His suggestions are given and accepted in the right spirit, and if there are occasional differences, as there must be, there is no difficulty in settling them in a sportsmanlike spirit of give-and-take in a personal interview, perhaps after a polo match or a review of Imperial Service troops.

As another type of the old-fashioned State, may be mentioned the small Muhammadan principality of Palanpur. The ruler bears the hereditary titles of "Diwan" and "Zubdat-ul-Mulk," both of which recall passages in the stirring history of the family. Their ancestor was an Afghan of the Lohani tribe, and distinguished himself in Behar in the reign of Humayun. Akbar bestowed the government of Lahore and the title of "Diwan"; Aurangzeb gave a large slice of territory in Gujerat, which

Portrait by] [SAIYID SHARFUDDIN.

ZUBDAT-UL-MULK, H.H. DIWAN SIR SHER MUHAMMAD KHAN, G.C.I.E.

"He knows his villages personally, as a shepherd knows his flock, and he knows his hills and forests as a sportsman knows his game"—p. 87.

To face p. 87.]

has since been somewhat restricted in the north in the vicissitudes of warfare with the Rajput clans. The majority of the population consists of Hindus, but the relations of the chief to his subjects are entirely patriarchal.

The present chief, Sir Sher Muhammad Khan, is a good type of the Muhammadan nobleman, and has ruled his little state for eight-and-twenty years. He knows his villages personally, as a shepherd knows his flock, and he knows his hills and forests as a sportsman knows his game. He is a man of wide reading in Persian and Urdu, and a poet himself. Though the family is strictly Moslem and the Saiyids are held in the highest esteem, the law of succession in the State is that of primogeniture. The heir has been trained in the Imperial Cadet Corps. The chief's time is spent in placid domesticity, or in the pursuits and pleasures of a country gentleman and a genial host, when famine or plague does not claim his attention for more sombre duties.

These are not the only types of the Native State, nor are these types even largely represented numerically. But they are the types that get hold of the imagination, and fasten on the memory for their old-world associations and romantic history. Such types merge by slow gradations into what we might call the intermediate stage, between the old world and the new. This stage is represented by a somewhat more complex state, with territory in which a certain amount of industrial development has taken place. The interests of the people are not purely martial, but partly agricultural and partly also industrial. Where this is the case there are more forms and formalities at Court, but there is still an easy bearing, and the simple manners of a people free from the cautiousness of commercialism. They show the usual hospitality to strangers. Their rule of social life is theoretical equality among all members of the sept or clan. In a state like Bikanir, where the camel-hair industry has been developed to a fine art and agriculture flourishes, the code of government includes a rough-and-ready set of rules, determining the rights of the sovereign in relation to his subjects, and of the subjects among themselves. There are agricultural or revenue settlements, but they have neither the complexity nor the exactitude of the British system, and the Government revenue taken from the agriculturists is more elastic. The State demand is more in times of prosperity than in times of adversity. Such agricultural calamities as hail, frost, or drought are generally followed, as a matter of course and without any long formalities, by a well-understood and automatic lowering of the scale of demand, or by an entire omission to collect the Government revenue. On the other hand, there is less fixity of tenure in theory, and the Government due is liable to revision from year to year. The immediate cultivators of the soil are more directly in touch with the State, and that growing middle class, with some affluence and influence, which is a marked feature of British administration, is entirely wanting. The ruler has his clansmen and his relatives. The people with any claim to position are connected with the land. The merchant class are not of much consequence. The artisans have their own separate life. The beautiful arts are practised without much competition, and freely patronised by the Court. Instinct and heredity take the place of technical schools.

The most complex type of state is such a one as that of Baroda, or Mysore, or Hyderabad. Here you have a large territory in contact with some of the most fertile and most populated portions of British territory. The problems here presented are of the most complicated character. In Mysore there is an enormous mining industry, and also a large number of European planters, who produce coffee. The mining industry carries in its train the installation of electric works, and the utilisation of natural forces such as the Cauvery waterfalls. The social problems of the mass of the people have also received a great deal of attention in the progressive administration of these states. In Baroda there is an act to deal with the early marriage question. In Mysore there is a representative assembly which is consulted periodically, and before whom a record of work is laid for information. The members are permitted to ask questions and make suggestions on the points in which they are interested.

Hyderabad is a unique centre of literature and social activity among the Muhammadans. Many of the most brilliant lights of Hindustani literature find a home and a centre of encouragement in the Nizam's Court. The industries, too, are being slowly developed, and the efficiency of the Imperial Service Corps is one of the objects claiming the Nizam's personal attention. This corps was organised in Lord Dufferin's viceroyalty. The Panj-Deh incident evoked an outburst of patriotism in the Native States, and they voluntarily asked the Paramount Power to allow them to be associated with the defence of the country. Hitherto their armies had consisted of unwieldy groups of retainers, armed with picturesque but obsolete weapons. The new idea was to have in every state which desired it the nucleus of a highly organised and efficient modern force, small indeed—much smaller than many of the chiefs would have wished—but able to give an excellent account of itself, both as regards its *personnel* and *matériel*, its organisation, equipment, uniforms, and weapons. This idea took root and grew, and has borne abundant fruit in twenty years, under the fostering influence of successive viceroys.

All the feudatory princes of India hold their thrones under treaties into which their predecessors entered. In the eyes of the law the more important of them are independent sovereigns in subsidiary alliance with His Britannic Majesty, and bound by the engagements entered into at different times in their history. They are free to try any experiments in social or domestic legislation, but they owe it both to themselves and the British Government, which guarantees their power and relieves them of the burden of maintaining a large army to repel external aggression, that there should be a feeling of tact, harmony, and mutual trust, in the broad lines of their policy as settled in consultation with the Paramount Power, which affords them friendly counsel and a practical example. The cordiality with which they are received and visited by the Sovereign's representative depends, not upon their personal habits or prejudices, but upon the degree to which they show themselves ready to become co-operating units in the great Empire of which they form such worthy ornaments and pillars. Their feelings of loyalty and devotion have been exemplified on many occasions. Ceremonial occasions, such as those of the Delhi Durbar and the Coronation of His Gracious Majesty King Edward VII., have found them vying with each other—almost beyond their financial resources—in adding lustre to the pomp and splendour which symbolise power and dominion. Their splendid equipages and noble bearing have been applauded by crowds which knew nothing of the generous enthusiasms which lurk beneath their calm exteriors. In times of great stress, such as the South African War, and the operations of the Allies in China, they freely came forward with help in the matter of transports, hospital ships, and ambulance appliances, while many of them were ready to go personally and serve with their swords in defence of the Empire with which their destinies are so closely connected.

It has been suggested that they should be invited to join the Privy Council in England, or to sit in the House of Lords, under some scheme by which the Indian Empire will be represented by her own sons. The main difficulty lies in the fact that their administrations are distinct from the administrations of the Indian Provinces, and their advice would naturally be more valuable in the matter of those wider Imperial problems with which the Privy Council usually does not deal, and which in the House of Lords are generally merged in the party politics of the Empire. In questions connected with the policy of the government of India in India, it would be invidious to ask their advice, as the internal administration of the British provinces does not directly concern them, but their aid has often been asked, and their advice freely given, on matters closely connected with their own order and class, such as the organisation and government of the chiefs' colleges, and the determination of the ceremonial and precedence which have to be observed on important State occasions. Their association, however, in more serious affairs than questions of ceremonial would doubtless do much to cement the bonds of our world-wide Empire.

The status and dignity of these feudatories were expressed so happily by Lord Curzon in his farewell address to the chiefs assembled at Indore, that I will take the liberty of quoting his words:[1]

> "Long may they continue to hold their great positions, secure in the affections of their own subjects, and assured of the support of the Paramount Power. May they present to the world the unique spectacle of a congeries of principalities, raised on ancient foundations, and cherishing the traditions of a famous past, but imbued with the spirit of all that is best and most progressive in the modern world, recognising that duty is not an invention of the schoolmaster but the law of life, and united in defence of a throne which has guaranteed their stability and is strong in their allegiance."

The next class for consideration is that of the great land-holders, men who have titles scarcely distinguishable from those of the ruling chiefs, but who, nevertheless, exercise no ruling powers. They merely hold land in the same way as English noblemen hold their estates. They have the titles of Rajas, Maharajas, and Nawabs; and some of them—for example, the Maharaja of Benares—are entitled to be addressed as "His

[1] "Lord Curzon in India," by Sir Thomas Raleigh, p. 241.

Highness." They take principal parts in ceremonials on State occasions, but have no power of life or death on their own estates, and they do not have any work of government administration properly so called. The important work of estate management, however, is dignified enough to give full scope to their organising talents. They control very large establishments of bailiffs and managers. The selection of tenants, the provision of suitable holdings for them, the grant of a fairly fixed title of occupancy in the land, and the determination of questions of rent, are subjects which, if properly attended to, are quite enough to occupy the whole of the time of the most leisured land-holder in existence. I know of a young and promising Maharaja land-holder, who is occupied for weeks together with the work of seeing that the leases are properly renewed to his tenants. These gentlemen form the aristocracy of British India. Nominally without any legal power, in reality they wield a vast amount of social influence. They can make or mar the lives of thousands of people who live and work on their estates, and the agricultural prosperity of the whole country depends on whether they are enlightened or are pursuing a selfish policy.

There are many of these great landed proprietors in Bengal, but they seem to be concentrated in the part of the country known as Oudh. This has been called the "Land of Barons," because the Taluqdars form a compact body, and both by history and tradition, are capable of acting together and assisting the general administration of the country. By their good sense and direct contact with the agricultural population, as well as their conservative instincts, they are marked out to be the pillars of the State, and useful auxiliaries to all movements that make for peace and order. Selected individuals among them are vested with magisterial powers, which they exercise to the relief of the overburdened stipendiary magistrates, and for the benefit of their own people. In many cases the quarrels of the rural population are simple in the extreme, and instead of fighting them out in the heated atmosphere of a court, with two sets of lawyers exercising their wits in a legal combat, the tenantry do far better to settle them in the unruffled atmosphere which surrounds their own landlord. He holds his head secure from the whirlwinds which vex the lower strata of the social air. He may be able to quietly suggest some means of compromise which may be accepted, thus doing an amount of good which cannot be measured by words.

The life of these landlords is made up of the usual routine of estate management, combined with such magisterial work as they have, and such ornamental work as falls to them in the *levées* and durbars organised by the ruling power. Some of them are fond of travelling, and undertake journeys through different parts of India, and occasionally to England, thus enlarging their own ideas and fitting them for a larger part in the work of raising the tone of their own people. Many of them are honoured members of the Legislative Councils, and they exercise their privileges and perform their duties in a manner which has won the highest commendation from their colleagues. The sons of many of them are being brought up in the "new light," that is, the more strenuous ideals of the West, which are associated with English civilisation. Many of them send their sons to be educated in the chiefs' or noblemen's colleges, which are unique institutions provided for their special class. These will be described when we come to speak of student life.

We now come to the men of the old learning, a class which is more truly the leisured class of India than any other. They are, among the Muhammadans, the Kazis and Maulvis, and among the Hindus, the Pandits and Upadhyas. These men live as book-worms, but their learning has very little market value, although the reverence attached to old traditions is so great that many people become their pupils, and at least nominally try to conform to the precepts they give. The precepts are generally impossible for any everyday mortal. They are either too formal, or "too good for human nature's daily food." If a very orthodox Pandit tell his pupils not to drink water from the waterworks made by the municipality, because the pipes are contaminated by the touch of people not of his caste, the advice is absurd, and cannot be carried out by any dwellers in the cities. The answer given to that by the book-worm, who holds to a creed outworn, would be, "So much the worse for the dwellers in the city." These fossils of an antique civilisation generally take refuge in some out-of-the-way place. They dream away their lives in extracting omens from an impossible system of astrology, to find out the precise moment when their learning and their prayers will bear fruit, little suspecting that the sad, sad answer has already been pronounced by the weird and wise Raven of Edgar Allan Poe—"*Never more!*" They waste days and nights of deep study and silent meditation in trying to discover the hidden meaning of old-world texts, plain and sound enough in their day, but now overlaid by the rust of ages, which it takes longer to remove than to construct a new system.

The kind of pupils they get tend to become fanatics—not the sort of fanatics that would use force in disseminating their doctrines or in fighting with their opponents, but the mental fanatics, who refuse to see any other side of the question than their own. As the more progressive sections of the population get more and more aloof from these people, they become the teachers of the very poorest and hungriest classes. Their pupils, after acquiring distinctions and diplomas not recognised in the practical world, find very little encouragement with the large outside public. This leads to great discontent and galling bitterness, not only against the men who fail to appreciate them, but with the social and political institutions actually existing in the country. It also leads to a mental and moral pessimism darker than that of Schopenhauer, and more despairing than that of Max Nordau. In the teachers there is a high-bred courtesy and an undercurrent of tolerance for a flood which they cannot stem. But in their disciples the stream of ideas tends to acquire a corrosive poison from the fact that they have no experience of life, and exaggerate tenfold the mysticism and introspection of a detached existence.

Their mental faculties get blunted by not having the advantage of being sharpened by actual facts or by contact with human life. Their astronomy is old-world, and based on the Ptolemaic system. They believe that when the sun or the moon is in eclipse it is due to two terrible demons who want to swallow up these luminaries, and it is necessary to make large gifts to Brahmans or beggars, to offer up lengthy prayers, and perform repeated ablutions, before the threatened calamity can be warded off. The science of medicine is with them divorced from the art of surgery, which is treated as simply the art of the barber. The science of chemistry is left to the dyer to study, or rather to learn by rule of thumb practice. Theoretically, they write pages of books dealing with the sciences, but they never have any apparatus to enable them to perform experiments to test their theories or even to understand them in all their bearings.

Poverty has spread its pall over them. They live in close, musty, badly-lighted rooms. Their books are very old manuscripts, which would be of priceless value in a Western library; but here they are handled and thumbed with the carelessness born of common use, and they are frequently eaten by worms, or destroyed by fire. When such a man dies, the fate of his books and papers is truly pathetic. His disciples are no longer with him, because they have been scattered all over the country, in search of their own means of livelihood. They are rarely men with families; but if they are, the go-ahead members have already gone into the large material whirlpool for which they have such utter contempt, and the backward ones among them have failed to reach *their* standard of learning, or *their* devotion to an ideal inherited as an heirloom of antiquity, before it was thrown out of fashion by an age of shallow sentimentalism and self-advertising show. The ladies of the family are generally uneducated, although they may be literate. Cases have been known in which a box laden with precious manuscripts and papers has been allowed to lie in a damp, mouldy room, until all its contents were practically destroyed. In some cases the books are sold at the price of waste paper, and thus that link of continuity which connects their learning with olden times is broken. It is sad to reflect that worms should be the only eager heirs to the old learning!

Can nothing be done for this class? Their character is generally weak but venerable, wanting in stamina, but full of idealism; and their actions, although they savour of pedantry, often appeal to the imagination. Their services used to be utilised not long ago in the educational institutions of the country, but they are being ousted and replaced by men who are more adaptable to new conditions, and who, if an hour is fixed for a lecture, would not hesitate to come punctually, merely because the astrological signs were unfavourable. The good that is in them can only be drawn out by giving them such responsibility as they can sustain, and helping them out of their abject poverty. They can earn their bread by no other means than their out-of-date learning, and the respect in which they are held is not sufficient to keep the wolf from the door. It is difficult to see how they can be made to fit into the scheme of modern life. They have been tried as sub-registrars of documents, but even there they have failed on account of unbusiness-like habits and the temptations engendered by a comfortable position, without the stamina that would keep them from taking advantage of the illiterate people they have to deal with.

Perhaps their appointment as celebrants and registrars of marriages might do something towards giving them a self-respecting and a fairly comfortable position during the last flicker of their existence as a separate class. It must be understood that whereas the registration of births and deaths is carried out by the civil agency, the registration of marriages is only carried out in the case of Christian marriages, or marriages celebrated in what would be called registrar's offices in England. These represent a microscopic minority for the huge population of 294,000,000 who inhabit India. Practically, we may say that all Hindu and Muhammadan marriages are ecclesiastical marriages, and, as far as the State is concerned, are not registered at all. Unofficially the priests (the Muhammadan Maulvi or Kazi who celebrates the marriage may be called by that name for convenience), no doubt, keep a note of these; but such notes are not systematically kept, and precisely in those cases where litigation arises and disputes take place, a great opportunity is offered for forgeries. In a large number of cases, however, even these unsatisfactory notes are not available, and oral evidence is all that can be adduced by either party. The priests have no official status, and in many cases are poor, struggling men, and scarcely distinguishable from loafers.

What I think can be done is that every district should be partitioned into circles, for each of which there should be an officially recognised Brahman registrar of marriages for Hindus, and an officially recognised Muhammadan registrar of marriages for the Muhammadans. In many cases two for each circle would be sufficient, but, as there are legal divergences of custom, and it is possible that some sections of the population may not acknowledge the validity of either of these two authorities, it should be provided that on due cause being shown, a separate registrar might be appointed at the discretion of the District Magistrate for any section of the people whose case is not met by either of the two registrars. But the number must be limited as far as possible. The men selected would be men of some education and character, and for misconduct they could be dismissed. The Muhammadans would, as far as possible, be selected from old Kazi families, and the Hindus from Pandit families. Their income would consist of a small compulsory registration fee, with such optional fees as are customary for celebrating ecclesiastical marriages. For the celebration of ecclesiastical marriages, option would have to be allowed to the parties to have recourse to whomsoever they like, but in the majority of cases, if there is an officially recognised registrar, the two functions would, if proper care were exercised in the selection of men, be performed by the same man. The registers could be moved, according to prescribed rules, at periodical intervals, into the Chief Registrar's (Judge's) offices of the different districts. Some sort of order would then be evolved out of that complete chaos which surrounds a case now when a birthday, a marriage, or a divorce comes into dispute in a civil court.

We may now consider the leisured merchant class, who have made their pile by a life of hard commercial activity, and have retired to a life of ease and dignity. They have not the interest of the ruling chiefs or the aristocracy in estate administration or in field sports. They have not been disciplined in habits of learning, and brought up in the reverence for books, which fill up so large a part of the thoughts and lives of what we have called the men of the old learning. Their life from a social aspect generally shows a great void. They are not often men of culture, excepting those in the Presidency towns, and their hobbies or interests it would be difficult indeed to describe. A general inertia takes hold of them, and they pass their hours in inglorious ease. It would be a veritable Godsend if some means could be devised for interesting them, and at the same time advancing the welfare of the community. If they have children, they no doubt feel a justifiable pride in seeing them lifted up to the best positions to which they can attain, but in many cases that interest fails them. In any case, their minds are so uncultured that they can find little rational enjoyment from such occupations as presiding at functions, or holding social gatherings, or attending or getting up popular lectures. Their purse is open, but they do not know when and how to open it to works of popular philanthropy. Sometimes on account of ignorance of social conditions their charity is wasted on barren soil. Sometimes advantage is taken of them, if, indeed, the process to which they are subjected should not be called blackmail. In any case, they are not able to put their own personality into the scheme they wish to aid, and the gift without the giver may be charity, but it is not philanthropy. There are no theatres to which they could go for amusement which would show them the mirror of life, as it is lived with its chequered lights and shades. They cannot travel much, because their physical energies are spent by the time they arrive at mature age. The climate, too, has undermined their constitutions. It has often struck me that if Cicero's ideas in his essay on old age were adapted for their special behoof, they might find a great deal to amuse themselves with, in spite of their general languor. If little schemes of public amelioration which they could grasp, and over which they could grow enthusiastic, were started, not requiring too much in the way of brains, but capable of utilising their matured experience of business, they could fitly take part with those who help to move the wheel of the social machinery. It would be a very good thing if there were unions of school children looked after by such men, and they were expected and encouraged to provide them with the expenses of little treats in neighbouring villages or towns, and altogether to take a fatherly interest in the rising generation.

The retired lawyers fill a very large place among the useful and active members of the leisured classes. The law is the one profession in which the highest distinctions are accessible to the humblest man and to the large class of mediocre celebrities from town and country. To such men, who have fought their legal battles, but not attained to the rare and coveted dignity of a High Court Judgeship, there are still many avenues of public and private usefulness within reach. Many of them become Honorary Magistrates, and serve as members of Municipal and District Boards. Some of them take part in all the gatherings which are organised in their towns of a public or semi-public nature. They wield a ready pen and a facile tongue, and command a graceful oratory, which can not only move the hearts of men, but also untie their purse strings. To any organisation of a public nature their help is invaluable. They show tenacity of purpose and independence of judgment, and yet none can be readier in appreciating "the case for the other side," as their whole experience is built on the art of seeing (and covering) the weakness of their own side. Their resource and shrewdness give life and spirit to new social movements. Is it a subscription being raised for a local famine, or a campaign being organised for the distribution of free quinine among the poor, in a malarious and fever-stricken district? Are fireworks and illuminations to be displayed on an occasion like the King's birthday? Is a new library to be opened, or systematic plague preventive measures to be adopted? At such times the retired lawyer is to the fore with his bustle and energy, which are at least as useful as the money which is largely contributed by the silent members of the community.

In plague and sanitary administration, and indeed in any administrative campaign, even if directed against the criminal classes, our chief difficulty in dealing with the mass of the people and ensuring their co-operation, is their ignorance and suspicion of the motives of Government. Now a lawyer understands these, or can be made to understand them; and if his sympathies are enlisted by the right kind of personal treatment, he is a most valuable auxiliary. The man in actual practice will not run counter to popular prejudices, because he is afraid of a falling away in the number of his clients. But the retired lawyer comes forward readily — if he is approached in the proper spirit.

The question has often been raised as to the

measure of culture to be found among the higher classes in India. Different opinions have been held on the subject. It is contended, on the one side, that true culture has almost vanished from a land which boasted at one time of a splendid chivalry and a nobility of the highest refinement. It is pointed out that there has been no Montaigne and no Abul Fazl in the India of the last two centuries. The conditions of transition from one state of society to another, from one system of thought to another, from one type of civilisation to another, are pre-eminently suitable to the rise of great intellects such as those of Montaigne, or Bacon, or Montesquieu, but no universal intellect of that kind has appeared in recent years. On the other hand, it is asserted that the culture of the East has permeated through all the grades of society, and that, man for man, the individual of the humblest classes in India is far more refined in his habits, manners, and ideas than an individual of a similar class in the West. The last statement is true. But the phenomenon equally prevails in such countries as Italy, where the traditions of civilisation reach back to earlier centuries than in Western Europe. Moreover, many of the classes in the humbler grades of society in India are only submerged representatives of the culture and distinction of a century or two ago. I have met a Chaukidár who traced his ancestry from the once ruling family of Oudh, and who had a seal and documents in his possession which proved his claim beyond doubt. There are many clerks in Government offices, whose pedigree connects them with ministers and statesmen who played a leading part in the history of the seventeenth and eighteenth centuries. It is not uncommon to find among the literary classes those whose families were overwhelmed by the political revolutions of the eighteenth century, and who now earn a scanty pittance, where under more congenial conditions they would have shone by their pen and their intellect. They refuse to put themselves in line with the more progressive ideas, and they only find themselves superfluous in the times in which they live. Poverty or humble living does not necessarily show that an individual belongs to the lower classes in the sense in which the term might be used in this country.

On the other hand, the opportunities of true culture understood in its highest sense are rare in India. Culture, I take it, is the carrying out of religion, art, and poetry into social life. Neither leisure nor money can, by themselves, supply the means for that humanising culture, which is born of the clash of mind with mind, and the play of intellect upon the practical affairs of courts and princes or nations. Of reading there is a great deal, but the dry bones of book-learning require to be vivified by a living human intercourse free from ceremonial, yet carried forward on the wings of that Time Spirit, which breathes over society taken in large masses, and gives shape to the institutions and ideals that move the world.

There is a passage in Goethe's "Wilhelm Meister," which describes the difficulty of an aspiring soul in India, if we only substitute "India" for "Germany," "Indian" for "burgher," and "European" for "Nobleman."

> "I know not how it is in foreign countries, but in Germany a universal, and if I may say so, personal cultivation is beyond the reach of any one except a nobleman. A burgher may acquire merit; by excessive efforts, he may even educate his mind; but his personal qualities are lost, or worse than lost, let him struggle as he will. . . . Since in common life the nobleman is hampered by no limits—since kings or kinglike figures do not differ from him—he can everywhere advance with a silent consciousness, as if before his equals. Everywhere he is entitled to press forward, whereas nothing more beseems the burgher, than the quiet feeling of the limits that are drawn around him."

This represents Goethe's difficulties in raising himself to the state of intellectual culture to which he aspired. He surmounted them. The difficulties are the same or greater in India at the present day; but there is no doubt that master minds are, and will be, able to surmount any difficulties whatever. It is well, however, to recognise the obstacles that exist in judging a people or their culture.

The palace of knowledge (to use an Oriental trope) is mounted on the ladder of curiosity; the palace of culture is attained by steps in which all the climbers feel, on the one hand, a sense of equality with those climbing like them, though not quite up to their level, and, on the other hand, a sense of welcome from those who have climbed a little higher, but whom they might claim as kindred spirits. The aim of human culture is to refine the pleasures of life and strip them of all their grossness. The intellect is not the only instrument for that purpose. Character and social gifts all have their part to play; but the noblest instrument for the attainment of this aim is the society of cultured women. Until woman's sphere is drawn concentrically with man's; until the idea of love is ennobled through the magic light of poetry and chivalry, and marriage ceases to be an affair of convention, and becomes an affair of the heart; until then the salvation of the higher classes, or, indeed, of any of the classes in India, will be a mere chimera — a dream which will vanish with the shades of the night. It is only when these conditions have been fulfilled that we shall have learnt the art of living. The dream of beauty will then merge in the realisation of duty, and the use of leisure will be felt to be the opportunity it gives for a higher personal and social culture. Without such culture — not only personal, but social — we can but live vacillating and wasted lives, and should well deserve the following epitaph[1]:

> "He revelled under the moon,
> He slept beneath the sun,
> He lived a life of going-to-do,
> And died with nothing done."

[1] For the source of this prize epitaph, see *Calcutta Review*, No. 229, p. 196.

IV

STUDENT LIFE

"An ignorance of means may minister
To greatness, but an ignorance of aims
Makes it impossible to be great at all."
—E. B. Browning, *Casa Guidi Windows*, ii. 212-214.

"Tell him that when he is a man,
He must reverence the dreams of his youth."
—Posa's last message in Schiller's *Don Carlos*.

"The educational harvest will increase as years go on, and the healthiness of the nourishment it gives will depend on the careful administration and distribution of its products."

—Lord Minto to the Muhammadan Deputation
at Simla, 1st October 1906.

STUDENT LIFE

THE greatness of a people depends on the education, culture, training, and opportunities afforded to its children. Educational ideals, therefore, and the life in the school can be a matter of indifference to no one who seeks to examine the hidden forces of social life, or to influence the stream of a nation's history. In India the problem acquires extreme complexity from the fact that there is no educational uniformity in different parts of the country, or among different sections of the people. There are no ideals to work up to. There is not even a definite understanding as to what is to be aimed at. There is great confusion as to the relative places to be occupied by Western and Eastern culture. Schools scarcely ever tackle this problem, colleges usually degenerate into a machinery for the training of clerks and Government officials, and post-graduate study entirely falls into the background. What is worse is that culture in its highest sense does not even figure as an object to be aimed at. It is talked about by educationalists in high places; but if you examined a private in the vast army of teachers to whom the early training of youth is committed, you will find that it forms no part of either his practice, his experience, or his ideals.

Let us take a survey of the actual conditions existing, that we may understand the difficulties of the situation and the gaps which have yet to be filled before the educational machinery can be said to have become comprehensive and efficient. Let us begin at the bottom and take a peep at the village school. The building is of the simplest description. In some villages there is not even a separate building used exclusively for the school. The village headman's public apartments are used for the school by day. Many of the parents come and gossip with the teacher while the school is supposed to be going on. The school hours are supposed to begin at seven o'clock in the morning in the summer months, but it is rarely that the school is at its full strength till nine or ten. There are no clocks or time-pieces in the schools, or, indeed, in the village. Most of the boys, as well as their elders, get up at home like the lark with the sunrise. So does the teacher.

But there are a number of personal, religious, and social duties to be performed before either the one or the other is free for the mundane affairs of life. Some boys come quite early in the day (even before seven o'clock), and help the teacher in cooking his breakfast. There is no separate kitchen for this purpose in many

Atfer a Photo.] [*By* Mr S. Athim.

A VILLAGE SCHOOL.

Near the gate is the village Chaukidár (p. 49) in uniform.

To face p. 116.

schools. One corner of the room is set apart for the teacher's kitchen, and sometimes he smokes the walls of the whole room as brown as a smoker's favourite pipe. Sometimes the boys all come with a rush before he has finished his culinary duties. If the teacher happens to be a high-caste man, of course he cannot admit the pupils of lower castes into the room until he has not only finished his cooking, but also has done full justice to his frugal meal, composed of unleavened bread, rice, pulses, and vegetables. This morning meal is to serve him for the whole day. He, like everybody else in the village, has only two meals during the twenty-four hours, and therefore he cannot hurry over his breakfast-lunch. At the same time, it does not take him long. If he is not ready at the regular hour, the pupils all play about outside until he has finished. He then dresses himself in a garb becoming the needs of modern life—for it must be distinctly understood that the Hindu, while he is cooking or eating, must clothe himself as scantily as possible. It is a matter of personal cleanliness. Clothes are liable to get dirty, and therefore you must divest yourself of them as far as possible. The body, of course, has to be washed immediately before the meal, and can be washed cheaper and with less trouble than clothes. It is even suggested that this custom is due to a reversion to old habits, carrying us back to the times when the wearing of clothes was supposed to be a mark of disrespect to the gods of hearth and home.

Having donned his practical everyday garb, the teacher also dons his ordinary everyday look. From a cook who personally attends on himself, he now becomes the grave dominie who has to instil knowledge into the minds of the young. It is quite likely that he has no desk or table, but he has probably a cane stool on which he sits holding the elementary books from which he is supposed to teach. The children all come and sit on the floor. There may be long strips of gunny cloth spread out to keep them warm if the floor is cold. These are sometimes made by cutting up the bags from the shop of the nearest Banya, who, if his son attends the school, naturally makes a present of them. But let it not be supposed that it costs him a very large sum, for you can get four gunny bags for six-pence. The boys have all come with a book and a wooden board which serves for a slate. The wooden board is about a foot long and from 4 to 6 inches wide. At the top it has a little knob, which is perforated with a hole that carries a string. When the boy goes home, his slate, as we shall call it, is hung up by a nail, except when he wants to do his lessons. When he is ready to practise the art of penmanship it is taken down for him. He squats on the ground, puts the board between his knees, and begins to write on it. It is not a pen or a pencil he uses, but a sort of brush, and for ink he has a composition of diluted lime or chalk water. He dips his brush into this and begins to write on the black or dark surface of his board. The figures he produces are pure white when they dry up. After he has shown what he has written to his teacher, and heard the criticism or praise his teacher has to bestow, all the writing can be effaced by means of a damp cloth rubbed over the board. No sponge is used or carried, but the more stylish of the children carry a piece of cloth tied to the board, which can always be dipped in water and used for cleaning the board. The first thing the child learns in the village school is not the alphabet, but the numerals. The Indian child has a marvellous faculty for arithmetic. He may be said to have been born with the multiplication table up to ten in his head. What he learns at school is the multiplication table up to over a hundred. When he has learnt that, he can multiply 27 by 35 without any mental effort, simply by the elaborate tables he has learnt by rote. He also learns simple formulæ, which help him to calculate without the least difficulty the price of an article in seers and pice, given the wholesale price in maunds and rupees. In his second or third year the Hindu child knows more of rough and ready arithmetic than boys of a very advanced form in an English school.

The use of the memory is the great feature

of elementary education. The teacher pronounces an arithmetical formula in a sing-song way, and the boy is expected to follow him. When one such formula has been learned sufficiently, the boy is expected in a drawling voice to repeat and repeat it until he has got it thoroughly by rote. This process takes time. It lulls the waking intelligence to sleep by means of a lullaby, of which pupil, parent, and preceptor are equally proud. Usually a *pièce de resistance* is given by the teacher, and serves for the whole day's bill of fare for a particular child. The boy goes on repeating this in drawling tones, shaking his head and his whole body to the waist to and fro with increased energy, if he thinks he is drawing any one's attention. The more vigorous the shake the better is supposed to be the concentration of mind with which he is learning his lesson. The teacher passes on from boy to boy in this manner, until the whole class has got something to work with. This is the oral part of the lesson.

The writing is on the board that I have mentioned, and is practised more quietly. While the writing lesson is being performed you would think there were a set of juvenile artists all drawing elaborate figures, so great is the earnestness with which the eyes are directed to the writing-board, and the deliberation with which the pen-brush is moved. The picture of the teacher steadying the boy's hand without uttering a word, but using the wistful gaze which the boy directs into his eyes as a conduit pipe through which to pour into him something of his own knowledge and learning, would remind you of the famous picture of Swift and Stella, the Dean and his fair pupil, to whom a word is a sacrament and a smile a solemn offering to the goddess of learning. The teacher steadies his hand until it is able to take care of itself. Periodically the oral lessons are repeated *en masse*. The teacher says: "This is a day for revision, boys. You must repeat all together such-and-such a number of multiplication tables." The boys then all fall to, sitting in a row cross-legged. They begin to drawl out all the lessons which they have hitherto learnt. Louder and louder grows the noise, and more and more vigorous the shakings of the head and body all through, until the climax is reached, when the teacher himself joins in the closing bars of the drawl, to show that, the victory having been won, the general must lead them in person to the citadel.

When the time for reading lessons comes, the same mechanical method is followed. A simple story is read from the text book in drawling tones, until it impresses the boys and their simple parents at home (the drawl, not the story) with the idea that there is something grand, something truly noble and erudite, in this manipulation of the voice, as far removed from ordinary talk as possible. The reading goes on in a graduated course from the simple to the complex, but the question of spelling does not much trouble them. All the Hindu languages are written in an alphabet that is absolutely phonetic. You have only to know the sound to be able to write the word. The alphabet is the result of a long period of evolution. Grammarians have worked out the exact sound which each letter represents. All these sounds are classified, and the letters of the alphabet are grouped according to that classification. Hence you hear of labials, palatals, dentals, gutturals, and sibilants. The Muhammadan boys have a little more difficulty to contend with. They use the Arabic alphabet, which runs together the different letters when they are combined into words, in the manner of script or a running hand in Europe; but in Arabic the difficulty is that when the letters are combined they do not retain their whole shape intact. A letter may have one shape as an initial, another as a medial, and a third as a final. The learning of all these complexities takes some time, and six months or a year is sometimes spent in a Maktab school over the alphabet. But when these intricacies have been mastered, the pupil is in the proud position of knowing that he has not only mastered his alphabet, but has also learnt a system of shorthand, for with the Arabic alphabet written in a cursive hand you can write as fast as you speak.

The boys have not much life at school. They sometimes have their little jokes and get through a little mischief when no one is looking, but very little organised play goes on under the auspices of the village school. The *esprit de corps*, which looks upon the school as the rallying centre of juvenile life, is wanting. An attempt is being made to devote more attention to this aspect of education, and it is succeeding fairly well; but for thorough success it will be necessary to take the indigenous games and reduce them to such rules as will enhance their educational value. There are many such games. One consists in having a square of four lines with two lines running through the centre of the square, and cutting its sides into halves. This gives three parallel lines facing the invaders, and three parallel lines at right angles to them. The first three lines are each in the charge of a boy — this set of three boys forming the party in possession. The attacking party also consists of three boys, whose object is to get through the square. The defenders have both the right to run on their own lines, and also, under certain restrictions, on the cross lines, if necessary to prevent the attacking party from getting through. As there are an equal number on both sides, the game eventually resolves itself into a series of single contests in speed. The defenders are confined to their own lines, but the attackers may make any feints they choose, and on account of these feints and tricks a number of openings arise, which require some organisation on the part of both the attacking and the defending sides. As the front lines are captured, a more and more furious and organised struggle rages at the back lines, where the captain's post of honour and of danger is located. In our example we have supposed three lines and three players a side, but the number may be increased indefinitely. There is another indigenous game, which is exactly like hop-scotch, and another still, which may be called cricket in its most rudimentary shape. Drill has been introduced into the village schools, but the combination, smartness, alertness, and ease with which it ought to be carried out are rarely attained, and this is generally due to an imperfect appreciation on the part of teachers of what is required in drill.

Let us take a somewhat higher school — a town school. Here the building is of a superior order, and entirely devoted to the school. Instead of one teacher, there is a staff of teachers under a headmaster. The boys are expected to come punctually and leave punctually at stated hours, and altogether there is an air of business-like activity. The schools are formed more after the Western model, and the lessons are expected to be learnt in a way somewhat different from the ways of the village schools. What is lost in picturesqueness is gained in point of organisation. But some of the old habits acquired in village schools are not entirely got rid of, and you frequently see the reading aloud of lessons by all the pupils together, and the shaking of the head to and fro in the most approved village fashion. But you will notice a great difference in the teacher's attitude. He is no longer a benevolent man who calls his pupils "my children"—who now and again has a laugh with them or their parents—who thinks nothing of using the pupils' services for his own domestic affairs—who, moreover, being a part of the common life of the village, is sometimes seen in the pupils' homes, and in other and more homely relations than that of the schoolmaster to his pupils.

Instead of all this, the town teacher is a stone idol, without flesh and blood. The fibre of his composition is made up of four strands—viz., the Jack-in-office, the hungry place-seeker, the martinet, and the pedant, the whole tied together by a band of red tape, which he brought from the Normal School. The tentacles of officialdom hold him firmly in their grasp. The more highly placed he is, the more he thinks it his duty to keep himself aloof from pupils and parents, so as to keep up the "dignity" of the school. Not many opportunities of social intercourse occur between the teachers themselves. The head-master rarely calls them together, or speaks to them in a friendly, familiar way about their work, or advises them about their own reading. There is rarely a library attached to an ordinary town school. The libraries in the High Schools are scarcely worth the name, and in any case are little used. Many are the groans I have called forth by insisting on rummaging such libraries, and I daresay the only good I did was in clearing away the dust from their shelves. The boys scarcely read any novels or tales except those which may happen to come in in their school books.

They are beginning, however, to learn cricket and football, and other games in which the faculties of organisation and association are called forth. The beginnings of social life may also be seen growing in the town schools. If any of the boys come from villages at some distance, they live in what are called boarding-houses. It must be mentioned that, whether in a village or a town school, a distance of five miles or so would be considered quite insignificant. The smallest pupils would walk that distance from home and back every day, but in town schools some of the pupils come from a village, say thirty or forty miles distant, where they have already finished their elementary course. They must live in the town. If they have no relatives or friends with whom they can live, they go to the boarding-house attached to the school. Here they see something more of their resident fellow-pupils than they would do if they were day pupils.

But the name boarding-house is a complete misnomer. It calls up the idea of a place where the children are boarded together, and have a good social life during the hours that they do not spend at school. In reality it is nothing more nor less than a simple building with bare rooms, in which they live the primitive life they would live in the villages. The boys are generally expected to cook their own food and make all their living arrangements themselves. The only thing they get is shelter. As the Hindus all eat separately, and not at a common mess, even the pleasures of social dinners are impossible. A slight amount of supervision is exercised by one of the teachers, who is put in charge of the boarding-house as superintendent. But even this is purely nominal. What is required is that something of the old idea of Hindu student life should be revived in the boarding-houses. As is well known, the ancient Hindus divided the ideal life of a man into four parts: the first was childhood, the second, studenthood, the third, manhood (in which a person married and lived a household life), and the fourth was the life of an ascetic (in which the person retired from the world and became a teacher or religious guide).

It will be seen that the life of the student in those days was one of much discipline enforced by the preceptor, and of much social fellowship as amongst the pupils themselves. They lived in brotherhoods, and cultivated their intelligence by reading and writing under the common guidance of their saintly tutor. Their habits were governed by strict rules like those of monasticism. As marriage and family life were postponed to the third stage, the early marriages which sap the root of so much of the social and intellectual life of modern India were no part of that ancient system. The students did not come and go as they pleased. Their admittance to the brotherhood was a high privilege, and they were expected to live up to it under the ken of their preceptor. They did not live in crowded cities with the din and turmoil of city life, nor were they troubled with the fashions of Court. Secluded in some beautiful valley or some primeval forest, they lived in touch with Nature, and acquired the learning, arts, and sciences which were to fit them for their lives as householders, and ultimately as teachers and religious guides. Perhaps the practical side was left in the background as compared to the religious side, but a harmonious blending of the two would be possible and desirable in modern India.

The headquarters of every district contain a High School, generally maintained by Government. In this school the final class is what is called the Matriculation class, or the Entrance class. It is an English school—that is to say, the curriculum is English, the language in which the students are taught and in which they write out their examination papers is English, and the vehicle for instruction even in the Oriental languages, such as Arabic, Persian, or Sanskrit, is English.

Theoretically the Entrance Examination is supposed to form the gateway to one of the numerous Colleges affiliated to the Universities. In practice, a large number of students stop their education at this point. For this reason the old Entrance Examination has been partly replaced by what is called the School Final Examination. This is specially provided for those pupils who wish to go on no further, but desire to obtain the hall-mark of a certificate by which they can enter the numerous clerical appointments for which the recruitment is by the test of general examinations. Practically, as regards the amount of knowledge required, the School Final and the Entrance Examinations are of the same value.

By the time the pupil reaches this stage, he has spent about ten years of his student life. In a large number of cases it takes fifteen years to reach that stage. If the pupil started at seven, he will reach that stage at from seventeen to twenty-two years of age.

How does he compare with a pupil of equal age in the West? He has a smattering of his own language, but he is very little acquainted with its literature. He has had a glimpse into one of the Oriental classical languages, or possibly into Latin or Greek, but not enough to enable him to do an unseen passage, or to turn out even mechanical verses, such as those at which Public School boys try their hand in Europe. His knowledge of the sciences is of a wonderfully scanty description, if, indeed, he can be said to have any scientific knowledge at all. He has never been taken through a course of Nature study. He has had no access to any apparatus or laboratory for performing chemical or physical experiments. He knows nothing of industrial or economic problems. The history he has read has been in those small compressed doses which might be called crammers' tabloids. In geography he has learnt a large number of names, but commercial geography, or that higher science of which Herodotus may be considered the founder, has never entered his ken. Maps are not sufficiently used.

Into English literature he has had a slight peep through his books, but he knows nothing of current literature, or the larger movements of thought which mould contemporary literature. In his command of English he is a curious mixture of Johnsonian pomposity with the incongruousness of Mrs Malaprop. He will be unable to draft a simple business letter with correctness or accuracy, and from a purely practical point of view his education has so far done nothing for his mental faculties, but has merely taught him the mechanical arts of reading and writing, and the cultivation of the memory. In some respects he is actually inferior to the boy he was when, with his shining morning face, he crept unwillingly to school. He then had freshness, spirit, and energy. His outlook on life was healthy and bright. These precious possessions he has bartered away for a few ill-digested facts and fancies, which make him unlovely in the sight of friends and enemies.

The greatest gap to be filled up in our educational system is with regard to the teaching of science and a systematic scheme of technical education. The few Arts Schools that exist, devote their attention to the Fine Arts more than to the Industrial Arts. We want workshops where Mechanics can be trained on accurate scientific methods, not only for the more technical parts of modern engineering, but for the humblest departments of the smith's, the carpenter's, the builder's, and the dyer's work. The most practical mission of science in the early stages of education, as well as in its most advanced stages, is to stimulate and husband the productive activities of the masses of the people. This view has been insisted on by Sir William Huggins in his recently published history of the Royal Society. As early as 1660 it was noted "that the reason why Germany has been so eminent for mechanical inventions, is because there have been public lectures of this kind (on mechanics) instituted among them, and these not only in the learned languages but also in the vulgar tongue, for the capacity of every unlettered ingenious artificer." Germany's modern eminence in the Chemical Arts is due to similar causes, and India's barrenness in recent times in the field of the Industrial Arts may be ascribed to causes of an opposite nature—the break-up of the old apprentice system and the want of technical education.

Let us now turn to the life of the University student. We have seen the material with which we start. It must not be supposed, therefore, that the best examinations of the University can yield a result at all comparable to those in other lands where university education starts on a broader basis. It has been noticed that University students in India, although they study some of the most advanced text books, are scarcely in their mental equipment on a par with the Public School boys of England. Those who criticise University education and University government, even in its unregenerate days, forget that what is generally responsible for the disappointing results is the material supplied at the source.

You cannot make a silk purse out of a sow's ear. You cannot turn out advanced students after three or four years' study of difficult subjects if you begin with raw material which cannot assimilate or respond to your methods, and over the production of which you had no control. A vigorous attempt has been made in recent times to reorganise completely the government of the Universities, and to considerably raise the standards of the Colleges affiliated to them. A good start has been made in that direction, but no sanguine hopes can be entertained until the fabric of education is remodelled from its very foundations, and greater attention is paid to the social and intellectual environment of the pupils than is possible under the conditions of school life as it is now lived. For a higher advance in University life it will be necessary to insist upon the Entrance Examinations of the University being really what they pretend to be—namely, a test of fitness for the student entering the University. As a test for clerical fitness for posts in Government or other offices it should never be recognised. The curriculum should be of a character which leads to advanced study, more than to the practical requirements of a clerical life. It is not so much that the standard of buildings in which the institutions are housed requires to be raised, or that any good can come of the tendency to make the examinations too difficult or too expensive. A spark of the divine fire may lurk in the children of those most poorly endowed with this world's goods. Some of the world's greatest intellects have owed their activity and their achievements to their struggles against adverse circumstances. What is required is to raise the standard of equipment with which the teaching is carried on, the standard of the men who carry on the teaching, and the standard of preparedness with which the pupils commence their University course. What has to be aimed at is not so much the actual knowledge, as the capacity of acquiring knowledge and of using it in pursuing systematic research. If a boy can use the text books actually before him in such a way as to answer his questions in logical sequence, and in a form which shows that he is capable of arranging his thoughts, he is far better able to follow a University course of instruction than a boy who is given no books in the examination hall, but is expected to bring forth from his memory various disjointed facts over which he has been labouring throughout the year. When we talk of raising the standard of examinations we are liable to be misunderstood in India. The standard has been "raised" several times with disappointing results.

What was done was that more difficult text books were substituted for those which were supposed to have afforded too easy an entrance to students who were unfit. That did not mend matters. Students with a good memory were able to learn the difficult text books just as easily as the easy text books, and the mischief that was done was greater in proportion as the teachers and the students felt that it was hopeless to follow intelligently and thoroughly in a given time all that was contained in a difficult book. If you examine the standards of examination for entrance into the Indian Universities and compare them with those followed at Oxford or Cambridge, you will find that on paper the Indian standard looks formidable. The reason why it breaks down is because a higher standard, as applied to a poorly equipped mind, stimulates despair in the pupil and the crammer's art in the teacher. Educate your teacher in right ideals. Let him master method, the theory and technique of teaching, and the psychology of young minds. Let him take a pride in his profession. Give him a status of dignity, and leisure and large opportunities for self-improvement and self-culture. The quality of the teacher must set the tone to the teaching. Like other professions in India (excepting law), the teaching profession is largely merged in the services. The question of the educational services has been raised and examined more than once, and many valuable reforms have been initiated. But it must not by any means be supposed that the last word on the subject has been said. Every scheme of reorganisation raises fresh problems to be dealt with. The distinction between the Imperial and Provincial Services leads to some heart-burnings. The ideal system will be that which will attract the best minds of the country into the educational field, where there ought to be abundant opportunities for sowing good seed and reaping a rich harvest.

The residential system has been brought into great prominence during recent educational controversies, and, so far, nothing but good has come out of the discussion. But in order to render it perfectly efficient, it will be necessary for the authorities to take the lives of the students completely into their charge, and mould them according to the educational ideals which are already in the air. Any half-hearted system of residence, in which there is no discipline as to hours and occupations, will not work. A tender regard for the susceptibilities of narrow prejudices is most excellent in private life, where every one ought to be tolerant to his neighbour. But the teacher is not in the position of a tolerant neighbour to his pupil. He has far higher responsibilities. If he is to fulfil them he must exercise his right of discussing and disregarding those trivial prejudices which do not touch religion, but which exercise a very considerable influence on the formation of the students' habits and character. Where the student goes, what company he keeps, and how he uses his leisure—these are not matters which a truly earnest teacher can afford to neglect. It may be that education under these circumstances might receive a smaller numerical following, although that consequence is by no means certain; but the resulting quality will be superior. And, after all, we should aim at the best which it is possible to produce, in a carefully devised system of true education.

What is the life led by the average University student? At the present day there are five centres of University life—namely, Calcutta, Bombay, Madras, Allahabad, and Lahore. Madras and Bombay have a great many features in common, and so have Lahore and Allahabad. I will, therefore, describe the three principal and typical centres of student life in Bombay—Calcutta and Allahabad.

The Bombay University has on its rolls

between 1,400 and 1,600 undergraduates, of whom scarcely 200 take the B.A. Degree in a given year. The proportion of failures to successes in most examinations is as two to one. In exceptional years there are thrice as many failures as successes, so that the chances of an average student passing an examination would be as one to four. The students are distributed in a number of outlying colleges, the majority of which are situated in the presidency of Bombay, but at great distances from the city. Scarcely any of the undergraduates make use of the University library. More than half of them never see the University building, except on Convocation day. Officially there is no common life, and no common centre for lectures. Each College has to maintain as complete a staff as it can, and some of the Colleges are very backward in this respect. There is no special journal or paper which the undergraduates take in, and by which they may communicate their thoughts or their difficulties to each other. There is an Undergraduates' Association, and there is also a Graduates' Association, but neither has shown great activity in promoting a corporate student life, or in welding together the units into a mass which can feel any *esprit de corps*.

The majority of the students in all the colleges live at home, or in lodgings which are not supervised by the University or the College.

They come merely as day pupils. Their life at home is sometimes lived under depressing circumstances. They have to contend against the apathy or the prejudices of their elder folk, and against insufficient nourishment, badly lighted rooms, and insufficient clothing. It is a fallacy to suppose that you can never be insufficiently clad in a hot climate. Whatever may be the case with men who live by hard physical labour, the case of those who are engaged in intellectual work is different. Frequent ablutions without a thorough rubbing and drying of the body are responsible for many chronic colds, which take hold of a system imperfectly protected by judicious clothing. The tenacity with which the students pursue their studies under the numerous difficulties described is maintained from motives of material benefit, and the highest culture is scarcely possible in the circumstances. In some of the Colleges there are residential quarters, but residence in these is not compulsory. The students in these quarters have naturally more opportunities of seeing each other than the day students, but many of the latter attend debating societies, and are members of cricket, football, or lawn tennis clubs. Sports bring the students together on a footing of so much equality and manly self-respect that it is a pity that the devotion to them is not more universal among the Indian students. The physique of the working students is in many cases at a low ebb, and their eyesight in particular is usually bad, on account of the imperfectly lighted rooms in which they have to work at home. No records of the physical fitness of the students are kept, but it is certain that the generation of University students who are now in mature manhood is far weaker physically than their ancestors. The size of the pupil, too, has grown less in both stature and chest measurements. This is a result greatly to be deplored, and calls for immediate attention and a speedy remedy.

Many of these remarks apply to the life of the University student in Calcutta or Allahabad, but there are distinctive features in these two centres which require mention. In Allahabad (and more so in Lahore) greater attention is paid to Oriental learning than in the older Universities, and there is far less study of the Greek and Roman classics. The opportunities for the students, when they have finished their University career, are fewer on account of their greater distance from the large presidency towns, which are the hives of industrial activity. On the other hand, in the quieter and more patriarchal atmosphere which surrounds them, there is something more of that spirit of gentleness, humility, and erudition, which goes towards the making of a true scholar.

In Calcutta a greater feeling of *esprit de corps* has grown up within recent years. It does not always manifest itself in forms which can command approval. But, apart from occasional breaches of discipline — boys will be boys — there seems to be a far greater unity of student life in the Calcutta University than in any of the other Universities. A most encouraging sign of the times is the growth of an Indian school of thought and research. There is an Association for the Advancement of Science carried on in Calcutta under entirely native auspices. Two of the foremost men of science are professors in Colleges in the Calcutta University. One, Professor Bose, has already made discoveries in electrical science, which will stand out as landmarks in the educational history of India. The other, Professor Roy, had written a history of Hindu chemistry, which shows what results can be achieved by applying the equipments of modern science to elucidate and illustrate the history of ancient Hindu science.

We must now consider the special Colleges as opposed to the general colleges that we have so far discussed. One of them is the great Muhammadan College at Aligarh, founded by Sir Syed Ahmed in 1877. It has made marvellous progress during the twenty-eight years of its existence. Sir Syed Ahmed was not a man brought up under the English system of education, but he had thoroughly imbibed the English spirit. He saw the secret of English progress.

He realised the cause of the backwardness of his own community. He decided to found a college which, without excluding the Hindus, gave predominance to the Muhammadan spirit. This spirit may be defined as the spirit of the Humanities—the spirit which aims at the cultivation of the human Personality in its social aspect. This spirit pervades the dining-hall, the mosque, the cricket fields, and the polo ground, and in fact gives tone and colour to the whole institution. The founder's life was devoted to the working out of this ideal, and he was fortunate in the men whom he secured as Principals of the College. The names of Mr Beck and Mr Theodore Morison are as completely identified with the Aligarh College and the cause of Muhammadan culture in India as those of Nawab Mohsin-ul-Mulk and of Sir Syed Ahmed himself. The present Principal (Mr Archbold) is a worthy successor to those two great educationalists, and if the finances of the College are as ably administered as its educational policy, a still more promising future is in store for it. The aim of its leading spirits is to convert it into a University, and it is possible that the idea may commend itself to the Authorities, when the funds necessary to start the venture have been collected. In that case we shall have a new centre of educational influence which will be able to make its own laws and prescribe its own curricula without being hampered in its advanced educational ideals by a system in which it has only a faint voice.

Let us take a look at the interior of the Aligarh College. We enter through a beautiful iron gate into extensive grounds, which have not yet been laid out to the fullest advantage. The buildings, too, have not all been finished, and a unity of design is wanting if you take a general view of the whole from the standpoint of architectural beauty. But the large lecture-hall is a noble building, and the beautiful mosque at the side, with the tomb of the founder guarding the ideals which his zealous spirit conceived in this life, proclaims to the visitor the simple faith and the large hope on which the foundations of the College rest. The dining-hall has not the pretensions of many an ornate scene of mirth and conviviality in merry England, or sociable Germany, but it is full of memories for the old Aligarh boy who dines in later life at the Middle Temple Hall, or visits the Gothic Halls of Central Germany. The students' rooms are in a block by themselves, opening out of long galleries that suggest the flavour of mediæval cloisters—soon to be dispelled by the conversation and bearing of the up-to-date young men who emerge into the quadrangle. They are wearing long black Melton coats and red Turkish fezzes with black silk tassels, whose movements let you into the secrets of the energy and activity of the heads which they adorn. Their riding breeches show that they are wending their way to the riding-school. If you had seen them last night, ranged on opposite sides in debate at the Siddons Union, you would have thought they were high ministers of State, holding in the hollow of their hands the destinies of nations and continents.

The Hindu College at Benares has been founded recently by Mrs Annie Besant, with Dr Richardson as her able lieutenant. The mainspring of the movement was connected with the modern theosophical synthesis of East and West. Mrs Besant wishes to hold up before Hindu students the ideals of their own past, and insists, by a system of close personal touch with them and their lives, upon the formation of character. The College has not been quite as successful in games and athletics as the Muhammadan College, but its finances are on a far more sound and stable footing. The devotion of an Englishwoman who can sway large audiences with her persuasive oratory and identify herself with the ancient culture of India, has been an asset of incalculable value, although reactionaries have not been wanting to protest against her eminently sensible programme of reform along national lines. At my last visit to this College I was struck with the well-bred manners of some boys whom I addressed *incognito*. I was prepared to meet either the usual shyness of boys not used to conversation with outsiders, or the indifference born of a want of curiosity. I was agreeably surprised to notice an absence of both these boyish qualities. They seemed to have attained the Roman ideal of education, which we are told by Horace softens manners and wears away uncouthness.

But there is another class of institutions which is not hampered by financial considerations, or by the varying social grades of the students who seek instruction within their walls. These are the Chiefs' or Noblemen's Colleges, which only admit pupils of the most aristocratic families. They have sprung up under official patronage, and are still most closely supervised by Government. They have fine buildings, and each of the students in them has a special well-built suite of rooms, well furnished by the standard of taste as well as of comfort. In the Ajmere College each student has almost a separate palace to himself. The beautiful white domed buildings, which conform to the architecture of Rajputana, stand out as the glittering homes of the higher aristocracy, and give shelter not only to the student chief, but to the retinue which he brings with him, according to his rank and station. There are fine grounds all around, with tastefully laid out gardens, and polo, cricket, riding, and driving are indulged in *ad libitum*. The whole scene, as witnessed from the top of the tower, suggests a Homeric picture, in which the tents of the chiefs lie scattered over the plain, each having an individuality of its own, and showing by its size and adornment the rank and wealth of its occupant.

The social life in these Colleges is of a far more cordial, although leisurely and dignified, character, and though the literary standard of instruction is not very high, and examinations do not loom large in the student's mind, the cultivation of the body and the formation of character, both individual and social, are important features, and are thoroughly appreciated in these institutions. Here the students may mix with their fellows of equal social standing, and acquire the manly sports of England.

It was at such a school that Prince Ranjitsinhji obtained his first knowledge of cricket, and he was already distinguished in that sport before he left the Rajkumar College in Kathiawar. When he came to Cambridge and had the opportunity of meeting men of the highest distinction in the sport, he found his early training useful, though a further course of earnest preparation was necessary before he succeeded in getting to the top of the tree. It is in such schools that the young men cultivate the art of riding, for which the youthful nobles of India are famous, and which exercises so much influence on the social life of the country. It is there, also, that they come into contact with the true spirit of the cultured English gentleman in their masters, who are usually not only scholars, but men of social position, men of affairs, and men of insight into human character. The ordinary English official is so hedged round with formalities, and is such a busy man, that he has no opportunity of cultivating the intimate social intercourse with people who might take advantage of his official position, and put him in an awkward dilemma when official or magisterial work has to be done. The ordinary English merchant is too busy with his affairs of money-making to be able to meet with people other than those who, like himself, are engaged in similar pursuits. But the Oxford or Cambridge man who directs the destinies of a noblemen's college in India, and brings to his work the manly spirit, the social freedom, and the disciplined habits of the University, has, outside school hours, many an opportunity of influencing the thoughts and habits and inflaming the imagination of his pupils. The seed thus sown bears fruit in after life, when a Raja or Nawab, fully installed in his regal dignity, gratefully acknowledges the splendid influence exercised over him in his youth by his teachers.

It is true that the attendance at many of these Rajkumar Colleges leaves room for improvement. Many of the pupils are wards of Government, and their relatives often look upon their education in the school as an unpleasant duty to be got over as soon as possible. But Lord Curzon's reorganisation of the Chiefs' Colleges has effected some reforms which will probably affect the popularity of the Colleges with the classes for whom they are intended. The Taluqdars' School in Lucknow is full, and more buildings have to be erected for the increased accommodation required.

Perhaps the highest development of student life in India, in its all-round aspect, is seen at the headquarters of the Imperial Cadet Corps at Dehra Dun. This corps was raised and organised by Lord Curzon in order to give the youth of princely families in India an opportunity of learning something of military life, and fitting themselves for high command in the Imperial Service Troops. The recruitment has usually been made from the Chiefs' Colleges, but previous residence at those Colleges is not indispensable to enrolment in the Cadet Corps. There are the most perfect arrangements for military drill and discipline, and these act upon the social life of the young men in an entirely beneficial way. They are taken away from Zenana influences, which make for softness and indecision of character; and from that atmosphere of flattery and intrigue, in which courtiers flourish at the expense of the cardinal virtues. They are brought up, while they are being trained in the corps, in a healthy outdoor life of military simplicity, and while they are improving their minds and bodies, they are, at the same time, laying the foundation for that grit, that character, that social *savoir faire*, which are the principal requirements in personal rule. What limits are there to the possibilities of progress in a native State ruled over by a born leader of men, who has also cultivated an eye that can take in a critical situation at a glance, and unravel a tangle with tact and the coolest imperturbability!

The uniforms of the Cadet Corps are most picturesque and striking. The chargers are black, with trappings of the beautifully white skins of the snow leopard—at once rare, costly, and splendid. The uniforms and turbans are designed with an unerring eye to grace and colour. The Tyrian purple of old suggested opulence and pride. The pale, almost transparent, sky blue of the "first gentlemen of India," suggests the unclouded sunshine of youth, and the serene dignity of a sober and aspiring life. The appearance of the Corps created quite a sensation at the Delhi Durbar. Led by Maharaja Sir Partap Singh, they evoked the most hearty cheering, both from the native crowds and the European spectators. They form a sort of guard of honour to the Viceroy and Princes of the blood royal when they visit the country. They escorted the Prince and Princess of Wales at Calcutta in the course of their recent visit to India, and their introduction to the Heir-apparent under conditions of military honour and military *esprit de corps* will do much to add to the mutual esteem entertained for each other by the high representatives of both nations. It is a pity that such a corps should confine the opportunities of social, moral, and military education to such a small number of individuals in the country. Being restricted to selected members of the ruling houses, it is necessarily narrow in its limits. To jealously safeguard its select character is no doubt a wise policy; but the extension of

Portrait of Himself.] [*By* PRINCE TALEY MUHAMMAD KHAN.

A MEMBER OF THE IMPERIAL CADET CORPS.

"The unclouded sunshine of youth, and the serene dignity of a sober and aspiring life"—p. 148.

To face p. 148.]

the principle to the formation of other corps on similar lines, but open to the nobility and gentry of British India as a whole, would be a blessing to the scions of many great families, as well as a source of strength and security to the British throne.

We have now taken a survey of educational and student life from the humble village school to the proud aristocratic institution known as the Imperial Cadet Corps. We have found that nothing in the nature of a social student life begins to make its appearance until we come to the highest aristocratic institutions, and that it is wanting on the lower rungs of the ladder. The necessity of education for the masses has not yet taken hold of the minds of the people. Technical education scarcely exists. Evening classes have been started spasmodically in different places with varying success, but they have not yet established a firm hold upon the educational system of the country. The system of Vacation Schools, which has made such progress in England during the last five years under the zealous advocacy of Mrs Humphry Ward, is absolutely unknown. The University Extension movement, which has done so much in Western countries to bring the culture of the Universities to the homes of the people, has not yet been developed. There is a wide gap between those who have attained University distinctions and those who are the common toilers of the nation. The growth of a spirit of sympathy and union amongst all classes, by means of the superior culture which the Universities ought to impart not only to a class, but with a view to its filtering through the mass, is one of the ideals which educated India will have to place before it and work up to in real earnest. It is only by associating the large masses of the people with their ideas and their aspirations that their voice can fittingly claim to make public opinion and to demand acceptance from the Government. The opportunities and the privileges of student life are great, but the maturing of it in after life, by men who do not cease to be students when they leave school or college, is the most glorious privilege which culture can confer. A combination of practical common sense with idealistic sympathy is only possible if the seeds sown in student life germinate and fructify in the larger life of the world.

V

INDUSTRIAL AND ECONOMIC PROBLEMS

"Every nation
To every other nation, strange of yore,
Shall face to face give civic salutation,
And hold up, in a proud right hand before
That congress, the best work which she could fashion
By her best means."
—E. B. Browning, *Casa Guidi Windows*, ii. 587.

"When through the gates of stress and strain
Comes forth the vast event—
The simple, sheer, sufficing, sane
Result of labour spent—
They that have wrought the end unthought
Be neither Saint nor Sage,
But men who merely did the work
For which they drew the wage."
—Rudyard Kipling, *The Wage-Slaves.*

INDUSTRIAL AND ECONOMIC PROBLEMS

Some one has said that all the great movements in history are ultimately traceable to economic causes.

The movement of the ancient Jews into Egypt was due to a famine in their old home, and to a careful system of finance and agriculture under Joseph in the land of the Pharaohs. Their movement back into a Promised Land, "flowing with milk and honey," was due to the intolerable conditions of their economic life, in which their *rôle* was narrowed to that of hewers of wood and drawers of water. The first impulse in the onward expansion of Rome and Italy was given by the commercial and manufacturing rivalry between the Phœnicians and the Romans. The mediæval struggle between East and West among the Mediterranean nations, of which the outward embodiment was the Crusades, was in reality fought over the issue: who were to be the masters of the commerce and industries of the world? The combatants in the struggle have changed, but the struggle itself has gone on unceasingly ever since. The Italian Republics and the Hansa Towns, Spain and the Empire, England and Holland, France and Germany, have represented different phases in the ebb and flow of the tide of modern progress, of which the determining factor has been the operation of economic forces. The same course of reasoning can be applied to the internal history of a nation. The English Reformation was really an economic Revolution, and so was the coming and passing of the Commonwealth of Cromwell. The French Revolution was a stupendous cataclysm which completely upset the old stratification of the economic world, and compelled an entirely new grouping of the social forces which stir our modern life.

The great achievement of Economic Science is that it has discovered and tabulated the hidden economic forces which underlie the lives of organised communities, and has given a new interpretation to many social phenomena which were previously accepted as inexplicable. More than three generations of economists have been hard at work in England, Italy, and other countries of Europe and America to bring this science to bear upon the numerous complexities of modern life, and to solve the questions of labour and capital, commerce and industry, agriculture, banking, and finance, which vex the social and political atmosphere. The result is that a certain number of propositions have been established which may be accepted as maxims by an enquirer into some new or disputed phase of national life. They are the bed-rock principles which can always be appealed to with some measure of confidence.

But this resource entirely fails us in discussing economic problems in India. The science of political economy is not an abstract science. Its conclusions depend for their accuracy on the facts on which it works. Where the features of economic life are so different from those in Western countries as they are in India, the axioms and postulates of Adam Smith, Ricardo, Mill, Walker, or Marshall do not necessarily apply, at least in the terms in which they are usually expressed and understood, and we have to begin from the very beginning. There is no Indian School of Political Economy. Considering what a vast amount of literature connected with public questions in India is available, it is surprising how little there is in it that can be accepted by a trained economist as clearing the ground for those generalisations which alone are possible in a brief discussion. There is only one economic history of India—that by Mr R. C. Dutt; and that is a brief sketch, and only covers a short period. There have been many heated discussions of the economic interpretation of certain facts revealed by statistics, and a stream of acrimonious controversy pours forth through the press on individual aspects of the vast economic problems of India, but I know of no systematic exposition even of one-sided views as to the origin, growth, modern condition, and future prospects of the economic institutions of the country.

The reason for this absence of clearly defined views on broad, economic facts is, that those facts have not yet got crystallised sufficiently to permit of a reasoning on scientific principles. All we can do is to study the facts themselves, in as great a detail and with as much accuracy as possible; to put them in juxtaposition with parallel facts as known from our past history; to compare them with the facts and phenomena observed in other countries; to generalise with caution, and draw tentative conclusions; and to lay the foundations of a science free from current bias and prejudice, and yet not blind to the views which have been put forward on all sides by publicists and practical men, not only with reference to Indian facts, but with reference to the well-ascertained facts in all the leading countries of the world. India having entered into the comity of nations through the British Government, her history and her economics are no longer isolated, but are influenced and even interpreted by the events that mark the progress of the modern world.

The village was until quite recently the economic unit in the country. As regards the production, distribution, and exchange of wealth, it was absolutely self-contained. The food supply of the village was obtained from the grain, the pulses, and the vegetables grown in the village lands. The surplus grain in a given year was not exported, but was stored up in pits for future years. The people of the village were clothed with white cotton locally grown, which was spun by the village women, and woven into cloth by the village weavers. Even such articles as salt were manufactured in many inland villages from saltpetre, before the Government monoply in salt was established. Bricks were made in the village from mud excavated from tanks and hollows, and baked either in the sun or in kilns, of which a few succeeding one on the top of the other have made many a hillock round large villages and towns in India. Timber and fuel were both sought locally, either in the village lands or in those numerous waste patches covered with wild trees, which must have formed so characteristic a feature of Indian landscape in the time of Kalidasa, and for centuries afterwards. Animal food was little used, but the village cows supplied the different milk products which figure so largely in Hindu cookery, including that peculiarly Indian commodity called *ghi*, or clarified butter. The castor-oil seeds and the sesamum—besides some inferior oil seeds—supplied the vegetable oils which were burnt as illuminants, not to mention the *ghi* lamps, which were specially appropriate to sacred shrines. Indigo, *kusumb* (safflower) *harsinghar*, and saffron were a few of the vegetable dyes which produced the far-famed colours of the textile fabrics of India. Their rich, brilliant tones, their warm and delicate tints, their harmonious blending and their everlasting beauty won a name and a prestige for Indian textiles which the cheap vulgarity of the latter-day German aniline dyes has not entirely obliterated in the art world.

As in the case of commodities, so in the case of services and tools, the village was economically self-contained. There was very little of the employment of elaborate mechanical contrivances or of the forces of Nature in the service of man. The simple agricultural implements—the plough, the hoe, the yoke, the cart; the simple domestic implements and utensils; as well as those required by the village artisans, were manufactured locally as required. The sweeper, the potter, the basket-maker, the cobbler and shoemaker, the washer-man, the barber, the herdsman, and the tailor were all officers in the more or less socialistic economy of the village. In such an organisation there was no place for the merchant class. There was no buying and selling, and no middle-men's profits. No stocks were accumulated, and no commodities were made except to order. There was no bank-ing system, and no commercial law or custom. There was no distinction between the maker of an article and the seller of it, or between wholesale and retail business. Capital was not separated from labour, nor had the minute sub-division of labour in any particular manufacture, which is so characteristic a feature of the competitive system, been worked out. Merchants were not absolutely unknown, but they were a product of town life and of an extraneous civilisation. I can imagine the arrival of a merchant on one of his rare visits to the village. Loaded with his wares and cares, he would present the same aspect to the agricultural population that Odysseus, the man of many sorrows, who had known cities and men, presented to the simple Phæacians in Homer.

These considerations will help us to understand some of the elements in the industrial and economic problems that confront us at the present day. They explain how it was that there were no large industries or foreign commerce on an organised scale among the institutions of the country. They also explain the strong opposition which a forward railway policy has called forth among some of the leaders of the community. In the days of hand-manufactures and capitalist wage-earners, no great attention was required to the internal or external communications of the country. While there were some splendid trunk roads for military or administrative purposes, there were few that served the commercial and industrial needs of the community. Such needs can scarcely be said to have existed, and therefore no means were required for meeting them. In England, long before the introduction of railways, there was a splendid net-work of roads, and a beautifully organised system of coaching traffic and internal communication. The factory system was getting organised. When railways came they simply supplied one of the pressing needs of the country in a far cheaper, quicker, and more efficient way than the system which they supplanted. Apart from the temporary displacement of labour which they caused, and the outcry of the vested interests which they injuriously affected, they were welcomed as a new and potent factor in the development of industrial England, and immediately took their place as a national asset in the economic system. In India they have been built under State control, or State guarantee, somewhat in advance of the immediate needs of her commerce or her industries, and some of them were due to considerations of military strategy, or administrative policy. Some of them are just beginning to pay. But when the day of industrial expansion comes, their immense value as an indispensable factor in the life of an advancing community will be realised.

The impression prevails in some quarters, that India has more railways in proportion to her population than any other country which is purely agricultural. This is an error. The Argentine Republic has a purely agricultural population. The Argentine railways have been built principally with English capital, as the Indian railways have been. But in Argentina, with a population of 4,500,000, there is a railway mileage of 10,000, or a mile of railway to every 450 persons.[1] India has a population of 294,000,000, with a railway mileage of 28,000, of which an appreciable portion is due to the energetic policy of Lord Curzon within the last seven years. This gives the ratio of a mile to 10,500 people. On a comparison of areas, however, India is better served with railways than Argentina. The figures are: India, with an area of 1,600,000 square miles, has a railway mileage of 28,000, while the Argentine Republic, with an area of 1,125,000 square miles, has a railway mileage of only 10,000. With an area scarcely 44 per cent. greater than that of Argentina, we have a railway mileage approaching to three times as great as that of the Republic.

With all these facilities ready to hand, with a settled government, and with an industrious and fairly intelligent population, why is it that the country does not advance rapidly on the path of industrial progress? The reasons are many and various. First and foremost, there is a want of correct appreciation of the economic position among the people at large, and among the parties chiefly interested. Nowhere is it more true that knowledge is power than in the industrial and commercial field. We find that the very existence of problems which trouble the

[1] I take the figures from an article by Lord Avebury, in the *Standard* of 21st November 1905, p. 5.

minds of specialists is unsuspected by some of the classes chiefly affected. We cannot help recognising, in this state of things, a most important factor retarding progress. Misunderstandings caused not by any real conflict of interests, but because knowledge, which is in the possession of one side, is not in the possession of the other, are responsible for many evils, which only require a complete understanding and association between the different classes for their removal.

What could be simpler or more certain in agricultural economics—the basis of all economics and finance in India—than the fact that animal manure is being diverted from its natural function, the fertilisation of the soil, to its unnatural use as fuel in the form of what are known as cow-dung cakes? The waste of a valuable manure under the people's very eyes, and the consequent impoverishment of the soil, are enormous in their extent. But the agricultural population has not had its eyes opened, and the waste goes on. It is true that wood fuel is in many places scarcely obtainable, or is prohibitive in price. The unwise practice of cutting down forests in some places, and the wise policy of conserving the forests in others, are responsible for this result. But the phenomenal development of mineral coal in the country —from 4,000,000 tons in 1897. to 8,250,000 tons in 1904—suggests an alternative which has, in fact, been adopted in all the industrially advanced countries. Railways in India now mostly use indigenous coal. I look forward to the day when mineral coal produced in the country will become an article of universal consumption for domestic and village use. It is not so much that the prejudice against it has to be overcome; the first step is to get the agriculturists to realise the waste of resources that now goes on, and make them think out their own remedy.

Another illustration of the remarkable lack of appreciation of the economic position on the part of the princes and people of India is shown by the figures for the annual exports and imports of the country. Lord Curzon's reference, at the Delhi Durbar Fine Arts Exhibition, to the palaces of Indian nobles being stocked with Tottenham Court Road furniture, has become quite classic. But the Fine Arts industry is a mere flea-bite compared with the everyday industries which might, but do not, support the millions and millions of people who have to be clothed and fed in India. I wish that every one who is in a position to lead public opinion, or to direct the current of trade and industry in India, carefully digested the facts contained in a handy form in the admirable annual review of the trade of India, published by the Indian Government. Let us briefly glance at the review for the year 1904-5. The imports are valued at about 88 crores[1] of rupees, and the exports at about 146 crores. The balance of trade is 58 crores in favour of exports, because India is a debtor country, and has to supply an equivalent of 66 per cent. of her imports to pay for interest on borrowed capital, interest on her debt, cost of maintaining the India Office and the Secretary of State's establishment in London, and the pay and pensions of the officers and men of the Indian Services, civil and military, in England. Of the imports of 88 crores, 38 crores—or not very far short of a half—represent Lancashire cotton manufactures, viz., 33½ crores cotton piece goods, 2½ crores yarn, and 2 crores other cotton manufactures. Sugar represents about 7 crores, iron and steel 6 crores, and machinery and millwork (which are exempt from even the light tariff for revenue purposes) 4 crores. The figures for sugar are rather remarkable. Mr J. A. Robertson discusses them in his review in these terms:

"The growth of the imports of sugar is chiefly remarkable from the fact that India is the largest individual producer of sugar in the world. Well-informed opinion has put the annual production at 3,000,000 tons, which is about one-third as much again as appears in the commercial estimates of the crop. Taking the highest estimate as the outside limit, and adding the imports of 1904-5, which represent one-ninth of the home production, the quantity for consump-

[1] A crore of rupees may be taken as an equivalent of £666,666, 13s. 4d.

tion provides only 25 lbs. per head of the population, a rate less than that estimated for Germany (28 lbs.) during 1902-3, when the artificial restrictions on consumption were most powerful, and only 28 per cent. of the estimated *per capita* consumption of the United Kingdom in that year. A considerable advance on the present rate of consumption is therefore possible, and the material will be obtained by importation, so long as the home production fails, as it does now, to provide a sufficiency of refined sugar of good quality to meet the demand. During the four years following 1898-9 the area under cane decreased, chiefly from climatic causes, but last season showed a considerable recovery, and the yield was remarkably good."

The passage I have quoted throws some light incidentally on the popular fallacy that the Indians are great consumers of sugar. In fact, the average consumption of sugar per head in a prosperous year does not come up to one-third of that in England. The disastrous set-back to the sugar industry, which took place some years ago, was no doubt partly due to the unfair continental competition. The Cartel system subsidised sugar exported abroad from the countries in which it operated. Even now, Austria-Hungary is the principal supplier of foreign sugar to India. Legislation was undertaken by Lord Curzon's Government to impose a tax on bounty-fed foreign sugar, equivalent to the amount of bounty it had received. The object aimed at was not to shut out foreign sugar, but to remove some of the artificial advantages under which it competed with the sugar produced in India; neither protection nor retaliation, but an equalisation of the burdens of the home producer and the foreign importer. The result is not as striking as was anticipated. But the question is doubtless complicated by many other considerations which it is unnecessary to dwell upon here. It must be mentioned, however, that the system of local (municipal) taxation in the towns of India is not all that can be desired. The octroi imposts sometimes strangle or kill nascent industries, which usually seek a location in towns; at any rate, they hamper the free import of produce into towns for manufacturing purposes. Take a hypothetical case. If unrefined sugar imported into the town for a refinery pays an octroi of 2 ans. per maund, and refined Austrian sugar pays 3 ans. per maund; and unrefined sugar sells at a rupee a maund, while refined sugar sells at Rs.5 per maund; the result is that the local refiner pays a tax of 12½ per cent. on his raw material, besides the income tax on his profits as estimated by the Tahsildar, while the importer of refined sugar gets in with less than 4 per cent. paid to the municipality. Local taxation is, fortunately or unfortunately, in the hands of people who have received no training in finance or political economy, and they often unconsciously levy imposts against the interests of their own towns or people.

If, in the matter of sugar, which, in its manufacture, requires comparatively little capital and plant, and depends upon much less elaborate machinery and processes than the higher manufactures, we are unable to hold our own, it is small wonder that in the matter of textiles and yarns we should have to import 38 crores worth of goods. India, at one time, not only clothed her own people, but exported large quantities of textiles abroad. The movement has now been entirely reversed—not only are vast quantities of the cloth used by the masses of the people imported, but I have frequently found village weavers working at their hand-looms using imported yarn. Thus even a large quantity of the so-called indigenous hand-weaving industry depends upon yarns and twists manufactured outside the country. India produces more than enough cotton for her own consumption. Except what she uses in her decaying hand-looms, or makes into yarns in her own cotton mills, principally in Bombay, and the small quantities she weaves by means of power-looms, the greater part of the cotton she is content to export as raw material, and receive back in its manufactured state for her own use. During the American Civil War a large impetus was received by the cotton mill industry in Bombay, though the first mill was started as early as 1851. Since then this new steam industry has undergone remarkable vicissitudes. Three or four years ago the prospects were of the gloomiest, but a certain amount of revival has recently taken place. In the weaving mills the output of the finer classes of goods is increasing in greater proportion than that of what are called Grey Goods. But, taken as a whole, the progress of this industry in half a century has been neither as rapid nor as continuous as might have been wished. In fact, it has scarcely kept pace with the expansion of the population. It is doubtful, too, how far the social revolution which will be worked in the lives of the masses of the people, when once the factory system has taken a firm hold of the country, will really make for the greater happiness of the population. The alternative lies in the development of the hand-loom industry, if that is at all possible in its formidable rivalry with steam. The introduction of the fly shuttle into hand-loom weaving, promises, on the authority of Mr E. B. Havell, to give a considerable chance to the Indian artisan in his competition with outside forces in the modern home market. The fly shuttle has been adopted in various centres, principally in Bengal, and the results are reported to be more economical and more efficient (besides the saving of time and labour) with its use, than with the use of the ordinary shuttle. I have seen the shuttle, but I have not been able to work out its practical superiority over its rivals by means of detailed experiment or figures. However, it ought to be given every trial and encouragement in India, and it is the duty of all who gain any practical experience of it to publish the details with the greatest accuracy, as the matter has an important bearing on the economic development of the textile industry.

Cotton goods produced in the Indian steam mills are subject to an Excise Duty of an equal amount to the duty paid under the Customs Tariffs by imported cotton goods. In 1894 the "vanishing rupee" reached so low an ebb in international exchange that the Customs Tariff had to be revised, and a small duty was imposed on (among other goods) the cotton goods imported into India. No countervailing Excise Duties were imposed by the Indian Government on cotton fabrics, or on cotton yarns of a lower "count" than "twenties"—the Indian mills mostly manufacturing yarns of low counts. An agitation was immediately set on foot by the Lancashire Mill interest, as was only natural, in England, where the ultimate political power with respect to India rests. It was asserted that unless the countervailing Excise was imposed, a sort of bounty would be created in favour of the Indian mills as against Lancashire, which would be against the declared policy of Free Trade pursued by the Government. The countervailing Excise Duties were therefore imposed, but they do not apply to the hand-weaving industry.

Now it is contended by the Indian Mill interest —and I think personally there is a great deal in their contention — that the Indian Mills do not really compete with the Lancashire Mills in the classes of goods produced. It is estimated that only one-fifth to one-sixth of the yarn produced in Indian Mills is of counts above the "twenties," while only one-eightieth of the yarn imported from the United Kingdom was "twenties" and under. Thus the products of the Lancashire Mills and the Indian Mills do not compete to any great extent. This is a matter of opinion, but it is at any rate a legitimate argument. In such matters, however, the hands of the Indian Government are tied by the influences that rule in the political atmosphere in the centre of the Empire.

The Government of India, as far as the means at its disposal and the peculiar circumstances of the case permit, have made it a settled principle of their policy to encourage local industries and manufactures. If the people of India only knew it, the charter of the Swadeshi movement is embodied in a Government Resolution.[1] The Swadeshi movement has been much misunderstood and much misrepresented. Its unfortunate association with breaches of the public peace and with certain political propaganda has obscured the fact that, as originally conceived, its object

[1] Government of India, Finance and Commerce Department, No. 185, dated 10th January 1883.

was the very laudable and patriotic one of the support of home manufactures. Such a support in India is absolutely necessary for the country's economic salvation. The friends of India will, therefore, all the more regret that the word should have fallen into discredit on account of its being mixed up with extraneous issues, which may prejudice, but cannot advance, the cause of industrial progress. As the provisions of the Swadeshi Resolution are not well known outside official circles, I will quote from paragraph 28:—

"The orders of the Secretary of State make it incumbent on all officers of Government requiring stores of European manufacture, to obtain them by indenting on the Secretary of State, and permit of the purchase in the local market of articles made in Europe and America, only under special circumstances mentioned. The Governor-General in Council, therefore, desires again to invite the attention of local governments to the expediency of supplying the wants of Government by the purchase in the local market of articles of *bonâ fide* local manufacture. The Government of India is desirous to give the utmost encouragement to every effort to substitute for articles now obtained from Europe articles of *bonâ fide* local manufacture or of indigenous origin, and where articles of European and of Indian manufacture do not differ materially in price and quality, the Government would always be disposed to give the preference to the latter; and the Governor-General in Council desires to remind all officers of Government that there is no reason why articles manufactured in India should not be obtained locally, even although the raw material necessary to their manufacture may have been originally imported from Europe. . . . There are many articles which may not be immediately obtained in the local market, but which can be made in the event of Government encouraging the manufacture."

Can anything be more enlightened or patriotic than this policy? If only the people of India would act up to it in their own life, not in the spirit of fitful aggression, but with a firm and patriotic determination to put the industries of their country on a prosperous basis, many of the most difficult economic problems of India would be solved.

We have hitherto considered cotton as it appears in the imports and exports of the country. But if we analyse the whole of the Indian exports we shall find that the predominant share of the exports in all departments is taken by food-stuffs or by raw material, which forms the basis of manufacturing activity in other countries. The total exports of India in 1904-5 amounted to about 146½ crores of rupees. Of these, 60 crores consisted of raw material, principally raw cotton (17½ crores), oil seeds (14½ crores), raw jute (12 crores), hides and skins (10 crores), lac (3 crores), raw wool (a little under 2 crores), and indigo and raw silk (together a little over a crore). Then 52 crores consisted of food-stuffs, viz:—rice (19½ crores); wheat (18½ crores); pulses, millets, and cereals (3 crores); tea, coffee and spices (11 crores). About 22½ crores consisted of cotton yarn and cloth (mostly for the far Eastern and East African markets), jute manufactures (*i.e.* gunny bags) and oils. The remaining exports of 12 crores consisted of opium, principally for the China market (10½ crores), and wood and timber and provisions (about a crore and a half between them).

This export of food-stuffs and raw materials and import of manufactures would not be economically unsound if we had some manufactures of our own, in the production of which we specialised, leaving others to manufacture for us those articles which they could manufacture to greater advantage. Commerce under such circumstances benefits both parties to it: it blesses him who gives and him who takes. But when it becomes one-sided, when an old self-contained country becomes practically dependent on outside manufactures for its luxuries and necessities, so far as they include the reward of human manufacturing labour and the return on stored-up capital, it becomes necessary to enquire into the causes of such helplessness, and to remedy them as far as possible. It is a truism to say that a vast number of the Indian people are clothed with the product of outside looms, burn matches and oil prepared in foreign countries, use iron and brass vessels produced entirely or partly abroad, write on imported paper, and wear colours which were produced in German chemical works. Indian labour is almost confined to the production of agricultural produce, which requires a high degree of patience indeed, but does not call forth that highest form of human activity or organisation in which the ideals of good citizenship take root. This all but universal dependence upon agricultural industry produces those appalling famines when the rainfall fails and starvation stares in the face millions of people who live habitually from hand to mouth.

India's exports are bulky in character, being mostly raw material and produce. The imports, being mostly manufactured articles, occupy a very small bulk relatively to their value. As even the value of exports is about 66 per cent. greater than that of imports, it follows that in bulk the exports would be twice or three times the quantity of the imports. This has a curious effect on the freights in the sea-borne trade of India. In the export season ship-loads of bulky produce are found waiting for ship room, and the competition is so keen that the freights on the outward journey are exorbitant. On the journey *towards* India, with merchandise of relatively small bulk and of considerably less value in the aggregate than the exports, the ships have to go half empty or nearly empty, and the competition among shipowners to earn freights in that direction is so keen that the freights are almost reduced to a vanishing point. Now to a shipowner it is immaterial, if he earns a given amount of freight that pays him, whether this is divided exactly between the outward and return journeys, or is nearly all earned in one journey with only nominal freights in the return direction. The result is that in India the export trade practically pays the freights of the import trade, and thus the process called the "dumping" of foreign manufactures receives an artificial subsidy and stimulus.

This is not all. Industries such as oil-pressing get no fair chance at all. The Indian exports of oil seeds amount to 14½ crores, while the export of oils only amounts to a single crore, of which a great part is made up of the Burmah mineral oils, which do not enter into our argument at all. Now the extraction of the oil from the oil seeds in India itself would give employment to a considerable section of the population, and the processes involved are sufficiently simple, and the capital required sufficiently small for India to be able to undertake the industry. The value of the same quantity of oil seeds when manufactured into oil would be much greater, and the bulk being smaller, the freights ought in any reasonable system of freights to be smaller too. But practical experience shows that the freight difficulty is an almost insuperable barrier. Shippers are business men and not philanthropists. There is so much bulky cargo waiting to be exported that the lighter cargo of oil, which requires more elaborate arrangements for storage and precautions against fire, is either refused altogether or only accepted on prohibitive conditions. Thus a valuable nascent industry gets no support to enable it ultimately to stand on its legs. The freight problem is one of the most important for the industrial future of India. I speak with reserve and diffidence. But I see no reason why, if the railway freights are so largely regulated and controlled by the State, some sort of regulation or control should not be exercised by the Indian Government on the question of sea freights. The problem is complicated by the fact that most of the shipping companies are domiciled outside the jurisdiction of the Indian Government. It is enough to call attention to the problem. It is for responsible statesmen to devise a remedy.

While on this subject, the opinion of so weighty an authority as Sir Frederick Lely may be quoted on railway rates in India. Local opinion is frequently heard making out grievances against railway rates, but there is no subject anywhere on which local opinion has no grievances. When, however, the late Chief Commissioner of the Central Provinces pleads for a more effective control of railway rates by the State, his views are entitled to respectful consideration. And the parties which can least afford to neglect them are the Railway Administrations themselves.

"The Traffic Manager," says Sir Frederick, "wields an irresponsible power over the country commanded by his railway which should not be entrusted to any man, and least of all to one who, rightly from his own point of view, regards nothing but his master's dividend and certain wide limits set down by Government. By a slight readjustment of rates he can (and sometimes does) crush a rising home manufacture in favour of a foreign customer. An Amended Code of Civil Procedure occupies for days and months the wisest of the land, but is of less consequence to the people of a district than a new edition of their Local Goods Traffic."[1]

Closely allied to this are the questions of the shortage of waggons and a Railway Clearing House which have attracted a good deal of attention lately. It must not be supposed that Government is not alive to these questions. They recently brought over a specialist from England to enquire thoroughly into railway administration in India. Mr Robertson's Report is a masterly document, as comprehensive as it is lucid, and must be referred to for light on all questions affecting railway policy in India.

As I said before, if the people only realised accurately the economic position and the causes which hinder the progress of India in industrial expansion, it would be a very important step gained towards economic re-awakening. We have seen how an imperfect acquaintance with economic facts leads to apathy, or to misdirected activity on unfruitful lines. We must now review rapidly some of the other obstacles to India's industrial prosperity. India is very short of capital. It is not true that there are buried hoards of wealth in the country, which have only to be brought

[1] Sir F. S. P. Lely: "Suggestions for the Better Governing of India."

out and applied to productive industries. It would be strange, indeed, if half a century of perfect peace within the frontiers had still left so shrewd a population as that of India in the same attitude as that which was necessary in more turbulent times, leading to the concealment of wealth by the weaker party. Capital now fetches a very high return in India on account of its scarcity, and we may take it that the greater part of the available resources of the country are as fully employed as in any other country. And yet "more capital" is still the cry. In Bombay there is a large amount of native capital employed in the big modern industries, chiefly cotton mills and the Presidency Bank. But in other parts of India, the capital employed in the large industrial, banking, and commercial concerns is mostly European, and being usually expressed in sterling, and not in the rupee currency of the country, its earnings used to fluctuate according to the value of the rupee in international exchange. It was of the utmost importance, therefore, that the value of the rupee in international exchange should be kept as steady as possible. It varied greatly during the twenty years from 1873 to 1893, having reached, shortly before the latter date, to almost half the value it had held at the former date. These violent fluctuations naturally made foreign capital extremely shy; and though the fall of the rupee gave a certain amount of artificial stimulus to the exports (mostly grain and raw materials), it was an extremely disturbing factor not only in the trade and industry of the country, but in Government finance, which occupies a peculiarly pre-eminent position in the economics of the country. Bimetallism was suggested as one of the remedies for a constantly fluctuating exchange, but it did not finally win the field. A compromise was adopted. The mints were closed to the free coinage of silver; they had been previously quite open. The consequence was, and is, that the rupee attained, and maintains, a permanent value in relation to sterling, at about 1s. 4d., although the intrinsic value of the rupee is at least 25 to 30 per cent. less. The rupee currency is, therefore, now purely artificial, and the gold sovereign is legal tender at the rate of Rs.15 to £1 sterling. Whatever the other merits or demerits of this currency experiment may be, it has succeeded in its cardinal object of fixing the value of the rupee in international commerce.

A short survey of the modern capitalised industries of India will show the present position of the country in regard to the amount of capital invested in centralised industries. The foremost is that of the cotton mills. There are[1] 204 cotton mills, containing 46,421 looms, and 5,213,344 spindles, and giving employment to 186,271 persons every day. Of them, 113 are

[1] The figures in this paragraph are for the year 1903-4.

exclusively spinning mills. The capital invested is £11,000,000 sterling; 69 per cent. of the mills are in the Bombay Presidency and 19 per cent. in the Native States. Of jute mills there are 38, mostly in Bengal, in the neighbourhood of Calcutta. They have 18,406 looms, and 376,700 spindles, employing a daily average of 124,000. The producing capacity and capital employed have nearly doubled in the last decade, an eloquent testimony to the effect of the fixity of exchange in attracting foreign capital. The capital invested is about £5,000,000, of which fully one-half is in sterling. During the last decade the sterling capital has increased by 89 per cent., and the rupee capital by 63 per cent. After the cotton and jute industries, there is only one manufacturing industry (viz., brass and iron foundries), which employs as many as 20,000 persons. The woollen, paper, and leather industries have made a start, while tea and indigo have probably seen their palmiest days. The coal mines employ 88,530 persons, including 3,373 children. The production of coal has increased from 4,000,000 tons in 1897 to 8,250,000 tons in 1904, and is mostly confined to Bengal. These few figures will show that, while some progress has been made, the absolute amount of capital invested is not large for such an enormous country. The growth of native capital is an encouraging sign, but it has not kept pace with the growth of imported capital. There is room, however, for almost unlimited expansion in the investment of capital.

No modern industries can flourish without the predominance of joint-stock capital, and the small extent to which joint-stock enterprise has made headway in India is another retarding feature in our industrial organisation. Our commercial law, though based on English commercial law, is yet complicated by the *status* of the *parda-nashin* lady and the peculiarities of the joint Hindu family. Under these circumstances a great deal of business inefficiency results from the application of old ideas to new methods, and people are often unwilling to tie themselves to the clear and definite responsibilities imposed by statute upon joint-stock enterprises when they are free to follow the free and easy methods of the old days. A measure for the compulsory registration of partnerships has frequently been advocated by commercial opinion, and is, I believe, under the consideration of the legislative authorities.

It would distinctly raise the tone of commercial morality and inspire greater confidence in joint-stock enterprise on the part of the public if the Companies Act insisted on certain well-defined qualifications in the auditors whose audit may be accepted as meeting the statutory requirements. As the law stands at present, any man, with or without qualifications, may be appointed an auditor. A well-meaning man may pass over many irregularities which vitally injure the interests of a joint-stock company. A man not sufficiently acquainted with the tricks of the company promoter may, through ignorance, set the seal of his approval on a dishonest balance sheet. In either case the so-called audit may be worse than no audit at all, as it tends to lull suspicion, and to make the disillusionment, when it comes, all the more bitter. An auditor of recognised status, *e.g.* a chartered accountant, would have no excuse for falling into pitfalls through laxity or inexperience.

Banking facilities are extremely poor in India. The three presidency banks and eight joint-stock banks have their head offices in India, but there are eight exchange banks whose head offices are outside India. The capital of the former has increased from Rs.3,88,00,000 in 1893 to Rs. 4,37,00,000 in 1903—an increase of 49 lakhs, or 13 per cent. The capital of the exchange banks has increased from £6,000,000 sterling in 1893 to £11,500,000 in 1903—an increase of £5,500,000, or 91 per cent. Thus the banking facilities for the internal trade and industries of the country have not expanded in anything like the proportion in which the banking facilities for external commerce have expanded. And the sum total of banking capital, £14,500,000, can scarcely be called adequate for a country whose external trade alone reaches a value of £156,000,000. The indigenous system of banking is in a rudimentary stage. There is a large amount of customary law relating to Hundis or native Bills of Exchange, but it varies in different places. Hundis are distinctly falling into public disfavour. Joint-stock banking has at different times received some unfortunate checks, but the future rests with that form of banking enterprise.[1]

One of the greatest drawbacks to the establishment of large industries in India is the scarcity and inefficiency of labour. Though the population of the country is large, and the pressure of the population on the soil is extreme, it has been found almost impracticable to attract a sufficient number of labourers to carry on the mining and manufacturing industries. The tea-gardens of Assam are worked, though less and less so as time goes on, by coolies recruited under a system of State-aided and State-supervised emigration under the Inland Emigration Acts. The stream of emigrant coolies that used to be poured out to the British colonies under a system of State-

[1] A study of the relation between the external and internal trade of a country is of the utmost importance from the economic point of view. The social changes going on among the people are better shown by the internal than by the Foreign Trade This most interesting point was raised by Mr Percy Bunting, who presided when this Paper was read at the Passmore Edwards Institute. He pointed out that in England the proportion of foreign to internal trade was, roughly speaking, one-sixth to one-eighth. If the proportion was different in India, a study of the difference might be instructive as throwing light on the different social and economic structure on which the community was organised. Unfortunately, there are two drawbacks to this study in India. The statistics of internal trade are neither complete nor reliable ; and such as there are, are not easily accessible.

aided emigration is now[1] almost counterbalanced by the coolies who have to return to India (allowing for casualties), and therefore there is not the slightest relief to the congestion of the population. And yet mines and manufactures are alike calling for more labour, and cannot get it. The Conference of Indian and Ceylon Chambers of Commerce in 1904 carried the following resolution unanimously :—

"Whereas the supply of rank-and-file labour for organised industries is inadequate in many districts of India, and whereas the deficiency is seriously restricting the productive power of a large section of the manufacturing concerns of the country, it seems imperatively necessary to this conference that, in order to devise a remedy, measures should be taken by government commission or otherwise to investigate the causes which have led to a state of affairs inconsistent with the relative conditions of life of the factory operative on the one hand, and the agricultural classes generally on the other."

I have quoted the resolution *in extenso*, not only because it shows the serious situation which has to be faced by the captains of industry in India, but also because there underlies it an assumption which is of doubtful validity when all the circumstances are taken into consideration. The assumption is that the factory operative is better off than his agricultural *confrère* of the

[1]

Emigrant Coolies.	Sent out.	Returned.
1903-4	13,665	11,673
1893-4	13,735	5,844

same class. If the statement were made in this form, that the apparent wages of the unskilled hand in mills are better than the apparent wages of the landless labourer who earns his livelihood by working for hire in agricultural operations, the statement would be true. But it must be remembered that even unskilled labour in factories tends to be specialised and to form a definite class; that the cost of living in towns is higher, and the simple comforts, such as a coolie requires, fewer in the towns than in the villages; and that town labour is more exacting, and requires more punctuality and strenuousness than open-air labour in the fields. The agricultural labourer does not form a specialised class; many of the petty agricultural tenants get submerged into his class, and not a few industrious and capable agricultural labourers raise themselves to the status of sub-tenants, tenants-at-will, and even occupancy tenants in course of time. In the villages no rent is paid for houses, because no capital is sunk in them. A labourer is given a piece of waste land, and he builds a mud hut by his own labour, and thatches it with leaves or grass gathered by himself. To such a one the payment of house rent in a town appears at first as altogether an anomaly, and even if his income be nominally larger than in the villages, he has not learnt by collective or inherited experience to adjust his new expenses to his new form of income. Then, again, agriculture is a kind mother to all—the able-bodied as well as the physically weak, the wastrel as well as the efficient worker, the man of fitful lethargy as well as the man of grit. Of course the result is more or less successful according to the character of the husbandman; but in agriculture the mental and physical wrecks manage to find a livelihood, while in the competitive life of town industries they would be utterly and hopelessly lost. Thus the town industries in a way take a selected class even in the rank and file; a class that, if left on the soil, would probably be able to raise themselves a little higher in the social scale than they started. Further, there are the risks to life and limb in working with machinery or in mines. In the year 1903-4 there were employed about 98,000 persons in coal mines; but there were 68 fatal accidents causing 81 deaths, and 84 serious accidents causing injury to 87 persons. Now a casualty roll of 168 persons killed or *seriously* injured—taking no account of slight accidents or a gradual deterioration in health from working underground—is appreciable in a mining population of 98,000. Then there is no Employers' Liability Act, and no Workmen's Compensation, as such, is legally claimable. All these considerations apply in a different form, and perhaps in a different degree, to factory labour, when compared with agricultural labour, and yet they are apt to be forgotten. Thus the causes of the dearth of industrial labour go deep into the social fabric, and are not such a paradox as

Drawing by] [M. DHURANDHAR.

MILL HANDS IN BOMBAY.

"Thus the town industries take a selected class even in the rank and file"—p. 186.

To face p. 186.]

might at first sight appear. The matter is engaging the attention of the Governments of Bengal and the United Provinces, who have obtained the reports of officers specially appointed to investigate it. Let us hope that their enquiries will lead to healthier labour conditions, and will materially benefit both employers and employed.

An agitation was recently started in Bombay—strangely enough, by the mill-owners themselves—to reduce the working hours of the mill operatives to twelve. There is a Factory Act in India, but it does not limit the hours of work for adults, though it interferes for the protection of women and children. Stranger still, some of the *employés* are reported to have held a meeting in Bombay *against* the limitation of the hours to twelve. This would lose them the chance of earning overtime wages, and somewhat curtail their incomes. I am not personally acquainted with the currents and cross-currents of the movement in Bombay, and no good would be served by my attempting to discuss it. This I will say, that it is only one side, and in my opinion not the most important side, of the large question of the welfare of the working classes involved in a change of system from the old to the new. If we could only learn a little by the industrial experience of Europe—in both its moral and material aspects—and apply the lessons in constructing our own system of the future, we should be saved from much bitter social warfare, and many of the convulsions that rend the Western industrial world in strikes and lock-outs. The construction of houses for the workmen; the provision of free medical attendance; the payment of compensation for injuries; pensions in old age, and bonuses for regular attendance; and a careful regard to the comfort and well-being—moral and material—of the workmen—these are some of the points for the earnest consideration of both employers and publicists in India. I am happy to say that some enlightened employers of labour, such as Mr M'Robert, of the Cawnpore Woollen Mills, have already made a start in that direction; but in the country at large these matters have as yet received very little attention.

Not only is labour scarce in India—it is inefficient. Cheap labour, when there are no physical stamina, mental discipline, and skill behind it, tends to be costly in the end. The Indian labourer is mostly uneducated. I take education here not in the sense of literary education, which need not be expected in him, but education in habits, and in his own work or craft. He is not in touch with his tools; he rarely uses or knows of the best. He is not in touch with his employers or with his work. The labouring population of the towns is a flitting dilettante population. Any one who has examined the registers of factories knows how irregular any given individual usually is in his attendance. Now industrial and manual education would be the only means of creating a specialised, efficient, stable, industrial population. I am sorry to say that so far industrial education has not taken firm root in the country. The figures stand thus:—In 1896-7 there were 57 industrial schools, with 3,101 pupils in them, and the expenditure allotted to them was Rs.2,78,444. In 1901-2 there were 84 schools, with 4,977 pupils, and the amount spent was Rs.3,16,422. For an increase in pupils of 58 per cent. the increase in expenditure was scarcely 14 per cent. Lucknow supports a Government industrial school attended by about 100 pupils, and about Rs.11,000 is spent on it. The Rurki College in the United Provinces, and similar colleges in other provinces, are admirably equipped and give technical education of a very high order, but such institutions can by no stretch of imagination be described as Mechanics' or Working Men's Colleges. They cater for a very limited class. What we want is a network of institutions in touch with the actual working men of the land, leading up to the highest courses of instruction in handicrafts and the industrial arts. Within recent years a strong tendency has set in towards the encouragement of industrial education, and Government has recently instituted technical scholarships for selected persons to acquire a knowledge of arts and crafts in foreign countries.

A word in passing about India's position in a

possible system of preferential tariffs. All who are interested in the question should get a bluebook, published in 1904,[1] in which the Indian aspect of the question is discussed as fully as it can be in the absence of a clearly defined scheme or proposal. As we have already seen, the majority of the exports from British India consist of raw material and food-stuffs. Thus it is to the interest of the foreign countries importing them, to maintain a continuous supply of them. If they were to shut them out they would either injure their own manufactures in which the raw materials are used, or raise the price of food for their people by cutting off a source of supply. Again, of the exports from India, foreign countries take more than 61 per cent., while the United Kingdom and the Colonies take less than 39 per cent. If, therefore, there were any chance of foreign countries refusing India's exports on account of a tariff war with England, India would be the loser, but her hands would be tied, as her policy would depend on England's fiscal policy. Of the imports into India (exclusive of Government stores and treasure), foreign countries scarcely send 25 per cent., while more than 75 per cent. come from Great Britain or her Colonies. From an economic point of view India has not much in way of preference to offer to the Empire, and she has very little to gain in return from an

[1] "Views of the Government of India on Preferential Tariffs," price 5½d.

imperial inter-preferential policy. But she has a great deal to risk or lose if the balance of her exports and imports gets disturbed even temporarily, thus reviving the evils of an unstable rupee in her economic relations with gold-using countries which are her creditors. After long and anxious thought she has been able to build up a stable exchange, which is the foundation of her finance, and no advantage has yet been put forward as likely to accrue from the adoption of the new policy, which can at all outweight the possibility of a chaos in her fiscal system. From this point of view the danger to India of reprisals from foreign nations, even if eventually unsuccessful, is serious, and their results, as the Blue-book puts it, would be disastrous.

We have now reviewed the industrial and economic problems of India. We have seen how in the past the village was a self-contained economic unit, and how that fact explains many of the modern economic puzzles, and throws light on modern economic problems. We have gone through some of the causes which retard the industrial development of the country. We found that a want of appreciation of the true economic situation is responsible for many economic phenomena, such as waste of manure, consumption of huge quantities of foreign sugar, an unscientific system of municipal taxation, the dependence upon outside agencies for the cotton clothing of the mass of the people, although cotton is one of India's staple products, and a failure to make the most of our hand industries by the use of such simple improvements as the fly shuttle. We saw that the Government of India's attitude as regards Indian industries had been misapprehended. Analysing the export figures, we found that the question of freights was affecting unfavourably the rise of new industries in India. Other causes of our industrial backwardness we found to be shortness of capital; an indisposition to resort to joint-stock enterprise; a restriction of banking facilities; scarcity, inefficiency, and non-specialisation of labour; and an undeveloped system of industrial education. We glanced at the progress (such as it is) made in these several departments; and the moral and social aspects of labour problems. Finally, we considered India's position in a scheme of Preferential Tariff for the Empire. The creation of a commercial bureau by Lord Curzon will do much to collect and disseminate information on business topics in India. The holding of industrial exhibitions, which is becoming an annual event in connection with the Indian National Congress, and the generous grant of funds by the Government in aid of the industrial programme, will stimulate popular interest in economics and industry. If our fixity of exchange, and, therefore, the fiscal balance of Government finance, remains undisturbed, there is no reason why a period of industrial prosperity should not raise India from a somewhat low economic status to a position of considerable importance in the industrial movements of the world.

VI

PUBLIC HEALTH ADMINISTRATION

"Outer threshold ever clean,
Clean within let all things stand.

House all clean, might entertain
Angel from the Heavenly Land.

Clean the food, and clean the cup,
Clean the wall from smoking brand.

Son! thy outward cleanliness
Pledge of inward is, when scanned.

Clean let hand and mouth be kept;
Clean the garment's every strand."

—*Divan of Jalál-ud-din Rumi.* (Trans., Wm. Hastie.)

"It was not the cold, clear voice of one giving advice and warning from serene heights to those who were struggling and sinning below, but the warm, living voice of one who was fighting for us, and by our sides, and calling on us to help him and ourselves and one another. And so, wearily, and little by little, but surely and steadily on the whole, was brought home to the young boy, for the first time, the meaning of his life—that it was no fool's or sluggard's paradise into which he had wandered by chance, but a battle-field ordained from of old, where there are no spectators, but the youngest must take his side, and the stakes are life and death."

—"Tom Brown's School-days," chap. vii.

PUBLIC HEALTH ADMINISTRATION[1]

THE connection of public health with public weal is universally recognised in European countries. But a few facts may be advantageously put together to show how pressing the question of public health is in India, and to emphasise the conditions in that country which make for so appalling a waste of human life, human energy, and human efficiency.

The death-rate in England and Wales for 1903 was 15.4 per 1,000; the death-rate for the whole of India for 1903 was 34.7 per 1,000, which is more than two and a quarter times as high as the death-rate of this country. Fifty years ago the death-rate of England and Wales was 22.5 per 1,000—that is to say, the 1893 death-rate in India was 154 per cent. as high as the death-rate in this country was fifty years ago, before the splendid achievements of modern sanitary science had established their claim to universal acceptance.

[1] A Paper read before the London Congress of the Royal Institute of Public Health, 1905.

Think for a moment of what these figures mean. If the death-rate in India were on a par with that in England, there would be 19.3 fewer deaths per 1,000 than there are; or, in other words, taking the population of India roughly at 300,000,000, there are 5,790,000 lives lost annually which would be saved if the English death-rate prevailed in India. We may stand aghast at these figures for the whole of India, but what should we say of the figures for particular provinces whose death-rate is above the average? The provinces I know best are the United Provinces. The death-rate of these provinces in 1903 was:—

Urban . . .	54.9	per 1,000
Rural . . .	39.2	,,
Average . .	40.3	,,

In the big city of Cawnpore the rate was as high as 89.5. A high death-rate of that character not only means that so many millions of people died who would have lived under better sanitary conditions. It means, further, that for each million of unnecessary deaths there are so many more millions of debilitated living persons, whose lives (from a physical point of view) are a curse to themselves and to society, whereas in other conditions they might have been fruitful of results that added to the sum total of human happiness.

Again, take the figures of infant mortality. I

extract the following paragraph, which refers to the United Provinces, from the Annual Report of the Sanitary Commissioner with the Government of India for 1903 (p. 75):—

"Owing to the prevalence of measles, the death-rates of children were very high, 279.2 male and 269.1 female infants respectively having died among every 1,000 born; while boys and girls between the ages of one year and five years died at the rates of 89.71 and 88.49 per 1,000 living according to the census figures."

Compare this with the state of affairs in England. I take my facts from a paper read by Dr S. G. Moore, of Huddersfield, at the London Congress of the Royal Institute of Public Health. In the worst parts of the great English cities only 3 out of every 4 children born live for twelve months. On the other hand, in houses with more than five apartments in Croydon as many as 945 per 1,000 infants born survive for twelve months.

Let us put these facts in a tabular form. The chances of any particular new-born infant attaining the age of one year are:—

In favourable localities in England, $\frac{945}{1000}$.

In the most unfavourable localities in England, $\frac{750}{1000}$.

In an *average* locality in the United Provinces, $\frac{726}{1000}$.

Thus our average figure, taken from both rural and urban areas, favourable and unfavourable conditions, is far worse than the figure taken from the most unfavourable industrial urban areas in England. If Dr Moore is (and rightly) indignant at the latter figure, what would he think if the figure for infant mortality were placed before him for a city like Cawnpore, in which, taking the population as a whole, the chances of any average individual being alive next year are only $\frac{910}{1000}$? A baby in Croydon can look for ard to his first birthday with far more confidence than a factory youth can feel in being alive to bathe in the Ganges at the next annual bathing fair.

It may be objected that a comparison of English and Indian figures is hardly fair: first, because India is subject to visitations of famine and plague; secondly, because of the enervating nature of a tropical or sub-tropical climate; and, thirdly, because of the inferior physique and vitality of the people as compared with the hardier races of the North. As regards famine, I will only say that the figures I have taken are those for 1903, which was absolutely unaffected by any influences directly traceable to famine. As to the indirect influences of famine in lowering the vitality of the people who have suffered from it, though not to the extent of paying the extreme penalty, that, I fear, is a factor which, like the poor, is always with us. The measures for fighting this evil relate to a larger policy than that with which sanitarians are concerned. But after all, India is not the only country afflicted with the vagaries of nature or climate, with inequalities in the distribution of wealth, with periodically recurring depressions in agriculture, trade, or industry, or with the problem of the unemployed. The severest of our recent famines have been, not food famines, but wage famines —in other words, a phase of the Unemployed Question on a gigantic scale. If our economic calamities are more sudden, more acute while they last, and on a larger scale, it does not follow that economic evils in other countries, which are of a chronic if less impressive character, have not their weight in the solution of sanitary problems. India is not peculiar in being face to face with grave economic problems which require solution. Other countries have attacked the problem of sanitation side by side with the problem of poverty, and there is no reason why we should not do the same.

Plague is, indeed, a most disquieting feature in the sanitary administration of India. The last nine years' experience shows that it increases in gravity year by year. The recorded deaths from plague in 1898 were 89,265; in 1901 the figure rose to 236,433; in 1902 it was 452,865; in 1903 it was 684,445; and in 1904 the estimated figure was 1,021,600. The total number of those recorded as having died of plague from the autumn of 1896 to the end of 1904 was 3,250,000. The rate of increase, it will be seen, is alarming, and I am afraid that, as far as we can judge, plague has come to stay in India. But it must not be forgotten that plague raged furiously in London only two centuries and a half ago; and if this country is now immune the credit is due entirely, under God's providence, to the better sanitary arrangements and sanitary habits prevailing now. The disease is not entirely beyond human control. If the people could be educated up to this view, if they would adopt the precautions which have been used with so much success in the lines of the native army and in the gaols, it would not be a hopeless matter to extirpate plague. In 1903 the number of deaths from plague in the native army was 115 out of an average strength of 124,660, and in gaols only 23 out of an average gaol population of about 98,000.

A comparison of the death-rate of the gaols with that of the free population is most instructive. In the one case we have a high sanitary standard enforced under medical supervision; in the other we have the normal insanitary conditions of an ordinary Indian town or village. The results are strongly in favour of life in the gaols, even after all allowance has been made for errors in the vital statistics of the free population and for the particular age and sex limits to which the gaol population is usually restricted. The females in the gaols constitute so small a proportion that they may practically be neglected. It has been calculated[1] that the mortality of males of the free population of India as a whole, under ordinary conditions, is at the rate of 25.8 per 1,000 of the number at the age-period fifteen to sixty-six years, which may be held to cover the ages of the prisoners. The gaol death-rate in 1903 was only 21.38 per 1,000. The prisoners are drawn chiefly from the lowest and most unhealthy classes of the population. These results are striking enough, but they are rendered still more striking by the fact that they show a continuous tendency that has operated from year to year. Any particular year's figures might be due to some exceptional circumstances; but when we find that for the last few years the death-rate of the general population has been steadily rising, while that of the gaol population has been steadily falling, we get an incontrovertible testimony to the practical efficacy of the gospel of sanitary science even in India.

I think I have shown that it is not the racial tendencies, nor the climate, nor any irremediable conditions in India that cause so great a loss of life. These drawbacks apply, in some cases with greater force, to the gaol population of India, and yet the gaol population shows not only a better death-rate, but a *constantly improving* death-rate year by year. A comparison, therefore, with the facts of life and health in healthier countries

[1] P. 58 of the Report of the Sanitary Commissioner with the Government of India for 1903.

is not only legitimate, but is useful as affording a standard to which we ought to be able to work up ourselves.

Let us glance briefly at the causes of this sanitary backwardness, the agencies which exist for meeting it, and the further means which might be employed in aid of public health administration.

It is well known that private and personal cleanliness is one of the strong points in the habits of the native population. But there is no co-ordinated effort for public sanitation, no realisation of the fact that the individual living in a complex state of society owes duties, sanitary as well as social, to that society, which are not discharged merely by washing the body. In many cases poverty is a strong agent in keeping from the people the blessings of well-built, well-ventilated, and well-lighted houses, well-drained and well-swept streets, well-cooked food-stuffs, and a pure water-supply. But, besides poverty, there is a vast mass of ignorance and prejudice to contend with. If a certain fashion of dress, or a certain style of houses, or a certain arrangement for the disposal of sewage and night-soil has become stereotyped by caste or tribal custom, resistance will always be offered to any suggestions that are based on the teaching of mere outside experience or of abstract science. Not only the vested interests of the sweeper or scavenger caste, but the conservatism of the general population would view with alarm any energetic sanitary policy, and attribute the most impossible motives to those whose worship of hygiene drives them beyond the dictates of conciliating discretion. The fact is, that urban life in organised communities is, as has already been pointed out in speaking of town life, a new thing in India. There were so-called cities in India before the advent of the British, but they were collections of menials, artisans, and courtiers, camp fashion, round the person of a ruling monarch or chief. No corporate life was understood, no common action based on the good of the city community was ever deliberated upon by people for and among themselves. The village community was a living entity, but towns with all that town life implies are an innovation. The people have not had time to adjust their ideas and habits to the new development of social life, and it will need time and education to convince them that sanitary science and public health administration are the necessary corollaries of a state of things in which every individual's physical and social life is a source of comfort or of danger to thousands of other lives with which that particular individual does not come into personal contact. People must learn that municipal by-laws for the examination of cow-sheds, the disinfection of stables and wells, the supervision of slaughter-houses, and so on, are not merely whimsical or unwarrantable acts of interference with the liberty of each person to do what he likes, but are a necessary complement and condition to that liberty

—viz., that such liberty should not be exercised to the detriment of other persons in the community.

If a person sells unwholesome milk in a village community, he is recognised at once as an offender in relation to the individual to whom he attempts to sell it. The next step will be that he will be recognised as a *public* offender by *public* opinion, and the higher step will have been attained when the vaccinator, going round with his lymph, will be hailed as a public friend and benefactor, instead of as a monstrous ogre sent by a mysterious Government or a misguided municipality! Then shall we have some hope of successfully combating, if not extirpating, plague, when every error in plague administration will be looked upon by the people as a step on which to build a larger and more effective policy, and every public measure for isolation, segregation, and disinfection will be judged solely on its efficacy and thoroughness.

The present agencies for public health administration in India are mainly external to the people themselves. The motive power is almost all supplied by Government. It is true that there are some 763 municipalities, with 5,000 elected members, 3,800 members nominated by Government, and 1,418 Government officers serving as members *ex officio*. But, apart from the municipalities of the presidency towns, the main ideas of sanitation in municipalities are worked out and carried through by the paid officers of Government. In district municipalities the civil surgeon of the district is usually the health officer, and his advice and assistance are simply invaluable. He is the only professional expert available in the district, but he is a busy man, with the district gaol, the hospitals, the vaccination staff, and a variety of other matters under his charge. Municipal work is merely an episode in his official life. There is no private medical opinion to lead or form lay opinion on sanitary matters, and no press outside the presidency towns which can take an intelligent interest in public health and form a valuable link of good understanding and cooperation between the public authorities and the people.

There are no private societies or institutes, and no degrees or diplomas of public health. The servants of the district municipalities have usually no technical knowledge of hygiene or public health, and are mere ministerial agents for the carrying out of orders.

While the lower departments of public health administration are — as they must be in a poor and backward country — so unsatisfactory, every one who has had anything to do with the higher departments must recognise how admirably they are organised and equipped, what a large mass of theoretical knowledge they collect and publish, and what splendid opportunities they have for higher research. The sanitary administration of India has been recently reorganised, and those who are interested in its history will find a short *résumé* of it in the Government of India's resolution on the subject in the Home Department, of 8th September 1904. There is now a Sanitary Commissioner with the Government of India, and a Sanitary Commissioner with each Provincial or (as it is called) Local Government. In accordance with the recommendations of the Plague Commission, certain well-equipped institutes are in process of being established for the study of the wider problems of public health in India. Researches in bacteriology are being pushed forward with vigour under the able management of Colonel Semple at Kasauli, and the Parel and Agra Laboratories have done a vast amount of practical work in spite of the difficulties under which they had to labour. If this talent and organisation at the top were fed from more vigorous roots at the bottom, we might have a living tree with a prospect of abundant fruit in the near future. Unfortunately, the conditions rather remind us of a fabric with a golden dome and clay foundations.

In these circumstances it is now recognised that the surest means of progress will be somewhat slow in their operations. The people have to be educated up to a sense of duty in relation to public health, and this education can best be accomplished with the rising generation. The best method of overcoming the obstacles to public health is to enlist the co-operation and sympathy of the Department of Public Instruction, which has the privilege of giving a bent to the tendencies of future citizens. This is a point so strongly emphasised in the inaugural address of our noble President, the Marquis of Londonderry, himself the head of the Education Department in this country,[1] that it is unnecessary for me to do more than point out its application to India.

An ounce of practice is worth a pound of theory. I have no faith in a Sanitary Primer, glibly recited by a boy in dirty clothes, fed on ill-nourishing diet and polluted water, who reads about the benefits of pure air by wretched light in an ill-ventilated room. I would have the Department of Public Instruction take up the question of public health in their own quiet, practical way. I would allow no dirty little hovel to be used as a school-house for a State school or a State-aided school. I would not insist upon fine buildings or much furniture (except in the way of apparatus for games), but I would insist upon a place that was scrupulously clean, and properly lighted and ventilated. Half the school-houses in the interior are not rain-proof, and in the rainy season are full of a damp, muggy atmosphere. I would stop that. I would encourage open-air school in the cold weather, when open-air

[1] This was in 1905.

conditions are most pleasant in India—a practice which the open-air instincts of the people already adopt, except where some town-bred dominie considers it less dignified to sit under the sky than to sit under a roof. I would not promote a teacher who was not neat, clean, and orderly in his own habits. I would have bathing parades and tooth-washing parades wherever necessary, that is, mostly in towns. On account of caste rules it would not be possible to regulate the diet of the pupils, but some practical instruction and guidance might be furnished in the kitchens of the boarding-houses attached to the more important schools. I would pay special attention to the hours of work and the hours of rest or recreation in the schools. Games are receiving far more attention than they used to do, but it is necessary to systematise courses of physical education, and encourage those games which require organisation and discipline.

To carry out these objects, I would have a systematic periodical medical inspection of schools, and systematic hygienic records of the pupils. In every district there are qualified anthropometric measurers to record the physical data about criminals; in every gaol every prisoner is weighed and medically examined on admission, and at periodic intervals, and his physical history is compiled and recorded. Is it too much to ask that the physical history of boys and girls should be noted and examined for the benefit of the subjects themselves as well as for the advancement of a more intelligent opinion on these topics? For example, why should not a pupil's weight, height, chest capacity, lungs capacity, eyesight, and teeth be periodically tested, and the results recorded and used for the physical improvement of the pupils? If relative standards in these matters were fixed, and printed schedules hung up in every school-room, any intelligent master would be able to inform himself of the physical condition of the boys under his care, and would be able to regulate his discipline, and allot work to his pupils accordingly. Any difficult or abnormal cases he would bring to the notice of the medical officer at his inspection, and profit by his advice. We have a Factory Act which insists upon a quarterly medical inspection of factories. Is the health of factory operatives more important than that of the growing children of the community?

I have pointed out the enormous waste of life that occurs in India. I have shown the difficulties which all sanitary proposals have to meet with. I have endeavoured to prove that the waste of life and the difficulties can be prevented and surmounted, and instanced the striking results that have been obtained in the gaol administration. I have reviewed the agencies for public health administration in India, and suggested their weak points. Finally, I have tried to put forward what I consider to be the surest means of advancing the public health—viz., by directing our efforts to the growing children, and impressing some of these great needs of life by practical object-lessons, rather than by ready-made knowledge crammed from outside. If what I have said serves to stimulate the interest of sanitary authorities in Indian problems, or of my countrymen and fellow-workers in the splendid life-saving work that lies before us, I shall not despair of a day when centuries will be frequently heard of in India—not only the "centuries" of our Prince Ranjitsinhji, but also the "centuries and a little more" which Sir James Crichton Browne has told us are within the reach of us all.

VII

CIVIC LIFE

"Oh, what a joy this life would then be! No more hateful strife! Only emulation. All eyes turned to the same goal. Every effort, every nerve, straining onward—upward—each man in his own natural way. Prosperity for all—the work of all!"

—IBSEN, *Rosmersholm*, Act iii. (Trans., CARMICHAEL.)

"Commonwealths are not physical, but moral essences."—BURKE.

"The most worthy pursuit is the prosperity of the whole world."

—PIYADASI: Edict vi.

"Abject flattery and indiscriminate assentation degrade as much as indiscriminate contradiction and noisy debate disgust."

—Lord Chesterfield's Letter to his Son (10th August 1749).

CIVIC LIFE

THE average life of a citizen is made up of so many strands intertwined with one another, that it is useful occasionally to isolate one of them and examine it. We shall thus discover its strength or its weakness, and ascertain what strain it is undergoing under the stress of social forces operating on it, how it responds to that strain, and what can be done to render it more efficient as a binding force in organised society. The strand which we are now about to examine is that which knits municipal life together in India.

Some observers would doubt whether there is any active civic life in India. They fix their gaze on the predominating factor in the government of the country, the factor which has moulded its history for centuries past. That has always taken the shape of a central government, responsible only to its own conscience, and to religious and moral sanctions for its policy and conduct. When these were dormant, we had government of the most arbitrary and brutal type. When these were active we had an administration of the most beneficent and enlightened kind. But in either case there was no continuous growth of institutions, no evolution of the people guided by ideals which, whether successful or not at any given stage, supplied the motive power in the lives of communities. The people, as a factor in the commonwealth, were, for all practical purposes, neglected. It is true that the people (or realm, in Bühler's translation[1]) were one of the seven estates composing the commonwealth, as described by Manu. The father of Hindu polity enumerates those seven estates as the king, his minister, his metropolis, his people, his treasury, his army, and his ally. These have a sort of mystic union—*septem juncta in uno.* For, though the gravity to the commonwealth of the harm done to any of these estates is in the order in which they are named, it must not be supposed that any of these are of less importance than any of the others, so long as they fulfil their functions in the complex institution called the State. This noble conception of Manu is of the highest importance in dealing with the germs of Hindu political ideas; and yet, its practical working out is most disappointing, even in Manu. We have the amplest maxims for the king's life and policy; we have far-reaching regulations about the individual's life, ritual, and conduct; we have also full details about the constitution, history, rights, and privileges of the several castes and classes; but we look in vain for a definition of the rights and privileges of the

[1] Manu, ix. 294-7, "Sacred Books of the East."

of the most refined and high-thinking citizen, but, in the main, it is now restricted to a narrow circle of actions which come within the purview of criminal law or of municipal by-laws. My advanced citizen is governed, in his civic acts and ideals, by considerations like the following: "I am," he thinks, "more fortunately circumstanced than some of my fellows in the community. I have better education, a more refined up-bringing, more opportunities of travel, more wealth, a higher position, or more talent than some of those I see around me. Can I use these for the benefit of the less fortunate? Can they be brought to see things from the higher standpoint? Will it not strengthen the community as a whole, and therefore me, as an individual member, if the laggards can be made to march abreast of the active members, if the obstruction which stands in their way be removed, so that every one is able to make the best of himself, to his own benefit and the benefit of the community? Again, there are other members of the community who are somewhat similarly placed in respect of some of these advantages to myself. Will not the union of our efforts and resources produce a higher aggregate result in material and moral advancement than when some of the energy is wasted in individual and un-co-ordinated endeavour? Again, I see some persons better endowed than myself. In so far as it is in my power, is it not my duty to aim at bettering myself, not for personal aggrandisement or self-glory, but because the pursuit of the higher is the highest ideal, for myself individually, and for the community at large?" In such musings the individual is sunk in the community. If we must have a tangible formula embodying the incentive to such conduct, it would be: "If I do this, it will mean increased good to myself and the community." The hope of reward in its highest form here takes the place of the fear of punishments.

The prevailing notion that the ancient Indian village was based on communistic ideas of property and life is, I think, incorrect. The boundaries of a family are necessarily wider in an early than in a later stage of society. That being so, the unit which society recognises for purposes of ownership and possession is also wider and more indefinite. In movable property, however, we find nothing to justify us in inferring that anything like communistic ideas existed. In regard to land, the fact that periodical redistributions of land took place, and that no exclusive and permanent rights were recognised in individuals, has led to the reasoning that the property was joint. But perhaps it would be truer to say that no property in land was recognised at all, whether in the individual or in the community. Land was treated as a free gift of Nature, like light, or air, or the water of a river. As long as the population was scanty, and the quantity of land appeared unlimited, there was no occasion to create well-defined rights of property. When the demand first began to outstrip the supply, the rights which were earliest recognised were rights of cultivation or pasturage, or, to speak generally, rights of temporary possession. These were regulated by many provisions of customary law, designed, no doubt, for the common good, or for the good of the lord or chief, much in the same way as an individual's private conduct was regulated. A conquering chief parcelled out the land among his kinsmen or retainers, in the same way as he might detail his sentinels on duty at different posts, or assign different offices or functions to different members of his household. Here the question would not be one of property in the individuals, the community, or the chief, but rather one of discipline and organisation.

Nor was life in the village community based on communistic ideas. Equality among all the members was the last thing that would have occurred to a philosopher of the times, or been recognised by any one in touch with the actual government of the village. There was a splendid system of subdivision of labour, and a thorough understanding between the different classes into which the community was divided. The organisation was perfect; it promoted the greatest efficiency with the least waste of energies,—the greatest peace, concord, and contentment, with the least inducements to luxury or crime. It may be one form of the millennium dreamed of by the framers of fancy republics, but it is not communism. The bed-rock of the communistic principle is equality of enjoyment for all members, coupled with an equality of responsibility for the well-being of the whole society. The fundamental basis of village life in its palmiest days was the due subordination of castes and classes to a scheme which was nowhere, and at no time, worked out with feudal precision, but which acquired strength or weakness, according to the amount of resistance which village institutions were called on to exert in antagonism to a strong or weak central and military power. The village had no military organisation or history, but it had marvellous powers of passive resistance. And its relation to the central power was not usually that of branches that supply nourishment to a tree, or that of a large number of tiny rills, whose flow goes towards the augmentation of the strength and volume of some mighty river. On the contrary, the village community looked upon the central power much as a tree (if it could think) would look upon the parrots and mainas that feed on its fruit. There was no intolerance, and no chafing, so long as no more than customary contributions were levied, but there was distinctly a feeling of aloofness, a consciousness that the structure of the village community was quite independent of the central power.

There is, therefore, no paradox in the fact that the most beautifully-organised structure of the village community led to no advance in civic life—the life that uses the experience and organisation of local communities for the formation, development, and support of the wider and more human, as opposed to a theocratic or other mystic, conception of the State. Nor have any of the modern representative institutions of India any historical affinity with village institutions. The trade guilds of the towns and the *panchayets* of the castes were the institutions that most familiarised the plebeian portion of the population with the practical details of concerted action. The higher castes are, and have always been, comparatively weak in the matter of organisation and combination for wordly ends. The history of the Indian trade guild and of the *panchayet*—if it could be written—would furnish some of the most fascinating chapters in the annals of India; but, unfortunately, there are no materials (whether in the forms of records, grants, charters, or accounts) on which even the meagre outlines of a reasoned history can be based. The Mir Mohalla ("alderman of a ward" would be a fair translation of the term), or the Lambardár[1] of a Mahal (shall we call him "steward of a manor?"), if and where the representative character of these functionaries was recognised, and they were invested with fiscal powers, exercised a certain amount of authority in immediate touch with the people. They acted

[1] The *word* "Lambardár" is quite modern, but the office and the idea which it connotes, can be traced to the earliest days of Muhammadan land revenue administration.

as buffers between the representatives of the central government and the people. The lump sum of taxation payable by the community which they represented was fixed after consultation with them, and they were left to apportion this among the contributories in accordance with local rights and customs. But these institutions never flourished with a lusty and vigorous growth in directions in which they can be traced as leading up to the local self-government of modern India.

The growth of modern civic institutions can all be referred to the last half century. The ideas naturally first took shape in the Presidency towns. Calcutta was the first of the towns to discuss, but Bombay was the first to adopt, the elective principle. Before this principle was adopted, the city government had been carried on by means of a bench of magistrates or justices. The elective proposals of 1840 for Calcutta had to be dropped. But when Bombay took the lead in 1872 with an electorate that was practically based on household suffrage, Calcutta followed suit in 1876. The history of municipal government in those two cities has since been full of both interest and excitement. The constitution of the municipality has been altered in both cases. But it is to be noticed that in Bombay the change has been effected without much popular excitement, while in Calcutta the revision of 1899 was attended with almost as great a measure of opposition as the more recent reconstitution of the Province of Bengal. In Bombay there has always been a large deliberative body, with a smaller managing council, while the entire executive power has vested in the municipal commissioner, who is nominated by, and is in close touch with, the Government. In Calcutta the executive power was until recently vested in what was considered an unwieldy body by those who applied the shears in 1899. After the advent of the plague ten years ago, a separate body, called the Bombay Improvement Trust, has been called into existence, which exercises powers, independently of the Corporation's control, for carrying out gigantic schemes of public improvement, such as the sweeping away of overcrowded areas, the widening of streets, and the provision of sanitary buildings for the mill hands, while the æsthetic side of a town's responsibilities was not lost sight of for a city which prides itself on the title of Bombay the Beautiful. This great scheme was due to the enthusiasm and practical sagacity of Lord Sandhurst, just as the great Calcutta Improvement Scheme, which has not yet emerged from the incubatory stages, is due to the marvellous energy of Lord Curzon. In the city of Madras the elective principle was introduced in 1878, and though little of dramatic or popular interest has been heard of in the recent administration of the oldest Presidency town of British India, the legislators, administrators, and people of the Southern Presidency are unanimous in claiming for Madras the title of the best and cheapest governed city in India. I wish they could add to the claim some faint allusion to the goddess of civic beauty, for her cheery smile can surely never come near the Madras *parcherries*, which for gloom and squalor could give points to the much-abused *bustees* of Calcutta or Bombay.

Local government by magistrates existed in the Presidency towns almost from their first creation as vigorous and growing communities; it flourished until it was superseded in the 'seventies by representative institutions. In the Mofassil towns organised government by a magistrate and a consultative council began in 1850, with an Act respecting "Improvements in Towns." This Act authorised local governments to appoint a magistrate and such number of inhabitants as may be necessary, to be commissioners to prepare rules for levying and expending money for any special purposes of local administration. In form, this statement of the Constitution has undergone a complete and radical alteration; but in substance—in the living ideas underlying the new forms—this principle practically applies to municipal government in the districts to-day. In 1856 was passed the great Act which governs the smaller towns in Northern India to the present day. This makes the arrangements for local improvements permanent instead of occasional. The magistrate of the district is both the initiative and administrative authority. He fixes the sum required for a given year for town purposes; and he constitutes by nomination a small council, or *panchayet*, to distribute this lump sum among the different inhabitants, either on their local knowledge of the taxpayer's worldly circumstances[1] (which sounds vague), or (which is very rare) on a definite valuation of property. In either case the magistrate hears the appeal from an aggrieved assessee. Having finally confirmed the assessment list, the magistrate collects the tax and spends it on local improvements. Now I have some little experience of the assessment lists of these little towns—some of them decaying vestiges of what were once important centres of population. I have no hesitation in saying that the vaguer of the two principles — assessment according to position and means — works far better, both in justice and in smoothness, than the apparently sound principle of a formal valuation of property! There are other institutions in India in which a similar paradox occurs, and it is well to remember in drawing up paper constitutions that things are not *always* what they seem.

In the government of the smaller towns under Act X. of 1856, there is neither the election of

[1] This vague method of taxation finds its counterpart in the method of assessing rates *juxta facultatem*, which prevailed in mediæval England.

members, nor in theory local supervision by the people, in carrying out the works for which the town fund is levied. In practice, however, a sympathetic magistrate always arranges informally for local supervision by such respectable inhabitants of the town as are willing to charge themselves with the responsibility of "looking after other people's business."

The principle of supervision by local, though not necessarily elected, citizens, for Mofassil towns and rural areas, was strongly insisted on by Lord Mayo's Government in 1870. It was then recognised that funds devoted to such objects as education, sanitation, medical charity, and public works of a local character, benefited by the supervision of local agency. But the greatest landmark in the history of modern representative institutions in India was the action of Lord Ripon's Government in 1882. Certain broad principles were laid down by that Government which were afterwards embodied in the legislation of 1882 and 1883. The objects held in view by the far-reaching reforms then promulgated were stated to be twofold—first, to relieve the officers of Government from a portion of the duties and responsibilities which had gone on increasing as the machinery of Government became more elaborate; and, secondly, to introduce local interest in local affairs, coupled with local unpaid service as an instrument of political and popular education. The machinery with which these objects were to be carried out was provided by the creation of local boards for rural areas and municipal boards for the larger towns, with an assured preponderance of non-official members, elected by popular vote wherever the local circumstances admitted of the principle of popular election. Government control, it was laid down, was to be from without rather than from within, and the chairmen of the boards were accordingly to be non-official. The rural boards were to be for small areas about the fifth or sixth part of a district on the average; and there was to be in each district a district board exercising authority over the local boards and co-ordinating their action.

The result of these comprehensive proposals was that all the principal towns of India were granted municipal constitutions, in which the elected members usually preponderated, though room was found for some members nominated by Government, and a few *ex officio* members. The franchise of the different municipalities varied very widely, and was fixed according to local circumstances, often under bye-laws drawn up by the municipalities and sanctioned by the Government. The constitutions and the numbers of these municipalities have varied little since then, except in regard to two important points presently to be noticed, though a vast amount of progress has been made in those twenty-four years in grappling with the details, intricacies, and pitfalls of local administration, and in elaborating municipal codes in the different provinces. The points in which there has been in practice the greatest divergence from Lord Ripon's ideas are (1) as regards the *personnel* of the chairman, and (2) as regards the relation of Government to the boards. In practice the chairmen of most of the Mofassil municipalities are the magistrates of the districts in which they are situated. The magistrate is not *ex officio* chairman. The board regularly goes through the formality of electing its own chairman, and may, if it chooses, elect a non-official gentleman; but by a sort of unwritten law the board, in fact, elects the district magistrate as chairman. Whenever there is a change in the office of district magistrate, it is distinctly understood that the out-going magistrate resigns the chair, and equally understood that his successor in the magisterial office is elected to the chair of the municipality. Now the district magistrate being the chief executive officer of Government in the district, it follows that his election as the head of the municipality, introduces indirectly Government control from within rather than from without. It is true that Mr Smith, as chairman of the municipality, sometimes carries on a lively correspondence with himself as magistrate of the district; but the situation, though full of humour, has no significance whatever in practical administration. The fact that one man fills the two posts is a guarantee (in the case of an average man) that he will take the same point of view in both offices in all material questions of business. This may possibly appear to derogate from the independence of municipalities; but in the present circumstances of India it is necessary in the smaller municipalities, in the interests of efficiency and smooth administration. The chairman-magistrate, a man of affairs and experience, and yet on the spot, serves as a buffer between the amorphous opinions of an inexperienced board and the weighty but somewhat detached position of the Commissioner, to whom the control and guidance of the municipalities has been delegated by Government. That Government control and guidance are necessary at the present stage no one can deny; granting that necessity, the arrangement which the experience of two decades has evolved seems to be the best possible at once for present efficiency and for future progress.

In discussing the progress of the rural boards, we find the situation far less encouraging than in the case of the municipal boards. The two points of departure from the original conception of the boards, which we noticed in discussing the municipalities, are also noticeable, even with stronger force, in the case of the rural boards. The greatest diversity prevails in the different provinces in respect of the unit for the rural boards. It may be said of several of the provinces that they contain district boards only, and practically no local boards for the smaller areas.

The United Provinces are an instance in point. The local boards have not sufficient powers and responsibilities, and they rarely do any solid business. It is only within recent years that even district boards have been invested with any financial independence, and in public bodies, as in families, you cannot be said to have started house-keeping until you have separate accounts of your own to worry over. Another cause of backwardness in the local government of rural areas is to be found in the great isolation of rural interests from one another, and the slower susceptibility, compared with the towns, to the grip of that knitting force which is the chief glory of the British Administration in India. Madras is the only province in which the rural boards have shown signs of a vigorous existence. There the unit adopted is a small one—the village union, governed by a *panchayet.* Higher in the scale are the Taluk Boards, which correspond to the local boards of Upper India; and over them all is the district board, which flourishes because its constituent feeders live a growing and healthy life. The village union was not in the large and comprehensive scheme of rural self-government drawn up for the whole of India, but by its adoption in Madras the roots have penetrated sufficiently deep into the soil below, to give strength and vitality to the growth above. Another argument for calling Madras the "benighted Presidency"!

There are in the whole of British India[1] 763 municipalities. The population living within municipal limits is close upon 17,000,000. The total number of members of municipal boards is more than 10,000, or an average of 13 members to each municipality. The municipal boards of the Presidency towns are very much larger bodies, Calcutta having 50 members, and Bombay 72; but their constitutions, offices, by-laws, and procedure are in many respects entirely different from those of district municipalities. The proportion of official to non-official members for the whole of India is 2 : 7, that of European to Indian members is 1 : 7. The maximum proportion of appointed to elected members is fixed by statute. For example, in the United Provinces the number of appointed members is not to exceed a quarter of the total number of members. The aggregate income of the municipalities, according to the Return[2] published in 1905, is £6,579,094 — roughly speaking, six and a half millions sterling. This may be divided into three convenient heads, viz.: (1) Loans, deposits, advances, etc., three and a quarter millions, of which fully one-third is on account of the Presidency towns; (2) amount realised from rates and taxes, two and a half millions; (3) amount

[1] The figures that follow are principally taken from the "Statistical Abstract relating to British India for 1903-1904," published as a Blue-book in 1905.

[2] "Statistical Abstract," as above.

realised from rents, contributions, sale proceeds of manure, etc., three-quarters of a million.

It will be noticed that about half the year's income is derived from loans and other sources which can be classified as debt. The year's expenditure nearly balances the income. The municipalities are very properly not allowed to hoard their money, a tendency which some of the outlying boards showed at the earlier stages of their career. A sufficient closing balance is, of course, insisted on. It follows that about half the year's municipal expenditure comes from borrowed money. While the expansion of income under the second and third heads (taxation, rents, etc.) has been only about 33 per cent. during the last ten years, the increase under the head of debt has been about 600 per cent. These figures are startling at first sight, but it must be remembered that the process of sinking money in material and tangible assets—to wit, large public works—has been carried on very considerably in the last decade. Most of the large district municipalities have constructed their waterworks within that period. Large drainage and sewage schemes, the widening and paving of roads and thoroughfares, and measures for the prevention or fighting of plague, have necessitated large demands on the municipal exchequer. Perhaps in some cases a more cautious policy in the matter of borrowings might be advisable; but the expert supervision of the Government makes it impossible that in any case the financial stability or solvency of a municipality should be jeopardised by reckless borrowing. All the Mofassil municipalities have to get Government sanction for their loans, and their financial statements every year have to show clearly how their debt account stands, with reference to their assets, the state of the sinking fund, and the arrangements made for the payment of the interest charges. In the case of the Presidency municipalities there are statutory limitations to the aggregate amount of debt which the municipality can owe. In Calcutta, for instance, the cost of the interest and sinking fund is not to exceed 10 per cent. of the valuation of the city. At present I believe it is 7½ per cent. The debt of Calcutta is about two millions, against an annual revenue of half a million; that of Bombay is about three millions against half a million of revenue. The proportion of revenue to debt is therefore 1 : 4 in the one case, and 1 : 6 in the other. The proportion in the national finances of the United Kingdom is between 1 : 6 and 1 : 7. On the other hand, the interest charges in local finance are very much heavier than in Imperial finance, the Indian municipalities usually paying between 4 and 7 per cent. of interest on their loans. The question of debt in municipal finance ought to be studied more carefully than it is by members of Indian municipalities, as the expedient of throwing the burden of present difficulties on future generations may result in a serious crippling of resources, or a check to the expansion of activity, unless there is an expanding benefit derived from the works undertaken.

As regards the form of taxation the different provincial systems differ widely. In the Punjab, the United Provinces, and the Central Provinces, octroi forms the chief source of income, and in Bombay it forms a considerable item in municipal taxation. Bengal, Madras, and Burma, among the larger provinces, do without octroi. The system works thus. A number of octroi stations (ten or fifteen) are placed all around the municipal boundaries, commanding all the ways of entry into the town. There is a clerk in charge of each station, whose duty it is to levy a tax on all goods entering the municipality, according to a schedule fixed and notified by the municipality. The schedule contains a classified list of goods which are chargeable to octroi, with the rates shown against each. Some of these rates are *ad valorem*, and others are according to weight or measure. A set of scales and weights is provided by the municipality. The quantity or weight is often estimated by the cart or the load, or in accordance with local commercial usage. But if there should be a dispute between the importer of the goods and the clerk, the whole of the goods have to be taken out and weighed, counted, or measured, as the case might be. In the case of *ad valorem* rates there is most chance of a dispute. Where the importer is a large wholesale dealer, the invoice which accompanies the goods is often a sufficient indication of the quantity or value. But in India, where make-believe and collusion play so important a part in the machinery of life, this test cannot always be relied upon. To the petty trader or the private individual, however, the annoyances are numerous and vexatious. The clerk who collects the tax has a salary of from 9s. to 12s. a month. There is a strong temptation and opportunity for illicit gains. In all cases where he can reasonably count upon not being found out, he creates difficulties and differences of opinion. There is a machinery for settling these, but it is cumbrous in comparison with the nimble coin slipped into the clerk's hand, which solves all doubts and difficulties without trouble or loss of time. Octroi administration therefore demands constant vigilance on the part of members and officers of municipalities. The first requirement is to make a good schedule, simple and unambiguous, with as few items in it as would be consistent with clearness, and with due regard to the fostering, according to economic principles, of the local industries and manufactures; the next object of attention should be the appointment of as honest and efficient a collecting and supervising staff as possible; and the third is the careful periodical examination of the statistics, accounts, and practical working, with free opportunities provided to all who have specific complaints to make before the Board. Some boards maintain an overgrown supervising agency, drawn from the same class as the tax-collecting clerks. They forget the maxim, "the greater the supervision, the greater the collusion."

They are gradually abolishing octroi in the Bombay Province. It would be a good thing if it could be abolished altogether. In spite of an elaborate and carefully worked out system of supervision, checks by means of standards of consumption, refunds, and exemptions, it probably takes more from the pockets of the people than actually goes into the coffers of the municipalities. Its chief merit as an indirect tax paid on commodities, and not directly levied from the citizens, is neutralised by many delays and petty malpractices, and it is a fruitful source of harassment to the poor and uneducated classes who enter towns with even a small amount of belongings—the very classes who require most protection. The question of abolition, however, is not yet within the region of practical politics in Upper India, and it is all the more necessary for civic patriotism to be directed towards insuring its proper administration.

Apart from octroi the most important sources of municipal taxation are a tax on houses and lands, which is sometimes levied in addition to octroi, but which occupies the chief place where octroi does not enter into the scheme; a water-rate in large towns with waterworks; and a conservancy - rate, which is usually for public conservancy only. The system of private conservancy is still peculiar in most of the smaller towns. The mechanical appliances for sanitary conservancy have scarcely taken root even in the Presidency towns; in the Mofassil they do not exist. A caste of hereditary scavengers, who look upon the goodwill of their business as a marketable and heritable asset, claim the monopoly of service in private houses. The payments to them are not systematic, but are based on a set of elastic customary rights. The consequence is that private conservancy is the weakest feature in town life. Any radical reform evokes opposition, not only from the scavenging class with vested interests, but even from the citizens themselves, who are apt to forget the inefficiency of the present system in concentrating their attention upon its cheapness. Taxes of minor importance are: taxes on animals and vehicles; taxes on professions and trades; tolls on roads and ferries; and a lighting-rate, though the cost of lighting the town is usually defrayed from the general income of the municipal fund.

The incidence, per head of the population, of the amounts raised or (what is equivalent to it) spent by the municipalities varies greatly in the different Provinces, and the different kinds of municipalities. The Presidency towns are, of course, more expensive than the Mofassil towns, and among them Bombay leads the way as easily first. From rates and taxes Bombay raises 12s. 7d. per head, and from all sources, including loans, 14s. 7d. per head. The figures for Calcutta are 8s. 11d. and 10s. 8d. respectively; and those for Madras only 2s. 11d. and 4s. 3d. respectively. Rangoon is almost as expensive as Bombay, the incidence of taxation being 8s. 8d. per head, and of all municipal revenue 14s. 6d. per head. But Rangoon, as a municipal town, has a shorter career behind it than the Presidency towns, and its borrowings must necessarily be on a liberal scale to keep pace with the phenomenal rate at which the town is growing—in size, population, and commercial importance. These figures are comparable to the incidence of the rates levied in England for the use of the Poor Law authorities, which average to about 6s. or 7s. per head of population. The incidence of municipal expenditure in English boroughs furnishes no fair basis of comparison; first, because the scales of people's incomes are so different in England and India, and secondly, because the English municipalities undertake, on the whole, more duties, and are more in touch with popular sentiment than are the Indian municipalities. The incidence of municipal taxation per head of population in the borough of St Albans, in which I reside, is about 15s.

The figures of the Mofassil municipalities are, as might be expected, lower than those of the Presidency towns. The Province of Madras is again the cheapest, with an incidence of 1s. 6d.

for rates and taxes, and 2s. 5d. for total income in district municipalities. Burma is the most expensive, with 2s. 3d. and 5s. 1d. respectively. The variation in the figures for the district municipalities is small, and the incidence per head may ordinarily be taken to be about 2s. for rates and taxes, and about 3s. for total income.

An analysis of the main heads under which the expenditure falls may be of some value. From the figures in the statistical abstract already quoted I have prepared the following table showing the percentages :—

	Percentage to total expenditure.
Interest, debt (repayment), sinking fund, deposits, etc.	50.3
Public health and convenience	35.8
General administration and collection charges	6.7
Public safety (lighting, police, fire, etc.)	4.2
Public instruction	3.0
	100.0

It will be noticed that the debt charges absorb more than half the total amount spent by the municipalities, and exceed by a long way any other single item. Under the head of public health and convenience, which accounts for about 36 per cent. of the annual expenditure, are included a large number of items. Not only is the annual expenditure on water-supply and drainage debited to this account, but also the capital outlay under these heads. This amounts to a very considerable item, and when the public works expenditure is added to it (*i.e.* the outlay on roads, bridges, public works establishments, and stores), the amount left for conservancy is not very large, and is certainly quite inadequate, in most cases, for the needs of the overcrowded plague spots which are called Indian towns. Markets and slaughter-houses are also debited to this head, but the outlay is small, and is ordinarily more than counter-balanced by the tolls and dues levied in them. The municipal expenditure on hospitals, dispensaries, and vaccination is not large, and is a mere supplement to the funds contributed from private, district board, or Government sources.

The expenditure on services of public safety is insignificant, being only 4 per cent. of the whole. Very few of the municipal boards maintain fire brigades. Systems of fire insurance are unknown in the Mofassil, as indeed might be expected, considering that the majority of the proletariat live in mud huts with thatched roofs, and a man's personalty in many cases amounts scarcely to anything more than what he might carry as personal luggage on a railway journey. The police charges, which are included in the statistics, are no longer paid by municipalities in the United Provinces, where the stability of municipal finance under the stress of plague expenditure was threatened, and relief from the police charges was one of the liberal concessions made from provincial funds by the Government of Sir James LaTouche. In the matter of lighting there is little satisfactory result in the Indian towns. Kerosine oil, often of the poorest description, is the illuminant used. In the Cantonments and the Civil Stations, as opposed to the Cities, a respectable attempt is made to light the roads, but even there the magnificent distances which separate one house from another preclude the struggling street lamp's misty light from performing any other office than that of rendering the darkness more visible. The magnificent distances also render any thorough schemes of street-paving or well-constructed drainage so expensive as to be prohibitive. The best roads consist of a strip of metal 9 or 12 feet wide, with broad alleys on either side of a depth of 2 or 3 inches of dust or mud, according to the moods of Jupiter Pluvius.

The charges of general administration and collection of taxes amount to nearly 7 per cent. of the expenditure. This is the average. In many municipalities the proportion is higher. Considering that the majority of the servants paid out of the salary bill are entertained primarily for purposes of tax collection, the proportion is high, and might with advantage be scrutinised and reduced wherever possible. The salary bill in many of the English municipalities bears a much smaller proportion to the total expenditure. In the borough of St Albans it is about 5 per cent. It is an invidious task, especially where the servants happen to be nominees or *protégés* of the members, to cut down salaries or reduce establishments, and Indian civic dignitaries are as generous in voting money—other people's—as any in Christendom. What they ought to remember is that public money is not other people's money, but their own. Indeed, the standard of care and economy to be expected in regard to public money ought to be very much higher than that which people are accustomed to exercise in their own private affairs. If a man mismanages his own affairs he only hurts himself, and the ordinary promptings of human nature should in most cases deter him from persistently erring in that direction. But when he fails to exercise the utmost diligence in his power in the administration of public funds committed to his care as a sacred trust, he is a traitor to the interests of hundreds of poor tax-payers who have bestowed upon him the honour of being their representative because they trusted him. Such betrayal, if there were an active civic conscience, would be considered deserving of far more reprobation than any individual lapses in private life.

Economy, however, is not to be confounded with niggardliness. Economy makes for efficiency, while niggardliness is only a form of mismanagement. Now there are objects on which municipal boards might spend far more funds than they actually do. Such an object is education. Under this head the total sum spent by the municipalities of India amounts to a paltry 3 per cent. of their outgoings. This can scarcely be considered adequate. Free education in municipal towns may be a counsel of perfection. But there can be no doubt that a much larger amount than is actually spent is required to meet the existing demand for education, and that this demand is growing every year. It has always been the settled policy of Government to encourage municipal boards in making liberal grants towards elementary education, but it is remarkable that the response from the boards has not been as hearty as might have been desired. In the towns the demand is all for English education in Anglo-vernacular schools. These come rather under the description of secondary than of primary education. Now while primary education has received most attention, the opinion has frequently been held that secondary education—especially in English—should be paid for by those who desire it. Every town has one or two secondary schools, but they are generally overcrowded, and as the English course is of most material benefit to the pupils, it is the most popular branch of study. It is also the least organised. The names of many distinguished statesmen—none more than that of Sir Alfred Lyall—are associated with an attempt to encourage secondary and English education, and there are signs that the Education Departments are realising the importance of English in the early education of the children of India. But the municipalities would do well—while not starving elementary education—to lay out, judiciously, sufficient funds for meeting the demand that has vigorously set in for secondary and English education.

I think I have said enough to show the opportunities and the experiments, the performances and the shortcomings, the possibilities and the pitfalls of civic life in India. It is true that the qualification for voters, though low enough, still keeps a large number of the population outside the vortex of municipal life. In Calcutta, for instance, the qualification is threefold—viz., either the payment of rates and taxes to the amount of Rs.24; or the possession of a licence to practise certain trades and professions; or the occupation or ownership of land of a certain value. Under the last head a man may have as many votes as there are units of property. In any of these three forms property bulks largely (for India) in the makings of a civic elector, and the number of names on the Voters' Register bears a very small proportion to the total population. In the City of Calcutta, with a population of 1,000,000, the electors number scarcely 10,000. But, on the other hand, the interest shown by electors in contested elections is very keen; indeed, in some cases it might with advantage be moderated with some of that tolerance for opponents which introduces chivalry into the civic code. In 1895, as many as 75 per cent. of the electorate voted in the contested wards of Calcutta.[1] This makes a very favourable show when compared with the London County Council election of 1901, in which only 20.6 per cent. voted in the City of London and 56.8 in Stepney. The fact is that in spite of many failures and many gaps to be filled up in the future, a fair amount of progress has been made in building up a civic conscience in India. So acute an observer as Lord Curzon (then Mr Curzon), in piloting the India Councils Bill through the House of Commons in 1892,[2] used words which are truer to-day than they were fourteen years ago — words full of generous sympathy and penetrating insight. He defined the objects of that measure to be:—

"To widen the basis and to expand the functions of Government in India; to give further opportunities than at present exist to the non-official and native elements in Indian society to take part in the work of government, and in this way to lend official recognition to that remarkable development both of political interest and political capacity which has been visible among the higher classes of Indian society since the Government of India was taken over by the Crown."

[1] P. 83 of the "Moral and Material Progress of India for 1901-1902" (Blue-book of 1903).

[2] Hansard, fourth series, vol. iii. p. 53, 28th March 1892.

If comparisons are of any assistance, it may be useful to recall the fact that though some of the English towns had shown evidences of a vigorous municipal life in the Middle Ages, a long period of decay had followed. Most of the present forms of municipal activity in England have been created since the Reform of 1835. Prior to that a detailed enquiry into municipal life was instituted by means of a Commission whose conclusions form a scathing indictment of the depths to which English municipal institutions had fallen before the Reform. A perusal of these conclusions should at least save us from undue impatience or despondency with regard to the young nurslings in India.

"The Municipal Corporations were," according to Sir Somers Vine,[1] "for the most part in the hands of narrow and self-elected cliques, who administered local affairs for their own advantage rather than for that of the borough; the inhabitants were practically deprived of all power of local self-government, and were ruled by those whom they had not chosen, and in whom they had no confidence; the corporate funds were wasted; the interests and the improvements of towns were not cared for; the local courts were too often corrupted by party influence, and failed to render impartial justice; and municipal institutions, instead of strengthening and supporting the political framework of the country, were a source of weakness and a fertile cause of discontent."

[1] As quoted at p. 750 of the *County Councils, Municipal Corporations, and Local Authorities Companion*, 1906. Published by Kelly's Directories, Limited, London.

If some of these statements might be applied to Municipal Boards here and there in India, we should not be justified in losing faith, but rather stimulated to a more strenuous effort for the realisation of our ideals of public life.

The German philosopher Haeckel uses a felicitous phrase, "Communal Soul," in discussing the habits of the most primitive of Protozoan forms. Whether this communal soul exists in the unicellular radiolaria must be left to biologists to determine. But it certainly forms an important factor in the capacities of mankind. It is the centripetal force which binds families, races, and nations together. It is the element which lends pathos, dignity, and sublimity to epic poetry. It gathers the threads of isolated thoughts, floating dreams and visions, and unconnected deeds of gallantry and heroism, and weaves with them a tangible and splendid fabric, whose composite glory of sparkle, softness, and strength forms the outer robe of aspiring humanity in its stately march through the centuries.

VIII

WOMAN'S LIFE

"O gentle wives! your fondest wish is still
To have with him you love one heart, one will."
—KALIDAS, *Birth of the War-God.*
(Trans., GRIFFITH.)

"Partake, but never waste his wealth;
Or stand with smiles, unmurmuring by,
And lighten half his poverty." —BYRON.

"Forbid me not: with thee I go,
The tangled wood to tread:
There will I live with thee, as though
This roof were o'er my head.
My will for thine will be resigned;
Thy feet my steps shall guide;
Thou, only thou, art in my mind;
I heed not all beside.
Thy heart shall ne'er by me be grieved;
Do not my prayer deny:
Take me, dear lord; of thee bereaved
Thy Sita swears to die." —VALMIKI, *Ramayan.*
(Trans., GRIFFITH, Bk. II., Canto 27.)

WOMAN'S LIFE

It is difficult for a mere man to speak about woman's life in any country, but when you come to woman's life in India, which is hedged round with so much pomp and mystery, I do not know how I shall be able to acquit myself. But I have one consolation. Intuition is said to be one of the strong points in a woman's character. If, therefore, I am so fortunate as to have any readers of the fair sex, I shall appeal to their intuition. I shall expect them to interpret my remarks as those of "a mere man," not impertinent, not over-confident, but anxious to know and understand. They have already been submitted to the judgment and criticism of a ladies' club. If wit, wisdom, and beauty found them of some interest in oral delivery, they may not be altogether devoid of interest to the outside world. For the rest I can but say with Shakespeare: "Piece out our imperfections with your thoughts."

Let us first speak about the life of an ordinary Indian woman from the cradle to the grave. We will take not a woman of a particular class—a Muhammadan, or a Hindu, or a Parsee, a wealthy woman or a poor woman, a woman of the working classes or a woman of the leisured or literary classes; but a simple average woman. We will make of her a sort of composite photograph and discuss what are the chief events and stages in her life. If you are at all inclined to doubt the accuracy of the picture as too abstract or too remote, my excuse will be the same as that of the young curate who was lecturing on angels. His *fiancée* was, of course, present, sweetly expectant of some tender touches in the discourse which should enable her to see herself as others saw her. She was sadly disappointed, and showed her disappointment in her conversation when they were walking back home. "True," said the curate, "I might have drawn many analogies to enforce my meaning, but I did not wish to be personal."

In England and in the countries which have advanced far upon the path of unification—to call it by no worse name—the lives of many individuals are cast in a particular mould; their ideas, aspirations, fashions, and wishes all seem to run in a groove. If one woman wishes to wear a particular style of hat, perhaps all the other women, whether they actually succeed in their wishes or not, hanker after it. Nothing of that kind obtains in India. The conditions are quite different, the ideas are quite different, even the standards are quite different, amongst the different classes. How, then, am I going to make my abstraction, and to put before you this pattern of an average life from the cradle to the grave? I think that in spite of the great diversity of form in Indian life, there is, in many aspects of it, an underlying unity of substance which enables us to make general statements with a certain amount of truth. It is a commonplace to say that the Hindu women are different from the Muhammadan. So they are, but at the same time I think there is a basis of character that is common to them both, and if we can only take hold of the essentials and eliminate the accidentals, I claim that we can bring forward a picture that is, on the whole, faithful to the essence of woman's character in India.

Now we will follow the history of our imaginary woman. She is just born. "A girl! A girl!" cries the nurse. As she is not a boy you will be prepared to learn that the same sort of rejoicings do not usher her into this world of sunshine and storm as would greet the arrival of a boy. Why is this? Does that mean that the birth of a girl is supposed to be a calamity? Perhaps, speaking only of the unregenerate, unimaginative classes, it may be so; but you must not on that account put down the Hindus as an ungallant race, insensible to the charms of the gentler sex. In their mythology there is the story of the churning of the ocean by gods and demons; and of the fourteen gems they produced, none was more valuable, none more dazzling, than the bright, smiling, tender-eyed Sri — Sri, the lotus-born goddess of fortune, wealth, and beauty, the type of Indian womanhood. On the other hand, we must remember that a son implies much more in Hindu ideas and in Hindu law than he does in other social systems. A son in Hindu parlance is often called the giver of immortality. The idea is that a parent never attains to the higher life after he completes his life in this world, unless he has left a son who can perform his funeral obsequies and give offerings to the gods, which alone give him admission amongst the immortals. Thus it will be understood that the advent of a son means something that affects the whole of the immortal life of a man after he finishes his wordly existence. The advent of a girl to a certain extent also means that, but it means that for other people; because the girl when she is married goes into another family, and all her virtues and all her greatness are, as it were, imputed to that other family of which she becomes a member. Therefore, to the ordinary Hindu family, the birth of a girl, irrespective of how much they may in their frailty have wished for a girl, is not an event of the same importance, or an occasion for the same rejoicings, as would usher in the birth of a boy.

There are many ways of showing joy because a child has been born in the family. If it had been a son, we should probably have found a number of guns let off, however poor the family was. The neighbour who has a gun licence watches an "interesting" house when the event is near, and prays that it may be a son, as he can then earn a few pice by firing salutes to the future lord and master of the house. Formerly they used to sound the conch-shell, the Hindu equivalent to the trumpet. At this sound, neighbours, relatives, and dependents, flock to the house to offer congratulations, and receive gifts, for the stream of largess is flowing freely. When a daughter is born they do things much more gracefully and quietly, for they bring in a large tray full of sweets, and offer it first to the nurse, and secondly to the mother's sister — that is to say, the child's aunt—and thirdly to all and sundry. The mother, we must notice, is not allowed to have any sweets—perhaps because she has already got her reward in the addition to the family.

After the sweets are distributed and the congratulations have been tendered to the boy-husband and his parents, there is a horde of dependents whose claims have to be satisfied in hard cash. There is another set of people who are expected to come and have the privilege of looking at the child's face—at the price of handsome gifts to the nurse and the members of the family. The law of compensation is strong in Indian social life. Wherever gifts have to be offered, gifts are received to a nearly equal amount. The successful social leader is the one who contrives that the balance of gifts is always in his or her own favour. A good deal of this depends on the gentle art of issuing invitations, an art whose economic aspect is not entirely lost sight of by the bride's mother in England, when she wants an imposing array of wedding presents to dazzle and delight their donors. For surely poor lords, smart millionaires, and handsome artists must all feel, when their names are bracketed together, that it is as blessed to give as to receive! In my ignorance I once remonstrated with an Indian father who was going to borrow Rs.500 for his son's wedding. "Surely you cannot afford it," I said. "Oh, yes," was the disconcerting reply, "it's very good business. I borrow Rs.500 and lay it out in expenses and gifts. I receive Rs.700 in gifts from wealth and rank; paying Rs.10 for a month's interest. I clear Rs.190, and marry off my children into the bargain!"[1]

But I am digressing. It is necessary to take the child's horoscope. The Hindus are an extremely astrological race. They can do nothing in life without consulting the stars. Perhaps this partly accounts for the want of punctuality noted as a glaring defect in Indian character. There

[1] This must not, of course, be taken to imply that I approve of extravagant expenditure at weddings or birth or death ceremonies. The outlay is purely unproductive, and is often indulged in as a speculation. Moreover, at weddings, the gain of one party is a burdensome loss to the other. Rational social enjoyment is one of the pleasures of life, but when expenditure disturbs financial equilibrium, and cripples an estate or family for generations, no sensible person would call it rational.

is an old story of a stately Raja who was invited to a party on a certain day and arrived two days afterwards. It was not that he had missed the train, for he travelled with a train of chariots, horses, and elephants. The fact was that at the time when he should have started, the ruling planet was unfavourable and he had to wait until the wicked planet had got out of the way and a more lucky planet had come to rule. The Sun, Mars, and Saturn, are unlucky planets (the Sun being a planet in Hindu astronomy), while Venus, the Moon, Mercury, and Jupiter are lucky planets. The Hindu almanac shows for each day of the week minute subdivisions of time which have different astrological characters. One *ghari* is good for business, another is mortal, for it will kill you if you challenge it. A third is fraught with a happy issue to all you undertake, and a fourth with affliction. There are some *gharis* which are neutral: you may do things if you are compelled to do them, but not if you are free. Hence in some circumstances compulsion is welcomed; for the compulsion converts the ill-luck into luck for the person compelled—but woe betide the person who compels, for he doubles his own sorrow!

Such being the ideas that affect life, it is most important that the precise time of the girl's birth should be carefully noted, for on it will depend her name, her marriage, and her whole future destiny. Her horoscope is made out and her ruling planet and the cast of the stars carefully determined and recorded. Not only must the favourable planet be known, as pointing out her gifts and virtues, but the star in opposition is equally important, because on that would depend her conduct towards those whom she has any reason to suspect as enemies. Then a number of minor stars and asterisms will have to be noted, as they aid or warp the influence of the guiding stars and planets. When the configuration of the heavens at the moment of birth is completely and accurately recorded, the Brahman or Pandit will be able to construct exactly the history of that child from the moment of its birth to the time it will have to be called away. Is such history true? That reminds me of the story of a man who was to have died at forty. In his forty-fifth year he was still alive, and suspecting that there was something untoward in the heavens, he sent for the learned Pandit who had read the horoscope and asked him to account for the discrepancy. The Pandit was a cynic, and answered by a question, "What did you pay for your horoscope?"

Fortune-telling apart, the horoscope has important practical results. No name can be given to the child until the horoscope has been scanned and studied. What's in a name?—why, the whole history of a Hindu woman. Just as the stars dictate her destiny they also dictate her name. It is true that a name is often informally given which is a pet name, and in fact most of the

Hindu women have two sets of names. One name is the name by which they are vulgarly called, but the other name, the true name, is the astrological name, the name which you must know before you are able to reason about her qualities or about her destinies, either in this world or in the next. This ordinary name is the *apparently* important name, but the *ráshi* name does not figure in actual life because it is too sacred to be defiled by daily use. The *ráshi* name is known to the parents, of course, and the priest, but not to the child itself until she is grown up sufficiently to understand it, and sometimes not at all.

There was once a peculiar case in a Criminal Court. A woman called Rampatia was entitled to a pension from the Government, and that pension was not paid unless she appeared in person. She was a poor woman and every year, apparently, she came regularly and drew her pension, until an energetic treasury officer looked up the birth roll and found that if the woman who had appeared last was Rampatia she must have been ninety years of age. On this, enquiries were made, and it was found that the woman who should have drawn the pension had been dead some years, and that at each previous verification another woman had personated her. They got hold of this person who had appeared before the treasury officer and drawn the pension, and she was put on her trial.

Her defence at the trial was:—"Oh yes, it is true I am not ordinarily called Rampatia, but my astrological name is Rampatia. I am therefore the other woman Rampatia, and I am entitled to draw the pension." That defence was probably good in psychology, though it was bad in law. It was not a defence that would have occurred to a lawyer trained in an English court of law: she appeared to be firmly convinced that her *ráshi* name being Rampatia it did not matter what people ordinarily called her in real life, and that in some way she was continuing the life of the person who had died. She really believed that she was committing no crime, but was actually entitled to the pension which she was drawing.

The *ráshi* name is a matter of some importance, but it may be asked: what sort of names do they ordinarily give for daily use? In England the only name about which there is any choice is the Christian name: the family name has to be taken whether you like it or not. Amongst Indians a Hindu child has usually no family name at all: the system of nomenclature is quite different. Each person has a personal name, and there is the unknown *ráshi* name. The ordinary names run in a very curious system which I should like to explain. If you were given a name, you could pretty nearly tell to what class an Indian woman belonged. Of course you could not do this in England. If you heard the name of Alice you could not say whether she belonged to a humble working class family or was a daughter of Lady Vere de Vere. Hearing the name of an Indian woman you could, within certain limits, tell her class and standing.

Suppose I was told that there were seven Indian women in the next room, and that their names were Dhukia, Maryam, Shirin Bai, Saraswati Bai, Phul Mani Dasi, Karámat-un-nisa, and Parmeshri Debi. Among these I should at once pick out Shirin Bai as a Parsi woman, Shirin being one of the heroines of Persian history and romance. Saraswati Bai I should say was a Hindu woman of Southern India, probably a Maratha, the suffix "Bai" being characteristic of Southern and Western India, and Saraswati, the name of the Hindu goddess, showing that the bearer of the name is not a Parsi. Karámat-un-nisa is unquestionably a Muhammadan woman of the better classes, for they look upon it as a mark of gentility to adopt high-sounding Arabic names which are really titles, this particular name signifying "A miracle among women." Maryam might be a Muhammadan of the humbler classes, as it is an Arabic name with no flourishes, or she might be a native Christian, rejoicing in the Oriental form of the English Christian name Mary. Dhukia is probably a lower-class Hindu woman, maybe a peasant. Among such persons the every-day names are either nicknames or simple unmeaning words of one or two syllables, such as Ládo. Phul Mani

Dasi is probably a Bengali lady of the better classes, but a non-Brahman, the suffix "Dasi" (female slave) being attached to non-Brahman names to distinguish them from the names of Brahman ladies, which have the suffix "Debi" (or goddess). By that suffix we know Parmeshri Debi to be a Brahman woman. For aught we know she may be a servant of Musammat Phul Mani Dasi, who, in spite of her servile suffix, may be a Rani or princess, but the Brahman is a Brahman "for a' that an' a' that."

Thus a little close study of the names in India tells us so much. The name may tell us of the religion or race; it may tell us of the caste, high or low, and it may give us a hint as to the social standing, as measured by wealth or poverty. Some names, such as Ramzán Bibi, may tell us the month in which the person was born. Others, signifying the gift of a particular god or goddess, would show the vow which the parents took to dedicate the child, if one should be given them, to the deity or local godling to whom the desire of childless parents is communicated by many propitiatory gifts. But such vows are usually for a male child. Other names, again, have opprobrious meanings, such as "a clod" or "worth a farthing," to put off the evil spirits which are supposed to be ever ready to snap off good children, but are easily deceived into leaving the child called by an opprobrious name because they really think that that child is not worth having. Of course, if you must give your child an opprobrious name, you counterbalance it by means of a lucky and beautifully sounding *ráshi* name, which is kept a close secret. In Indian nomenclature the names run in moulds, types, or patterns, which reveal so much folklore that no one who wishes to understand the people intimately can afford to ask the hackneyed question "What's in a name?" and pass on without waiting for an answer.

The giving of a name is attended with ceremonies, religious and social, and the exact time when it must be given is determined by astrological rules. The auspicious moment having been chosen, the girl grows and thrives—not only as the child of the family, but as the child of the whole neighbourhood. The children are gregarious in India, and except for very small babies, who ride astride the mother's waist, the office of motherhood is usually in commission.

The next stage you would expect to find her in would be that of a school girl, but I am sorry to say that schools do not exist for ordinary girls in India. They scarcely mould the lives of the boys; but for the girls many people would actually object to school life. They would say: "What has the girl to do with learning, as she has not to earn her bread?" Of course that does not mean that every girl remains illiterate. A certain amount of education is given to the better class girl, but it is home education. When she grows up she is able to read her own language if she belongs to the literary classes, and perhaps she knows one of the classical languages of India.

Then comes the important time when she must cease to be seen; she must go into the *Pardah*; she must live secluded from the gaze of men. At what age does that happen? There is no age fixed; but it is generally expected that she should begin to rehearse the process at eight or nine, and completely adopt it at twelve or thirteen. Marriage is considered a good point to start from, but Pardah often begins before marriage. The age of marriage in India is very early; and betrothal takes place even earlier. Betrothal is a contract of marriage between the *parents* of the children, and in exceptional cases may be entered into even before the children are born. This may be for family reasons, or because the endogamous group — the group outside which marriage cannot take place —is so small that the anxious parents (or grandparents) have to think out family alliances for their expected progeny, before they are actually ushered into the world. If A and B both expect an addition to their respective families and consider the two families fairly equal for matrimonial purposes, A would say to B: "I will make a bargain with you. If I have a son and you a daughter, it is a match, and the same *vice versa*." But what if both the children are sons, or both daughters? Would the bargain be off? Not entirely. One of the family might already have a child of the right sex of an age sufficiently near to make a match possible with the new arrival; or they may wait a year for future developments. It is usually considered right if the bridegroom is about the bride's age or just a little older. Thus it sometimes happens that a betrothal contract is entered into even before the birth of the parties whose lives are bargained away!

But the ordinary betrothal, even when accomplished, means nothing beyond an arrangement for a family alliance. The actual marriage takes place at about twelve or thirteen years of age. The age limit varies among the different communities. The Mussulmans believe in a higher age limit than the Hindus; and the vast little-known population of races or castes, which are classed as Animists in the religious statistics, live simple, natural lives, and act in this matter with freedom and good sense. Their morals, if lax, have at least the redeeming grace of conformity with nature. Including them, the statistics show that out of every thousand males in India twenty-three are married under the age of fifteen, and as many as sixty-two out of every thousand females. Remember that the sixty-two wives under fifteen years of age do not include widows, of whom there is a goodly percentage. Among the better classes the universal age may be taken to be between twelve and sixteen, and most families would consider it a disgrace if the daughter is not married and "settled" long before sixteen.

What is the marriage ceremony? There are many picturesque and pretty rites, and feasting for days on end is the order of the day. But the chief incident of the better class Hindu marriage ceremony consists in what is called the Bhaunri —the sevenfold circuit of a tree or post, or the seven steps taken in unison. All this is symbolical. The seven steps are the seven grades of life. Compare this with the seven ages of man in your own immortal bard, or the seven sacraments of the Roman Catholic church, or the seven planets of ancient astronomy, after which the days of the week were named. The husband, a mere boy of fourteen, walks round and round solemnly with the end of his coat tied to the end of the sheet or cloth that his little wee girl-wife wears on her head, symbolical of their union in life. All the time they do this they must not look at each other, but above. The Hindu ideal —a relic from the times when the Hindu race was full of ideals — does not recognise even that refined or romantic form of selfishness which extends its circle of self-absorption and self-deception to two instead of one. It holds more to Mrs Browning's ideal :—

> "Lead her from the festive board,
> Point her to the starry skies ;
> Guard her by your truthful word
> From courtship's idle flatteries."

Not that the children know anything of these symbols or mysteries, but all Eastern life is full of symbols for those who can understand. They may take different shapes and sometimes degenerate into mummery, but they undoubtedly exercise a vague, dreamy influence.

Among the Muhammadans these picturesque ceremonies are not recognised. In the first place, the parties are a little older. In the second place, the Muhammadan marriage is a civil contract in which neither party merges its identity in the other. The Hindu is bound to invite his whole caste or community, within a reasonable distance, to his wedding festivities; the Muhammadan only his select friends. The Muhammadan ecclesiastical ceremony is of the simplest description—as simple as that among the Society of Friends. Many of the Muhammadan families restrict themselves to the ecclesiastical ceremony, but the majority have adopted or inherited in addition the customs of the country. Some even use a modified form of the Bhaunri. Prolonged feasts and ceremonies, with music or noise (whichever you prefer to call it) and martial-looking processions (a relic of marriage by capture), are quite common. A wealthy family's bridal party would be mounted on palanquins, horses, elephants, and chariots, such as Abhimanyu might have used in the Great War. Coins would be scattered on the march, to be scrambled for by boys and youths of the poorer classes.

Fireworks play a very important part in the rejoicings incident to an Indian marriage. Most of the firework makers drive a roaring trade in the marriage season, and earn the best of their profits during that time, hibernating during the the rest of the year. Thus marriage is good for trade. The marriage season is limited to two or three months of the year, generally in the spring; but the heavenly aspect varies in different years. When the stars are most propitious there is a regular marriage boom, with a concomitant boom in the trade in fireworks, cloths, and fancy articles. But the stars may also ruin trade if they frown to the astrologers and indicate a slump in the marriage market.

If we may trust to the fidelity of Hogarth, English popular marriage customs were not so very different in the eighteenth century from what we may observe every day in India at the present time. Take the wedding scene in the series of pictures entitled "Industry and Idleness." The industrious apprentice has at last won the hand of his master's daughter. At the festivities the proud bridegroom is seen offering the drummer —shall we call him tom-tom boy?—*bakhshish* in the form of hard coin. The butchers are there with the marrow bones and cleavers, just as you would find the representatives of different trades following an Indian bridal party, each with the emblems of his trade—the sweeper with his broom, and the barber with his bag. You have further in Hogarth the beggar with his merry ballad but mournful face. An Indian Bhat might well have sat for a model. But what is this?—a poor woman with a child in one wallet and "the crumbs that do fall from the master's table" in another. Evidently a Chamárin come to assert her claims on the lord of the feast.

How is the bride dressed, and what does she look like? Dare I attempt a word-picture? It would be more satisfactory if a gifted artist's brush were allowed to tell its own tale. I have the honour to possess a picture in oils, "The Hindu Bride," painted by Mrs Barber, which won a medal at the Simla Fine Arts Exhibition some years ago. It is a symphony in colours, but most difficult to reproduce. Let us try to gain an idea of the bride's appearance by means of a feeble description. There is the girl, with the brightest of black eyes, and a face more round than oval. The white of those eyes is of dazzling purity, like the modest little soul that looks out of them, but you can scarcely see the eyes. The cloth which serves both for head-gear and body garment is drawn closely over the face. It would be difficult to name the colour of this piece of drapery. It is semi-transparent, and lets you see the glory of the raven hair and the sparkle of the jewels worn on the person, but it adds its own contribution of colour to the general harmony. Perhaps we should not call it colour: *Pas la couleur, rien que la nuance*, as Paul Verlaine would say. It is a suggestion in light blue silk gossamer, with a border worked in gold and silver threads, which both stiffens and enriches the airy stuff. The jewellery errs on the side of profusion, but there is no trace of vulgarity. The drapery, which, in concealing it, heightens its effect, gives it a subdued tone where it might otherwise "cry aloud." A row of little pearls hooked into one of the plaits of hair covers the parting of the hair in the middle. From it hangs on the forehead a flat little pendant of pearls, rubies, and moonstones, set in gold. This pendant also fits into the scheme of the caste mark if the girl is a Hindu; otherwise it is artistically meaningless. The hair is gathered into a knot behind, and a garland of the sweet-smelling *bela* flowers is intertwined with it — snowy white on raven black, filtered through the blue of the drapery. From the nose hangs a pearl-drop, and there are sapphire earrings to match. The neck is absolutely loaded with ornaments, but you only catch a glimpse of them through an indiscreet opening of the veil. The upper arms carry amulets and charms, and the lower arms bracelets and bangles of many shapes and styles of workmanship. There are rings, not only for the fingers, but also for the right thumb, and one of them has a miniature mirror with a receptacle underneath for a plug of cotton wool saturated with otto of roses. There are anklets and toe-rings to complete the tale of ornaments. Such is the bride as she sits on her *machia*, a sort of low chair, made of wood turned on the lathe and lacquered.

From a water-colour.] [*By* M. DHURANDHAR.

TOILET OF A HINDU BRIDE.

"The hair is gathered into a knot behind, and a garland of the sweet-smelling bela flowers is intertwined with it"—p. 272.

To face p. 272.]

There are no wedding presents besides the ornaments and the trousseau, but these give ample scope for display. The donors' names do not appear on cards, but this is atoned for by their being talked about, sometimes with a gushing simplicity that heralds the approach of another marriage in the family. A portion of the jewellery is often borrowed for the occasion. The jewellery is rarely false except in circles affected by "modern civilisation."

I have devoted so much space to the marriage customs, because I find that they are of perennial interest to people of all temperaments among all nations. Did not Lady Augusta Hamilton write a book on the marriage rites, customs, and ceremonies of "all nations of the universe"? This was in 1822, but the world has not much changed since then—at least in this respect.

Between the celebration of the wedding ceremonies, and the going away of the bride to live in her husband's house, there is often a long interval. When the time comes, it means a complete change in her life. She is entirely lost to her people. With us the daughter is not the daughter all the days of her life; she is only the daughter *until* she is a wife. Then she enters into a new circle and new relationships, and she literally worships a new set of family gods. The Americans have a saying that a woman is independent before marriage in England, after marriage in France, and at all times in America.

From an Indian point of view it would probably be expressed thus: that a woman has a protector in her husband in England, and in her brother in France, while in America she has to fight for her own hand against all the world. The Indian woman is always protected—by the father in childhood, by the husband in youth, and by the sons in old age. "A woman," says Manu the lawgiver, "should never be independent." Whatever degree of freedom and initiative she had in her mother's house is lost to her in her new home. There she is the daughter-in-law. The new life brings many hopes to her, but, alas! where in child-marriage can there be the delicious romance, the first sweet ecstasies of a life united to another in all honour and admiration, ennobled by poetry and purified by all the ethical ideals of the race!

The mother-in-law is with us the chief butt of satire and comic poetry. In what country is she not? But in India *the* mother-in-law is the husband's mother, not the wife's; and the amenities between her and her son's wife are accentuated by the fact that the former is so much older than the latter and the two have to live together, with scarcely any influence on the part of the boy-husband. The girl-bride cannot say: "Daughter am I in my mother's house, but mistress in my own." From having been perhaps the pet of fond parents, she enters into the glare of a critical mother-in-law's observation and correction. She may not speak to her husband before other people. It is to her mother-in-law that she must bow the knee. She must serve her apprenticeship as a good and dutiful daughter in-law, until years and honours grow upon her, and in spite of fading youth she reaches the goal of her social ambition in being able to have several sons and daughters-in-law, over whom she may herself exercise her stern authority.

All this is possible on account of the peculiar joint-family system of the Hindus. Under this system the individual is nothing: the family is everything. The family is a close corporation, recognised by law. It may in exceptional cases number as many as a hundred individuals. The eldest male member is nominally the head, but it is the eldest female member who rules. There may be three or four married sons with their wives, and perhaps uncles and aunts, and grand-children and great-grandchildren to several generations. There is a saying which ascribes family bliss to the man who lives to see seven generations gathered under his roof. Of course no man would be equal to the strain, but the elder women revel in the authority which that implies. When you hear that woman is a slave in Oriental households, with sundry harrowing details, do not swallow the story without a pinch of salt. Place a woman anywhere, and she would know how to rule, or at least to assert her authority. It is true that the younger women — especially the young girl-wives—are drudges to the mothers of their boy-husbands. But they bear it all patiently, for do they not hope to rise to the position and dignity themselves in the fulness of time? And you may be sure, when their time comes to be mothers of the household, they will not bate an inch of their authority or relax the rigour of their rule one whit because they have themselves passed through the mill.

The position of a childless widow, on the other hand, is anomalous and not at all enviable. Widow re-marriage is forbidden among the higher Hindu castes, and, I am sorry to say, looked at askance among some of the Muhammadan families in Upper India. According to the Hindu conception a wife completely sinks her personality in her husband, and the marriage is indissoluble even after death. After the husband's death the dutiful wife has nothing to live for, and no doubt many striking cases of self-immolation were prompted by the widow's keen sense of desolation and desire to join him in the next life. The courage of the deed and the applause of the Brahmans lent a note of heroic self-sacrifice, which ever appeals to a woman's soul in one form or another. Mrs Naidu well describes the feeling in the heart of the ideal Sati when she puts these words into her mouth:—

> "Life of my life, Death's bitter sword
> Hath severed us like a broken word,
> Rent us in twain who are but one—
> Shall the flesh survive when the soul is gone?"

In course of time the practice degenerated into a family or social rite, in which the woman's consent became a matter of as little consequence as it is in the majority of marriages. In the darkest times, however, cases of enforced *Sati* must have been rare. The practice was abolished altogether by the criminal law in the Governor-Generalship of Lord William Bentinck, but even now the Criminal Courts have occasionally to enquire into the lurid details of a crime which, were it not for the superstition attached to it, is entirely opposed to the instincts of Hindu character. The discomforts of enforced widowhood cannot now be so terrible after all, seeing that the Indian Census shows that widowhood tends to increased longevity.

It is no paradox to say that the happiest and most fascinating age of a woman in any country is her old age; but this applies peculiarly to India. Purged of her passions, invested with the dignity of motherhood, uplifted above the trivialities of life, she wears the crown of her pure white hair with a calmness and a protecting grace impossible to younger women. Modesty is the charm of young womanhood; goodness is the quality that endears women at all ages; but can any but an old woman understand the heart of our struggling humanity in fairness and mercy, and in real helpfulness? The respect attached to old age is extraordinary in India. Every one is most anxious to please and do any little services possible. There is a charming old book of Indian folklore by Miss Frere, called "Old Deccan Days." The old Nurse in it—an Indian woman to the core—happily hits off the privilege of old age in her own direct, homely way. She would advise you, if you are getting old, to *look* old. Then people will do what you ask them. If you are young, they will say you are able to do it yourself!

Having watched the growth of an individual, let us briefly examine the characteristics and pursuits of women in the different grades of life. Agriculture is the basis of all Indian life. And the women of the agricultural classes form the backbone of the women of India. You will find in countries where woman's life is restricted, or less free than it ought to be, that the lowest social grades enjoy the greatest social freedom. The lowest castes in the villages know nothing of the Pardah. Even among the highest castes in a village, life is more natural, and the relations of the sexes less artificial, than in a town. The woman goes to help the man at the plough, and sometimes the baby goes too! But, alas! many a sad fatality has marred the simple annals of a village, because the baby was taken out in a basket to a field. While the elders were engaged in their work, a wolf or a jackal has lain in wait and carried away the child.

The working classes in the towns do not live quite such simple lives. In moral dignity they certainly do not approach their agricultural equals. The bane of seclusion begins to work on their women, who lose, in losing their homely resource and personality, their chief claims to the worship of men. Home life is less cheerful, and the eternal promptings of nature are more and more silenced in the roar and din of a restless crowd. Among the labouring classes the woman has often to go out and help to earn her living. But instead of the open-air picnic which the village woman enjoys when she takes out her midday meal to the man in the fields, resort is had to a confectioner or a parched-grain seller, who offers refreshments produced under conditions that are never inspected under any sanitary laws.

The middle classes, as we understand the term in England, do not exist in India. There are the higher classes and the lower classes—and nothing between them except a residuum of nondescripts, *nantes in gurgite vasto.* The lawyers and successful professional men buy land, and tend to be absorbed in the landed aristocracy. Even if they remain in the large cities, they form the cream of society (such as it is), and have not that strenuous life and that steadying influence which give to the English middle classes a tone and distinction all their own. In the floating shabby-genteel population, the women have the hardest task of all. This population is predominantly Muhammadan, and has been graphically described by a Hindustani poet.

"They are the men," says Sauda, "whose stables had countless attendants from Persia and Arabia—but that was in the days of long ago. Now I see that the hand of time has dealt heavily with them; for do they not go about begging the street cobbler to mend their shoes on credit?"

The men at any rate have some comfort or consolation in loafing about the market-place. But what of the poor women they leave behind at home? They are in Pardah, and see very few people, and none of the male sex except their immediate relations. They cannot make the home nice and bright, because they have no wherewithal, even for the ordinary decencies of life. They grind corn or work at sewing or embroidery, or teach children in their secluded corners; but life must be to them one long drudgery without a ray of sunshine, or a hope of rest or holiday.

That is the darkest side of the Pardah. If you go to the richest and most comfortable classes, you will find that a good deal could be said *for* the Pardah, which would not be obvious to an outsider. Here the Pardah is a privilege, speaking from a purely personal point of view, and apart from its far-reaching influence on social institutions. It means that the man may lead a hard-working life, and struggle through dust and rain, literally or metaphorically, but his women-kind are brought up in the lap of luxury. They have the best of everything: the coolest part of the house, a separate establishment of servants over whom the men have no authority, and, above all, complete freedom from the hurry and excitement which kill our finer sensibilities. If they go to visit their lady friends, they have a covered *palki* to ride in, with the softest of cushions, and the most luxurious fittings imaginable. In this stage of life it is the fair sex that clings most tenaciously to the Pardah, and you cannot blame them for it. A sensible life is not always the one most desired.

The life behind the Pardah is a subject of untold fascination in the West. It is usually associated with luxury and languor, but there is a good deal of dignity, domesticity, and religious sentiment behind it. The artistic use of the fingers is evident in everything around — the hangings, the gold and silver thread work, the silk embroidery, and the personal clothing and ornaments. The Moslem women are also great readers, principally of devotional books. I am told that the women among the Hindu *noblesse* are equally devoted to their Tulsi Das and their Stories of Saints. Hindu places of pilgrimage are scattered all over the country, and the women go freely to them, confirming their religious beliefs by the actual sight of relics and shrines. The wonderful story of Rama and Sita is told every year about the month of November in dramatic representations that last over weeks, and Hindu ladies have opportunities of discreetly viewing these from the windows of their houses, which overlook the square selected for the entertainments. These delights are barred to the ladies of Islam. Neither music nor painting is cultivated by the ladies, Hindu or Muhammadan, who cling to the old modes of life. But the intoning of the Koran among Moslem girls is carried to a fine art, and the delicacy of touch shown in their embroideries is sufficient evidence of the highest and most refined artistic talent.

Among Englishwomen, none has described life behind the Pardah with greater intimacy or fidelity than Lady Mary Wortley Montagu, the famous wife of the English Ambassador to Constantinople. Her "Turkish Letters," though nearly two centuries old, are as fresh and vivid as if they had been written for our own day. Her picture of the ladies in a "Turkish Zenana" would apply to the Zenana ladies of the higher classes in India at the present day. This is what she says:—

"That surprising harmony of features—that charming result of the whole—that exact proportion of body—that lovely bloom of complexion unsullied by art—the unutterable enchantment of her smile! But her eyes!—large and black, with all the soft languishment of the blue! every turn of her face discovering some new charm. . . . A behaviour so full of grace and sweetness, such easy motions, with an air so majestic, yet free from stiffness or affectation, that I am persuaded, could she be suddenly transported upon the most polite throne of Europe, nobody would think her other than born and bred to be a queen, though educated in a country we call barbarous."[1]

Take the picture of a modern Indian woman of the aristocracy of intellect, as drawn by a modern English man of letters. Describing Mrs Sarojini Naidu as Mr Arthur Symons knew her before she was married, he says[2]:—

"To those who knew her in England, all the life of the tiny figure seemed to concentrate itself in the eyes; they turned towards beauty as the sunflower turns towards the sun, opening wider and wider, until one saw nothing but the eyes. She was dressed always in clinging dresses of Eastern silk, and as she was so small and her long black hair hung straight down her back, you might have taken her for a child. She spoke little and in a low voice, like gentle music; and she seemed, wherever she was, to be alone."

To complete our survey, let us take a glance at a modern Muhammadan woman in India. Among the higher classes the majority observe the custom of Pardah. In appearance, manner, and dignity, they are not very different from the Turkish women so spiritedly described by Lady Mary Wortley Montagu. Many of them wear divided skirts and smoke the *hukka* in the most approved Turkish fashion. Many of them read

[1] Letters of Lady Mary Wortley Montagu, edited by her great-grandson, Lord Wharncliffe, London, 1893, 2 vols.; vol. i. p. 318. Letter dated 18th April 1717.

[2] Introduction to the *Golden Threshold*, by Sarojini Naidu. London 1905.

up-to-date literature, and are not, in this respect, far behind their Turkish sisters, as described in Pierre Loti's *Désenchantées*. Of course these habits and peculiarities are by no means universal among them, and Pardah women are responsible for much silent work and serious thought that the outside world hears nothing about. Her Highness the Begam of Bhopal keeps herself in touch with all the administrative details of her principality, and keenly interests herself in women's education, though she lives behind the Pardah. Another Muhammadan lady of equally exalted position, and living in the Pardah, is worshipped as an ideal of grace, wisdom, artistic taste, and matronly virtues, by a young lady who has known her intimately and in all her moods, and who told me of it herself in speaking of Muhammadan women. This admiration is all the more remarkable as coming from one of her own sex—a woman of culture, distinction, and refinement.

In Lucknow a movement was set on foot recently, mirrored in a vernacular paper that reflected its hopes and aims, to relax the rigours of the Pardah, and initiate a more liberal social policy among the women of the Muhammadan aristocracy. It was supported by some women of position. But the forces of social orthodoxy were too strong for the journal, which died after a short but brilliant career. The movement behind it, however, remains, and must gather strength as time goes on. The most practical achievements in that direction have been made by different members of the family to which the late Justice Badruddin Tyabji belonged. One of them, on a visit to London, won a coveted prize at a fancy dress ball at Covent Garden. Several of them can give a good account of themselves with pen or brush. Music, too, has been cultivated — not only on the hackneyed piano, but on the Bín, an ancient musical instrument of India, the classical Vina of the Apsaras. In conversation, artistic talents, and social gifts, they would hold their own in the most cultivated society of Europe and America.

Thus far of the stars of the feminine firmament. In considering the workaday women the colours will have to be more sombre. If I were asked to name and describe the women's professions in India, I should have to reply in the same strain as the lecturer whose subject was "Snakes in Ireland." "Ladies and Gentlemen," he said, "there are none!" When we come to think of it there are very few professions in England which are entirely (to use an Irishism) manned by women. The typewriter girl and the telephone girl you would not expect to find in India, as neither the typewriter nor the telephone is yet a feature of our commercial or official life outside the Presidency towns. You would also miss women at the post offices and shops. Even in domestic service you would be surprised to find mostly men. In those branches of domestic service in which women are indispensable (*e.g.* as ladies' maids and children's nurses), the supply is far short of the demand. This also applies to the teaching and the medical professions.

The fact is that a woman is not supposed, according to our social ideas, to earn her daily bread. This is a wholesome rule where (as in India) almost all women are married, and the men outnumber the women. But in the process of evolution and social reconstruction, a rigid limitation like this might be disastrous to woman's independence. She should have the freest possible opportunities of making the best of herself. If she cannot cultivate her mind and character by playing that part in the social organisation for which she is best fitted, society loses the full benefit of the intellect, character, and imagination of one half of its members. This is a strong argument in favour of opening careers to women. I know that many, even among the social reformers in India, would shrink from this suggestion, but to my mind social reform is bound up with the opportunities of usefulness which you give to women who do not marry, or before they undertake the responsibilities of marriage. After all, even if the true destiny of every healthy normal woman be marriage and the care of home and children, there must be many individuals of both sexes who are not fitted for these high responsibilities, and yet have talents which would do justice to great responsibilities in other walks of life.

For the legal profession a very energetic and all but successful attempt was made by one of the most brilliant of India's women, Miss Cornelia Sorabji. After a distinguished college career in India she went to Oxford and studied law. She passed all her legal examinations, but unfortunately the High Courts in India did not see their way to permit her to practise as an advocate on account of her sex. The loss of the legal profession was the gain of literature, for she has since published two charming books containing sketches of Indian life. But her legal knowledge was not acquired in vain; her services have been requisitioned by the Bengal Government. She is acting as legal adviser to the women under the Court of Wards. Her position is one of great responsibility and exceptional difficulty, for she is the interpreter between two languages, vulgarly held to be incompatible with one another—the language of a woman's wish, and the language of the law. But the wit of a refined woman may be trusted to translate from the one to the other, with a full combination of grace, tact, and business acumen.

In literature the women of India are specially fitted to excel. If it were permitted to dive into history, Miran Bai might be mentioned among the Hindus, and Aurangzeb's daughter, Zeb-un-Nisa, among the Muhammadans, and a great many other names besides. But to confine ourselves to modern

India, it is a singular circumstance that the only two Indian poets who have really made their name in English literature are girls. Miss Toru Dutt's book,[1] "Ancient Ballads and Legends of Hindostan," tells the tales of old India with all the charm of a woman's style. Mrs Sarojini Naidu is at the threshold of her career, but with her very first book she has established her reputation as an inspired singer. Sarojini Naidu, like Pope, lisped in numbers, for the numbers came. "One day," she says, "when I was eleven, I was sighing over a sum in algebra; it *wouldn't* come right; but instead a whole poem came to me suddenly. I wrote it down. From that day my poetic career began." Then there are journals in India—such as Mrs Satthianadhan's *Ladies' Magazine* in Madras and Mrs Mumtaz Ali's *Tahzíb-un-Niswán* in Lahore—edited and managed by women. Mrs Satthianadhan is a Master of Arts of the Madras University. All the Indian Universities admit women to degrees as freely as men, and in this respect they are certainly more advanced than the older English Universities.

[1] If Miss Toru Dutt were to come to life again, and had nothing better to do than go to the British Museum, she would never be able to trace her own book from the Catalogue. Her name is to be found neither under Dutt nor under Toru, but as Tarulata Datta. Mrs Naidu's name appears under S as Sarojini Nayadu. Perhaps some sympathy might be extended to the Frenchman who never could understand why names were treated so badly in England; there was one he knew which they wrote as Marjoribanks and pronounced as *Chumley*! To be consistent the British Museum Catalogue ought (especially after the recent spelling crusade) to spell the name of the President of the United States "Rôs-felt," and classify it under T as Theodoros—Theodore being only a modern corruption of a good Greek name.

"Woman," said Keshub Chunder Sen, "has been defined as an adjective agreeing with the noun man. I should rather say that man is a noun in the objective case, governed by the verb woman." This humorous simile may be read with the simile of the poet of the Veda when he compares the brightness of the god of fire to the shining of a woman in her home. Sita, in a celebrated passage of Valmiki's *Ramayana*, says to her husband:—

> "The world shall wake no care in me;
> My only care be truth to thee."

If we apply this noble saying in a reciprocal sense, and base the solidarity of human society on the truth of man to woman, and of woman to man, many of life's riddles would be solved—many of life's difficulties would disappear. I may be something of a dreamer, but I hope and trust that society in India—as elsewhere—will recognise the place that is woman's, not as a result of conflict and strife—not as a victory after the dust of battle—but as the natural symbol of Peace, Harmony, Union, Devotion, and Love.

IX

SOCIAL TENDENCIES

"—As by toil man winneth happiness,
Through tribulation he must come to peace."
—*Demeter*, by ROBERT SEYMOUR BRIDGES.

"The wealth of a man is in the number of things he loves and blesses, and which he is loved and blessed by." —CARLYLE.

"To improve a man's outward condition is not to improve man himself; this must come from each man's endeavour within his own breast; without that there can be little ground for social hope."
—Mr JOHN MORLEY'S "Life of Gladstone," vol i., p. 5.

SOCIAL TENDENCIES

THE study of the structure of human society is a comparatively new feature of modern progress. It has been rendered possible—in all but its empiric stages—by the growth and elaboration of the science of statistics. This science not only collects and tabulates figures, but reasons upon them, and its practical value depends precisely on the extent to which it succeeds in explaining phenomena and co-ordinating their relations one to another. The chain of causation which it establishes enables us to judge of the forces which bind together or divide the different sections of mankind living in a given geographical area. We may enquire into the operation of these forces on social strata horizontally or vertically. When we understand the relation in which the different members of the groups stand to each other, and similarly the relations of the different groups among themselves, we can go on and study the evolution of the structure in two ways. We may study it historically, and make our calculations for the future, or we may study it comparatively, and estimate its influence in the progress of the world.

All this presupposes that human society as a whole, and each unit of it, viewed as a separate community, is an organic structure. This feature was long recognised in regard to political communities, even before the time of Aristotle. The Stagirite philosopher worked out a clear and logical system of exposition for political societies which can scarcely be said to be out of date even now. But a political society may or may not coincide with a social organism, and the social organism obeys laws far more complex, and is subject to forces far more subtle, than political organisms.

The study of the economic structure of society, too, preceded the study of the whole of the social structure. Political science led to economic science, and economic science in its turn paved the way for that larger social science, whose birth is one of the chief glories of nineteenth century thought. The eighteenth century had already felt the promptings of this science, dimly and vaguely. But it had not been able to advance beyond somewhat crude speculations, for want of the reliable statistician, whose treatment of figures on a large scale eliminates as far as possible the results of accidental or abnormal variations in the phenomena of social science. The Industrial Revolution, too, which followed the political upheaval known as the French Revolution, brought to the surface vast problems that led to a revision of social ideas, and to an entirely new outlook on the social horizon.

The difficulty of studying social phenomena is great in all countries, partly because of the human factor which they involve, and which, if not taken on a sufficiently large scale, presents aberrations that would seriously vitiate the reasoning of any but a most careful, patient, and industrious observer. Social facts are, again, often utilised as weapons in the battle-ground of politics; and where so many human passions and prejudices come into play, where vested interests cross the currents of scientific thought and obscure their clear and limpid flow, it is not surprising that the results are so often disappointing, if not even misleading, to the dispassionate philosopher. English society has made unique contributions to the growth of human civilisation; its insular detachment and its freedom from foreign invasion for eight centuries and a half have enabled it to pursue its bent along national lines with wonderful continuity; while the length, completeness, and accuracy of its records, to a period even anterior to the Domesday Book, afford rich material to the student. If, nevertheless, the difficulties which confront the social student in England are great, what shall we say of the difficulties in the way of a student who deals with a country like India —about which there is not a single statement which can be made of universal application, and in which political unification, the greatest of all cements for holding society together, and enabling it to concentrate the play of social forces, is a matter as of yesterday? How shall we generalise or deduce sociological laws when there are no well-defined atoms or molecules, cells or nerve-centres, in the whole organism? How shall we picture the whole mass, when portions of it have begun to crystallise, but large portions have not—when the whole body, politic and social, is still in the condition of the inert matter described by Virgil, which had just began to take shape in response to the spirit of law, order, aspirations, and ideals, which was breathing through and through it?

> "Spiritus intus alit, totamque infusa per artus
> Mens agitat molem et magno se corpore miscet."[1]

It is not that we are just beginning to construct our social system. In that case the problems would be simple, and the study of the primitive tendencies comparatively easy. We are heirs to a number of civilisations and social systems, to the fruits of countless seeds sown in history. Some of these seeds died even before germination, but they mixed with the soil and helped to form a mould which gave a more luxuriant growth to the trees which grew from more fortunate seeds. Among these, again, some died as seedlings; some grew up, but were choked by more vigorous

[1] Virgil, *Æneid*, vi. 726-7.

growths; some braved the storms and withstood the shocks of political earthquakes, but found no congenial nourishment in the new soil with which their roots have been banked up, and are showing signs of decay in branches basking in brilliant sunshine and a bracing atmosphere. There are others which are dead or dying—it is sometimes hard to tell if there is any sap left—from pure senile decay, and which no amount of care, pruning, or banking up, will save, except as ugly, dried-up timber artificially supported. We have thus to deal with a system not complete or homogeneous, not fed by similar roots or grown out of similar seeds.

The Aryan invasion of India already found a social system which the invaders did not replace or modify organically. In trying to place their own system side by side with the pre-existing system or systems, they thought they were conserving the growth of their own mind and genius. This was impossible. Where there was a conflict they tried to substitute their own institutions and destroy the older ones. This, too, was impossible. Instead of a compromise or a peaceful development of institutions, there was piecemeal destruction, and a loose agglomeration of the parts that were saved out of the wreck—without organic unity or structural symmetry. I have said that this happened at the Aryan invasion of India. But in truth there were many Aryan invasions, as there were many Germanic invasions of England. They followed each other in such quick succession that none of them was able to "set": the constant state of flux prevented the shaping of crystals.

It is often assumed that Aryan society in Vedic times was homogeneous — that it was governed throughout by the same laws and customs, and animated by the same ideas. This is not correct. The Vedas themselves grew up piecemeal. There is as much difference between the language and spirit of the Rig Vedas and the language and spirit of the Atharva Vedas as there is between Virgil and Dante, or between Piers the Ploughman and the *Earthly Paradise.* In each Veda, again, the different parts — the hymns, the ceremonial directions, and the philosophical disquisitions—were the products of totally different minds and social systems. Each Veda formed a school of its own, but within the school there was the greatest freedom and diversity of thought. Even the priestly organisation — usually labelled Brahmanism — was not characteristic of all the tribes of the ancient Hindus. At a time when it was well established in the Gangetic Valley, it was repugnant to the Vratinas, or Western Aryans, who, according to Professor Weber, probably developed the Atharva Veda.

The teaching of Buddha, the invasion of Alexander, and the establishment of Scythian kingdoms, all brought in new elements into the social structure.

Buddhism may be called a religion of human

personality as opposed to nature worship, Animism, and the cult of myths, which had held the field before the advent of the Enlightened Teacher, and which still enter so largely into the religion of the masses. It raised the human personality at once to kinship with the world-spirit. Its aim is not to destroy the human personality, owing to a weary hate of life, but to lift it to a region of peace, and to realise everlasting life—free from delusion and change. These ideas exerted an enormous influence on the social life of the country. It must not be supposed for a moment that they were entirely new. They had been floating vaguely in the intellectual atmosphere of India, but with the life of Buddha they took definite shape. They introduced freedom instead of formality into the social organism. They substituted for a priesthood of birth a priesthood of renunciation. They also gave an immense impetus to the inborn tendencies of the Hindu mind towards monasticism and asceticism.

The invasion of Alexander brought the Hindus into contact with Greek civilisation. While Persia was overwhelmed by the Greek conquest, India was internationalised by Greek influence. From the vague dreams of her forest devotees she turned to listen to the voice of the merchant and the diplomatist from foreign countries. Her political ideals changed from the shapeless freedom of what would now be called Tolstoyanism to the masterful organisation and orderly government of

Greek cities. Only the Indian horizon was always wider. It refused to confine itself to cities. In its formula of CHAKRAVARTI kings it cherished the dream of universal empire, and anticipated in theory the imperial policy of Rome. The subjugation of the earlier populations of India by the Aryans must have produced an influence on the Aryan system which has never been sufficiently determined. But it was backdoor influence, and though overwhelming, was kept in the background. The influence of Yavana ambassadors of culture like Megasthenes was exerted on the highest social circles, among whom types of thought and manners have greater fixity, and changes have a correspondingly greater significance. A very striking instance of Greek influence on the higher thought of the Hindus is furnished by the contact of Greek with Hindu astronomy. The Hindu Zodiac had been divided, in a most original manner, into what are called the twenty-seven lunar asterisms. The Greeks brought their less elaborate system of the Twelve Signs of the Zodiac. These were adopted in conjunction with the lunar asterisms, but in their names they retained unmistakable evidences at first of their Greek origin. If such was the influence in so abstruse a science as astronomy, we need not doubt that the Yavana merchants and the Yavana servants, whom we read about in the dramatists, produced an important influence in the social and domestic life of the people.

The Scythians exercised a far-reaching influence, not indeed on the science and literature of the country, but unquestionably on its art and manners. They probably form a more considerable element in the ethnology of India than the Danes in the ethnology of the East Coast of England. Who they precisely were, we need not stop to enquire. Nor are the materials for such an enquiry too plentiful. They, too, probably comprised different branches and practised varying social systems. But they were a frank, soldierly race, who did not despise the philosophy of wine, woman, and song. They sought the obvious and the direct in art, and eschewed the abstruse and the mystical in thought and religion. In their hands Buddhism became a religion of war for the preservation or conquest of sacred relics. To them snake worship or tree worship would be mere symbols of power and freshness—the strength in which youth rejoices, and the growth which goes forth out of the smiling face of Nature. Life has no problems, and Nature no mysteries. Is it not sufficient to live and be glad? A social system based on such ideas would have many points of contrast with one in which ceremonial purity becomes an obsession, and respect for animals almost a disease. We have pictures of the freedom of such life in the sculptures of Sanchi and Amravati. Let us take as an illustration a very simple habit, which shows both the persistence of a type through heredity, and the easy change in domestic manners which can take place in India. We find that during the epochs which these faithful records in stone portray for us, the habit of sitting on stools or raised seats had become fairly common. Now it is uncommon except in regions reached by English influence. People prefer to sit or squat on the ground. The old-fashioned Raïses or magnates who affect chairs, never feel comfortable unless they tuck one leg up on the seat, leaving the other either to hang or to rest on the ground. A book has been recently published in Bengal on "Etiquette for Indian Gentlemen." It seriously warns the reader, when paying visits of a ceremonial character, against the practice of tucking up a leg on the chair, and advises him to sacrifice comfort to courtesy. But the trick is not as recent as might be imagined. In the sculptures of Sanchi and Amravati, the typical attitude of a Hindu sitting at ease—with one of his legs tucked up—is seen in all its unconscious humour. Truly, heredity has much to answer for.

It is the fashion to speak of the Dravidian element in the Indian population, as in some way representing a lower plane of civilisation than the Aryan. In the matter of intellect the Dravidians of the Southern Peninsula are in no way inferior to other sections of the population. In social life they seem to me to have some points of superiority. The weakest point of the social system of Southern India—its extreme horror of the Pariah class—is probably an importation from the north. Dravidian tendencies have had the freest play in the social systems of such out-of-the-way Native States as Cochin and Travancore. There we find education flourishes, and the proportion of literacy, especially among women, is considerably higher than in the general population. The lower classes are not ground down. There is freer contact between the intellectual aristocracy and the horny-handed sons of toil. The age of marriage is not quite so low, and the status of woman is more frankly recognised. Their kinship with the Brahuis of Baluchistan may or may not be proved, but there is no doubt that the race and its social characteristics must have extended over a wider area and exercised a more permeating influence on the whole of the Indian population than is generally recognised.

The Mongolian element, too, has to be taken into account. It is appreciably strong in the hillmen of the Himalayas and in the districts immediately bordering on them. The historic sense of the Assamese, embodied in their valuable chronicles, is also derived from a semi-Mongolian descent. Had it not been for the barrier of the Himalayas, the Mongolian influence in India would have been predominant. As it is, it represents a larger factor in Indian systems and institutions than is usually allowed. According to Mr Risley, the Mongolo-Dravidian element is predominant in the ethnology of Lower Bengal.

The earnest, militant Puritanical spirit of Islam, the quiet, commercial, philanthropic, and (until recently) non-political habits of the Parsis, and the active, energetic, materialistic tendencies of European civilisation, have added important elements to our social ideas, which can in no way be measured by the numerical insignificance of the people who were responsible for their introduction into India. These three streams have poured their waters into the broad river of Indian civilisation within historical times, and have not themselves been free from the reflex influences which so passive and catholic a system as that of the Hindus was certain to exert on everything that came into contact with it. I have not mentioned the Syrian Christianity of the south and the interesting Beni Israil community of Bombay, because they have completely assimilated themselves to Indian conditions, and were it not that they were labelled with the names of Christianity and Judaism respectively, they would easily pass for a sect or school of thought in the all-absorbing Hindu system. Modern Christianity, as represented by post-Muhammadan missionary effort, is represented by the influences of European ideas, which we have taken into account. Those influences are dominated by the feeling of a complex pride of race and nationality which has stamped itself on the movement, in spite of the silent or express protest of not a few of the most zealous believers in the brotherhood of mankind.

We have taken a survey of all these diverse elements which went towards the building up of our modern social ideas and tendencies. An organic structure, with specialised parts subordinated to a common centre, may have existed in the village communities, but it has long been broken up. The crumbling process began long before the political organisation of the village began to show any marks of dissolution or decay. It has resulted in a complete social chaos. It would be too much to say that in social matters every man is a law unto himself, but it may be said truthfully, that the social unit which influences a man's conduct is so small that its atmosphere is close and unhealthy. If the individuals in a given unit multiply, there is no chance of a healthy circulation of ideas being set up. The fissiparous tendencies of the unit assert themselves, and it breaks up into other units which readily fall off from the parent stem. Instead of a slow and continuous evolution of types, with a steadying tendency in all the numerous changes, we have one uniform type, with constant and spasmodic changes within itself, which obey laws too minute for the study of the student of general sociology.

The diversity of social phenomena in India is a fact visible on the surface. But the ground-work on which that diversity is traced—the underlying uniformity of life from the Himalayas to Cape Comorin—is often lost sight of. There are really three stages in one's education about India. First, the enquirer is struck with the enormous difference between Indian life and thought, and the life and thought of the rest of the world. This is most striking in the salient thoughts and institutions, habits and methods, as viewed from a distance. It is as if an observer from a balloon were to view an Indian landscape in October. He would see a vast dull plain, with no hedges to mark the boundaries of fields, no great patches of forest or meadow land, no vast expanses of brick and mortar, no ungainly palls of smoke to mark out the haunts of men's luxury or men's industry. All would be one dull brown or russet, and the observer might in his haste conclude that the place was devoid of life or motion or interest, because it was so different from some other landscape with which he was familiar, in which the green relieved the grey, the infinite varieties of undulating surface furnished points on which the landscape painter might seize, and the busy trains and motor cars wandering in all directions gave evidences of life and activity. The second stage is reached when our imaginary balloonist descends from the heights and pursues his enquiries at close quarters. He finds extreme, almost bewildering, diversity. The dull, limitless expanse of fields turns out to be a number of fields with different soils and different crops. There are several kinds of millets, there is maize, there are the late varieties of rice—almost more numerous than he can count. No two fields are the same. He may be surprised and puzzled if he had to define the boundaries, but those concerned with them can distinguish them without difficulty. The human habitations, too, have all sharply defined individuality. No two of them are alike. Perhaps he can discover no common principles of classification. If he meets other enquirers similarly situated to himself, and compares notes, he is shaken even in those provisional theories which he had adopted. This revision of ideas goes on until, with extended knowledge, he gives up any schemes of generalisation in despair, and looks upon the social system as a hopeless chaos from which it is impossible to evolve any order. But in adopting this attitude he looks at things too much as an outsider. In the third stage we will suppose him to have plunged himself *in medias res.* He does not pretend to be a philosopher, a director, or a guide. He has no advice to give, no *nostra* to recommend, no experiments to try on others than himself. He simply makes himself one of the mass. He enters into their feelings, shares somewhat in their difficulties, and experiences a little of that patience and passive heroism with which God endows souls born to much suffering. Then he realises how much of the common heritage of humanity is shared by the silent masses of India — the sin, the pain, the sorrow, the misunderstanding, "the whips and scorns of time," "the proud man's contumely," and "the spurns which patient merit takes of the unworthy" set in the balance against the beauty, the truth, the fidelity, the unselfishness, the heights of noble enchantment, and all "the touches dearest prized" of a free, happy, and love-encircled life. In realising this he is made conscious, not only of the unity of Indian life, but its kinship with the whole world. The unity of Indian life, however, is not confined to those points which it shares in common with the rest of the world. All its infinite variety hangs on a common thread of a somewhat distinctive Indian colour.

Monsieur Gustave le Bon, a French student of Eastern civilisations, saw this clearly. He devotes a special chapter of his book on this country[1] to a consideration of the moral and intellectual characteristics common to the diverse races of India. He ascribes this common feature to the common physical and intellectual surroundings, and (he might have added) to a common history for at least a few centuries. He lays emphasis, it is true, on our common defects, our lack of precision, initiative, energy, and critical insight. But every defect has its qualities, and it is certainly so in India. Even his brilliant

[1] "Civilisations de l'Inde," par M. Gustave le Bon, Paris 1887. It is a pity that this book has not been translated into English or Hindustani.

epigram about "the astonishing aptitude of the Hindus to see things as they are not" might be translated, in more sympathetic hands, into something that connotes the virtues of resignation, patience, forbearance, and a determination to make the best of everything, to forget, in the rosy colours of the imagination, the hard or paltry realities of life. But it is in the investigation of the highest and most serious problems of life that the Indian sages and seers — Hindu, Buddhist, Muhammadan, and even Christian — seem unconsciously to have worked, and to be working, on a common basis. The ground-work of Buddhism may be said to be inherent in the Vedas. The stern, iconoclastic character of Arabian Islam has always been subordinated in India to the reverence for Saints and the embodiment of religious virtue in sacred persons and places. Both Madhu Sadan Dutt and Father Gorey were good Christians, and the latter was animated with an exceptional zeal for proselytism. The one represented the plastic Bengali spirit, and the other the vigorous, incisive intellect of the Maratha. And yet they were both inspired in an intense degree with the characteristics of Hindu genius and Hindu methods, the one in his mythological plays, and the other in his subtle theology.

It is the failure to grasp this elementary fact that leads to so much heart-burning, jealousy, and antagonism among the different sections of the

Indian population. Where they do co-operate, they find that there is much in their ideas that is harmonious if not identical. But the power of labels and Shibboleths is strong in Eastern countries, and can only be removed by a careful study of the ideas that lie in substance behind differing names and institutions. Kabir has seized this point with wonderful clearness, and expresses it with his usual virility when he says that a Muhammadan's ideas of *Nimáz* do not differ more from a Hindu's ideas of *Puja*, than does the gold in a bracelet from the gold in an ear-ring.

> "*Gahna ek kanak te gahna,*
> *Wa men bhdo na duja:*
> *Kahan sunan ke dui kar thápe,—*
> *Ek nimáj ek puja.*"

Nor has the point escaped those Europeans who have an intimate practical acquaintance with life and thought in modern India.

"India," says Mr Vincent Smith, "encircled as she is by seas and mountains, is indisputably a geographical unit, and as such, is rightly designated by one name. Her type of civilisation, too, has many features which differentiate it from that of all other regions of the world, while they are common to the whole country, or rather continent, in a degree sufficient to justify its treatment as a unit in the history of human, social, and intellectual development."[1]

This peculiar feature of variety in uniformity having been pointed out in the Indian social

[1] "Early History of India," by Vincent A. Smith, Oxford 1904 p. 5.

structure, we shall now be in a position to notice some of the leading tendencies in social life without the risk of misunderstandings. We call them tendencies rather than characteristics. The whole structure being in a transition stage, there are no fixed types yet. The old types, which have shown such vitality during centuries, and are still at the bottom of social changes, are gradually merging into new adjustments. The solvent of modern life is affecting India far more powerfully at the present day than in Western countries whose economic system has gradually been subject to revision *pari passu* with religious ideas, laws, political organisation, and foreign discovery.

The chief subject that will suggest itself for our consideration is Caste. Under that one word may be grouped most of the phenomena of our social life. How is this hoary institution, "Caste," holding its own in the new social struggle? And what effect has it on the social regrouping that is sure to follow the altered circumstances of the internal structure of Indian society? Into the origin of caste we need not enter here. There are the tribal or racial castes, the functional or occupational castes, the sectarian castes based on religious divisions, the mixed castes based on departures from hard-and-fast theoretical customs with respect to marriage, and the territorial castes based on migrations. The different views that have been held on this and cognate subjects have been admirably summed up by Mr Risley in his chapter on Caste in the last Census Report. But in discussing the present position of caste we must take account of two opposing tendencies operating side by side.

One is in the direction of a relaxation of the rules of dress, contact, food, and other ceremonial observances. The dress is about the most unstable part of Indian institutions. It could not have been possible at any time to indicate each minute subdivision of caste by outward dress, but there were well-marked types indicated by customary rules and conventions. It used at one time to be considered the right thing for the Moslem noble to tie his coat on the right side, while his Hindu brother had the tying strings on the left. There was a similar distinction which marked off the sexes in the matter of the side on which the buttons were fastened in mediæval costume in Europe. Again, the shape and style of the nether garments, the form of the shoes, the style of the hair worn—on the head, on the upper lip, or on the chin, or whether any hair was allowed to grow at all—depended upon the clan, or sept, or class to which one belonged. These matters have ceased to have much practical importance now. The *Achkan* is tied on either side by a Hindu or a Muhammadan, and there is even a bastard *Achkan* with a row of Birmingham buttons running down the middle, which bids fair to oust all old-fashioned attire. The *dhoti* is retained by the Hindus, and rarely worn by any of the Muhammadans except among the lower classes. But there are many Hindus in trousers. Even the beard, the symbol among Moslems of all that was venerable and manly, has been openly abandoned by the Aligarh dudes, who may be seen glorying in thick and bushy moustaches, much to the scandal of the Maulvis who prescribe a thin streak of hair on the upper lip "for greater cleanliness in eating and drinking." The last stronghold of dress traditions remains in the head-dress. By the shape, weight, and material of the turban, you may easily pick out some of the well-known types among castes and clans. A dashing young Maharaja, with the latest shape in collars and ties, and the latest cut of frock coat from Bond Street, would yet in an Indian assemblage probably carry a turban that would proclaim his pride of ancestry, and prevent the veriest tyro from mistaking a Rajput for a Sikh or a Maratha. Similarly you would know the clan or sept of a Muhammadan nobleman if he wears his turban. But even here the reforming spirit is abroad. The majority of educated Muhammadans have discarded the picturesque variations of the turbans in favour of the lighter and more comfortable Turkish fez. The Moslem students almost invariably wear the fez all over the country. A similar movement in favour of Delhi embroidered caps is spreading among Hindu students.

In the matter of social contact, the rules can never have been very strict in a mixed population like that of India. The story told of Nana Fadnavis, that he used to bathe from head to foot after an interview with a foreigner, to wash off the contamination, is probably exaggerated, and, in any case, is meant to illustrate his political intolerance in the waning days of Maratha supremacy. Of a similar nature are probably the tales of how a low-caste man in Southern India had to make a *détour*, because a high-caste man happened to be walking and would not tolerate the passing of the other on the opposite side of the road. But it is perfectly true that any familiar intercourse between the higher and lower castes must have been impossible, so long as exclusive ideas were allowed free play in the social system. Even now there are some castes in Southern India, numbering about four million souls, which are supposed to be so low that they pollute even without touching. Probably the "twice-born" never thought anything of coming into contact with each other in an ordinary way, even though of different castes. But the repugnance to the son of a chamár or sweeper attending the same school as the children of those who wore the sacred thread, was, and still remains invincible. This objection would not be altogether unintelligible in England, where a case was recently brought to public notice, in which a publican had to withdraw his child from a Sunday School belonging to a church of which he was a member, at the instance of a clergyman who professed to preach the Gospel of Christ. This prejudice may be all very well in schools—although I do not defend it—but in general life it has completely crumbled away. And the chief agent which has helped to "ring out false pride in place and blood, the civic slander and the spite," has been—not the press nor the pulpit, not the schools of philosophy or ethics, but the humble railway train, and the levelling yoke of the factory and the workshop.

The strictness of caste regulations in the matter of food and drink is well known. There are wells in villages from which no low caste man is allowed to draw water. Where there are other wells exclusively set apart for the lower castes, this restriction may not operate harshly; but in the absence of such wells, the lower castes have to shift for themselves as best they can. This prejudice ceases to exist with the introduction of waterworks into the larger cities. When the waterworks were new, some very old-fashioned Hindus attempted to boycott them, even declaring that sacred rivers like the Ganges or Jumna would refuse to flow into the mains. But considerations of practical convenience soon overcame all obstacles, and now waterworks are as freely used in cities (even if there *is* an alternative water supply) as wells and streams are in rural districts. The objectors, to save their face, have thrown the responsibility on the sacred streams themselves. As most of the waterworks are taken from the large rivers, and as most of the large rivers are held sacred, there can be no objection to drinking the water of the sacred streams—even if it comes through mains and pipes. The restrictions in the matter of food, too, are breaking down gradually and unobtrusively. Theoretically no caste can touch the food or water which has been touched by other castes. Indeed, the restriction would narrow commensality down to single families, so that there can be no social dinners among the Hindus. The first relaxation of this rule was in the matter of caste dinners, which, especially among castes not quite at the top of the tree, have been an institution for centuries. No plates, or bowls, or vessels of permanent material would be used, lest contamination should creep in. The guests would sit in the open air, and a Brahman or Brahmans would go round distributing the food on the leaves of the banana tree, or some other tree capable of yielding leaves large enough to serve as platters. Cups made of such leaves and stitched with twigs are not entirely unknown, but virgin earthenware vessels may be used for liquids, to be thrown away as soon as they have been once used. A Brahman cook may be employed by any of the castes, but as the monopoly would in many cases be attended with much inconvenience, a fiction was introduced. The Kahar caste, which draws water, though not a high caste, was made pure for purposes of contact with food and drink. The highest in the land may now drink water brought by a Kahar, or even eat food cooked by a Kahar. Similarly the Halwai, or confectioner caste has been neutralised. A man on a railway journey or out at work may eat the simple food sold by a Halwai without prejudice to his caste. Then, again, foods have come to be differentiated. Fruit you may take from anybody, and probably this has always been allowed. But now cooked foods, too, have been classified, so that there are some kinds which even a Brahman may take from a large number of specified castes, and a Rajput from an even larger number. The rules are in their nature indefinite. They are nowhere reduced to writing. No person can give an authoritative ruling on them, which may not be challenged by some person or other of at least equal authority. In this seeming confusion, a silent or gradual social revolution is being worked out, and the boundaries of groups and the definitions of foods are being gradually enlarged as necessity and social convenience may require.

The history of tobacco-smoking in India furnishes the most striking illustration of the changes in sentiment which have taken place at different times under the caste idea, and of the marvellous ingenuity with which fictions have been invoked to justify habits which the people had a mind to. The introduction of tobacco is comparatively recent in India. The Emperor Jahangir issued an edict against tobacco-smoking about the same time that his brother of England, James I., forbade the fragrant weed in the Western isle. The founders of the Sikh organisation put tobacco under a ban. But the people of the East could no more resist it than the people of the West. Devout Moslems said that the grape of the juice was forbidden by the prophet, but he could not have meant to forbid tobacco, as it was unknown in Arabia in his day. Puritans replied that of the two, tobacco was the more insidious, the more seductive. "Nicotia," as Lowell has said, is "dearer to the muse than all the grape's bewildering juice." Nicotia, therefore, won, and the *narjilch* and the *hukka* are now household gods in the East. Nor were the Hindu castes slow to recognise the power that resided in the *hukka*, as a symbol of peace and social understanding. It is not probable that they had ever heard of the American "calumet of peace," but they adopted the smoking of the *hukka* as a symbol of the bond of unity within the caste. In all caste councils the *hukka* is prepared as a necessary adjunct, and passed from mouth to mouth among the brethren. The ceremony of excommunicating a member who has broken the caste rules, is not "with candle, with bell, and with book," but consists, as the phrase goes, in "stopping his (share in) *hukka* and water." This phrase—*hukka páni band karna*—

is fraught with more terror to the villager than all the Proclamations issued by the Honourable High Courts. But tobacco is essentially a sociable weed. What is to be done when two men of different castes want to fraternise "over a smoke," as they often do among the lower castes? The *hukka*, being exclusively adopted as a symbol of caste unity, has come to have a sort of official status. But the *chilam* (the pipe) may be smoked between an Ahir and a Gujar without the slightest risk of contamination, although the two men's lips touch the self-same mouthpiece. The fiction is that the *chilam* is dry!

The baneful habit of cigarette-smoking has spread with more rapidity than any other form of smoking. Fifteen years ago scarcely any cigarettes were smoked by Indians, except those made with native tobacco, and rolled in kachnár leaves, whose distribution was quite local. But recently, a flood of cheap American cigarettes has come in, usually of the lowest grades. What would the Hindus think of them if Mr Upton Sinclair were to throw the search-light of his pen on the deleterious mixtures which masquerade as tobacco? And yet they seem to have been adopted in India with astonishing rapidity. Last year—the year of the supposed birth of Swadeshi and of foreign boycott—the foreign cigarette was more rampant than ever. As many as 666,000,000 were imported in Calcutta, which was an increase of 82,000,000, or more than 14 per cent. on the previous year's figure.

They are hawked about in the streets, and on railway platforms, and are offered to guests in Indian houses in supersession of the betel leaves and betel nuts, whose virtues have been so enthusiastically sung by the Sanskrit poets. Even little boys have fallen victims to the habit. I should not be at all sorry to see the cigarette placed under an uncompromising ban by all the caste authorities (if there are any still) which regulate such matters.

It is curious to observe that caste councils—or *panchayets*—sit more to adjudicate than to legislate. They pronounce upon the conduct of particular individuals on particular occasions: they do not make rules of general application. They deal with what has already occurred, and do not provide for future conduct. Their substantive law is nothing like the elaborate structure of the text-books called Hindu and Muhammadan Law: it is a body of customs, a mass of floating opinion as interpreted by the wisest of elders gathered under a village tree. The subject-matter of their decisions possessed at one time an unlimited scope, but as they are absolutely ignored by Anglo-Indian law, their authority has gradually weakened, and it is doubtful whether their action, even in those small matters with which they still habitually deal, can be justified in law, if called into question. They chiefly confine their attention now to such matters as breaches of caste custom in the matter of food and drink, or in the matter of marriage—in short, anything which is held by public social opinion as conduct unbecoming a true caste-fellow as such, and not as a man or a moral being. But even in such matters there is a tendency on the part of the beaten party to question the authority of the caste council. A Kurmi having enjoyed the hospitality of one not entitled to entertain a Kurmi, a panchayet of the caste is held, and it is resolved to lay an interdict on his eating and drinking with well-behaved Kurmis. If he is a rich man, and conversant with the bye-ways of the English courts, he immediately files a suit for libel against the leaders of the boycott against him, or, which is more expeditious and more like summary vengeance, lays a criminal information for libel. There may or may not be a good case for libel, but as the caste panchayet is not recognised by law, the position of the defendant is extremely weak, and the initial proceedings have the desired effect. The case is invariably compromised, and another nail is driven into the coffin of caste organisation.

The procedure observed in convening a caste meeting and passing its resolutions is interesting, and throws light on the ideas of self-government which lie dormant among the people. Mrs Grundy is personified in Indian rural life as a male, who hangs about the village well or the village chaupál. A casual remark is dropped by him as to such-a-one's relations with a woman of another caste. This is passed from mouth to mouth until it reaches the ears of the man concerned. Even if he is thick-skinned, and takes no notice, his candid friends are sure to add point and piquancy to the tale, and put him on his mettle. If the story is untrue, the victim denies it, and offers to prove his character before the panchayet. Even if it is true there are always extenuating circumstances, and in any case the offence may be compoundable with a fine or a caste dinner, which must be decided upon by the panchayet. The man will therefore ask the elders to summon a meeting. If he lies low, his enemies may take the initiative, or his candid friends may wish to "clear his character"—anything for a good, lively meeting, and a dinner to follow! The elders send round a verbal invitation to all the people of the caste in the village and neighbourhood. How far the "neighbourhood" is to extend would depend on the gravity of the offence, the area in which the interest in it has spread, and the number of guests to be fed at the subsequent caste dinner, signifying the expense in which it is desired to mulct the culprit. Always assume that the man is guilty until he is proved to be innocent. All the male adults of the caste flock to the trysting-place. Manhood suffrage is taken for granted, although I fear the "suffragettes" would find difficulties in getting a hearing. There are no delegates or representatives. Every one who is interested can come. And most of the men do come, for it is a sort of caste holiday, and who will miss a comedy or tragedy in real life?

When the assembly is gathered together, the proceedings are generally monopolised by five or six leading spirits. The man at whose instance the assembly is convened — whether he is the accuser or the accused — states his case. The opposite party replies, generally in person; but if he is not gifted with the power of tongues, he may put forward a more persuasive friend on his behalf. These constitute what would be called pleadings in a maturer system of jurisprudence. But as the whole of the talking is done, not in set speeches, but in assaults and parries, and asides and exclamations, with suggestions from the elders and cross-examination from anybody, the case has already proceeded a good deal further at this stage than you might suppose. In fact in many cases the decision is given at once in the form of a resolution which is proposed by some man of experience and carried by acclamation. Sometimes, however, witnesses are heard. Any one in the assembled throng is at liberty to say what he knows or thinks, and the functions of witness, judge, and jury are not at all differentiated. The resolution takes some such form as the following: We think that you, A. B., are guilty of a breach of caste rules, in that you did so and so, and therefore you should pay a fine of so many rupees to the caste funds and (in some cases) so much to the injured party, or that you stand a dinner or drinks (if the caste may drink liquors) costing so much. It is understood that if the penalty is not satisfied, the culprit would be outcasted: that is, an interdict would be laid on his sharing the caste *hukka* and water as already explained.

Thus the panchayets are primarily judicial tribunals with a limited and indefinite jurisdiction entirely unrecognised by law. But they also meet occasionally as an Executive Assembly to carry out some object in which the whole caste is collectively interested. This is particularly the case in regard to the occupational or functional castes, which are really trade-unions. Sir William Hunter described these trade-unions or trade-guilds, as he called them, as existing in strong force in Ahmedabad. But in reality Ahmedabad is in no way peculiar in that respect. All over the country there are trade-unions and commercial guilds, with funds and energetic executives. Only as they combine the functions of Friendly and Benefit Societies worked on somewhat indefinite lines, and marriage or social groups, the world at large looks upon them as castes in the same sense as the social or family groups which have nothing to do with business. A strike of sweepers, for example, is never carried out without careful deliberation in a panchayet, and as the decision of the local executive is arrived at in a meeting of all the members, it is carried out unflinchingly without a blackleg belonging to the locality. Blacklegs, however, can be found in abundance as soon as you go beyond the area in which the panchayet has jurisdiction, which is generally extremely limited, often not extending beyond a few square miles. That is why strikes are invariably unsuccessful except as a demonstration to call attention to grievances. This embodiment of the trade-union and co-operative principle—what the late Mr Thorold Rogers called the joint-stock principle in labour—must be carefully noted if we would understand all the characteristics and the vitality of the functional castes. And it is precisely in these castes—which we are generally pleased to call the lower castes—that the principles of organisation and cohesion have any vitality left. The "higher" castes have practically decayed, except in regard to the narrowing influences of social exclusiveness. But it should be noted that the regrouping of the industrial system in India is also making serious inroads into the vigour and authority of the hitherto flourishing caste-cum-trade-union systems.

We have discussed so far the tendencies that make for the weakening of caste ties. But, on the other hand, there are opposing tendencies which make for the strengthening of the caste idea, which we must now proceed to consider.

It must be remembered that the caste idea is so strongly rooted on Indian soil, that whatever changes of form or name it may undergo, it completely takes possession, and runs through the life of all the peoples who live or even sojourn in the country. The remarks which I have hitherto made may be supposed to refer principally to the

Hindus, but they apply to the Muhammadans with very slight alterations. It is no exaggeration, though it will create surprise at the unexpected terms in which the matter is put, to say that Muhammadan society in India is, generally speaking, based on caste organisations, although they have been diversified by many anomalies proceeding from the fundamentally different nature of the social system which theoretical Islam presupposes. Let us invoke the aid of Mr Risley in his latest Census Report.[1] Speaking of marriage customs among the lower class Muhammadans he says :—

"The functional groups, such as Joláha and Dhunia, which partake most thoroughly in respect of endogamy and general social organisation of the character of Hindu castes, and consist mainly of converts from Hinduism, are much more prone to the practices of infant marriage and compulsory widowhood than are the better classes of foreign origin, and than the converts who call themselves Shekh and live by cultivation."

Speaking in another place[2] he says of the better class Muhammadans :—

"Speaking generally, it may be said that the social cadre of the higher ranks of Muhammadans is based on hypergamy with a tendency in the direction of endogamy, while the lower functional groups are strictly endogamous, are organised on the model of regular castes with councils and

[1] Vol. I, Part 1, p. 451.
[2] *Ibid.*, p. 543.

officers which enforce the observance of caste rules by the time-honoured sanction of boycotting."

The Hindus and Muhammadans form the vast bulk of the population of India. But even amongst the Christians in India—whether native or foreign—the caste idea is paramount, especially in respect of marriage. At the Missionary Conferences, the question of caste observances among the Indian Christians is frequently brought forward and discussed, and Christian opinion is by no means unanimous in favour of doing away with caste. European society in India is practically divided into endogamous groups, with just a little bias in favour of exogamy in the matter of bringing brides fresh from Europe. Indian Christians rarely marry among European Christians. In the exceptional cases in which Indians of non-Christian creeds have married Europeans the alliance has generally been contracted in Europe, and with families of no Anglo-Indian connections.

It is in this question of marriage that the caste feeling is so strong and shows no sign of weakening. Indeed it may be said that it tends to be strengthened by three causes: viz. (1) the increasing facilities for travel and territorial intercourse; (2) the marked revival of Hinduism, and its sharp differentiation from other forms of religion; and (3) the greater precision given to legal definitions, and the enlarged scope of the influence which they tend to exercise upon social life.

The influence of improved communications in

the direction of strengthening endogamous and *à fortiori* exogamous groups is exerted in this way. Originally these groups were somewhat undefined, and arose from vague recollections of consanguinity, or family, tribal, or racial relationships. With the movements of communities in newly settled countries, all customs would be in a fluid state. When they were well established in a tract of land, and territorial barriers made communication difficult, the groups would tend to be restricted to certain areas. As long as the supply and demand of brides and bridegrooms of a given area were equal, no difficulty would arise. But in process of time these were sure to be inequalities, especially if the groups were small. Even taking the whole of the 294,000,000 of the Indian population, the males outnumber the females by about five millions and a half,[1] and there are provinces in which the deficiency of females is higher than 1 in 9. If we take smaller groups, no matter what the lines of division may be, the disparity would be still more striking. Now such disparities very seriously upset the equilibrium of the marriage market. In such cases various shifts are resorted to. One of these is exemplified by the marriage customs of the Kulin Brahmans in Bengal. But the one most in favour in rural circles is to import brides of unknown or doubtful origin, and by a fiction to get over

[1] In England, with a population about one-sixth that of India, the females outnumber the males by about a million.

the paucity of brides without apparently breaking caste rules. You simply make no awkward enquiries, and need not tell any positive lies. In some cases the marriage groups are revised, or the boundaries are made professedly more elastic, or—as usual among the lower castes—a higher and a lower form of marriage come to be definitely recognised. With better means of communication the necessity for these subterfuges becomes less as the area of choice becomes very much widened, and the wider the area, the smaller and smaller becomes the chance of glaring inequality in the numbers of the sexes.

The improvement of communications and the slow but steady growth of the press and a popular literature have also tended to solidify the structure of Hinduism and make it less elastic. This has often been spoken of as the revival of Hinduism. Formerly Hinduism was an amorphous system, but the tendency recently has been to define its rites and ceremonies, its ideas and institutions. Not that the general term Hinduism is still capable of exact definition. Even the two tests proposed, viz., veneration of cows and of Brahmans, fail in detailed application. But the different castes have begun to formulate their claims and customs, and by means of discussions and conferences have attempted to reach definite ideas as to what should and should not be recognised in their social code. The position of Kayasths and Khatris is very different in this respect to-day from what it was fifteen years ago. Even though this process gives rise to divisions, each division is evolved with a better-knit unit, and can run a better race in structural development. Formerly many non-Hindu tribes found a sort of entry into Hinduism by a back door. Now, although the process is still going on rapidly among the Animists and Aborigines, it is attended with greater precautions as regards the formation of caste groups and exclusive marriage circles. There is a greater tendency in Hinduism to stand on its dignity, and to assimilate nothing without carefully modelling it on its own ingrained institutions—preserving its own individuality while absorbing obscurer groups within its all-embracing system.

The action of the law courts has considerably strengthened this tendency. There is no system of law of general application in India, except Penal Law and Commercial Law, and Commercial Law is still in a somewhat rudimentary stage. In the matter of marriage, divorce, succession, and family rights, the law is personal. Given a party, you have to determine what law applies to him. You come to two main divisions when you come to Hindus and Muhammadans. But among the Hindus there is the Dayabhaga and the Mitakshara Law, and among the Muhammadans there are the Shias with sects, and the Sunnis, with four orthodox schools of law. Some of the Muhammadans, for example the Khojas of Bombay, follow the Hindu law of succession.

Some of the Muhammadan Talukdars of Oudh follow the rules of primogeniture in the devolution of their estates. The Hindu law, again, as laid down in the ancient text-books, is not free from either vagueness or practical difficulties. In the first place, it is not always easy to say whether the Hindu law should be applied to a particular individual or family or not. Like the famous recipe in the cookery book, which began with the very pertinent advice: "First catch your hare," a preliminary question is often put before a court: Was the party a Hindu? No lawyer of any eminence would stake his reputation on his definition of a Hindu, although various attempts have been made at it, and some important decisions on the subject will be found to have been reported. Supposing you have found your Hindu, it is not clear what Hindu law you are to apply to him. There is no authorised statement or "codification" of modern Hindu law as there was, for example, of Visigoth law in the Roman Empire, in the Lex Romana Visigothorum. But then the Visigoths were a simple people, with a few customs which could be defined with the assistance of their tribal leaders. They had neither the ingenuity to multiply infinitely the relationships of human life, nor the subtlety to indulge in close reasoning from abstract concepts. What was possible with their system would not be easy with the Hindu system.

Further, Hindu law is mixed up with religion,

and the British Government has given and faithfully kept its pledge of non-intervention in matters of religion. The result is that questions of the highest importance relating to personal law are only decided as they arise. As litigation usually runs in a groove, the total number of decisions given since courts of British jurisdiction were established scarcely touches more than a fringe of the subject. But it must be said that the definitions have in many cases become clearer, the floating opinions have become fixed. But in the process, it was inevitable that larger generalisations should be made than were warranted by local customs, and a greater uniformity insisted upon than would have been possible under a growing system of Hindu law as developed from the living opinions of the people concerned. For the best Hindu text-books—the Dayabhaga or Manu—probably represent philosophical speculations, and modern practice would depart widely from them if the Hindus had opportunities of developing their jurisprudence on their own lines. The decisions of caste panchayets often departed from the strict and cast-iron theories of text-books, or the opinions which learned Pandits would give, because those decisions were made by practical people confronted with the problems of daily life, and not by specialists interpreting dead text-books and time-worn formulæ. The caste panchayets would in this way frequently—though unconsciously—make what is called "judge-made" law, except that in their case the decisions would be in complete touch with caste opinion, and not be unduly hampered with either precedents or a law that came into conflict with the opinion of those most interested. Such a decision as that of the House of Lords, in the famous case of the Scotch Kirks, would in their case be quite impossible. The Anglo - Indian courts, on the other hand, have no alternative but to interpret as conscientiously as they can the scripture-made law of the Hindus, and to confine themselves strictly to precedents. In England this process is accompanied by a gradual course of legislation, which takes account of all the new needs and circumstances of the time, and the views of duly constituted organs of public opinion, but this course, as far as the semi-religious law of the Hindus is concerned, is out of the question for the legislative authorities in India. The tendency, therefore, of straining old *dicta* and interpreting them more and more strictly, as a greater and greater amount of judicial authority is attached to them by judicial decisions, leads to arrested development and want of progress. In this way, certain old ideas become stereotyped which would have been interpreted away in a purely native system of jurisprudence, or been brushed aside by the vigorous hands of legislators who felt themselves bound by no pledges, but were free to act on the maxim that the moral and material good of the people was the only test of sound legislation.

The science of Eugenics is quite young in Europe, but in the East it has been studied in all its various aspects. It has been studied from the point of view of philosophy, of religion, of heredity, and of social status. I believe the caste restrictions about marriage were consciously imposed from considerations of scientific expediency. If the system had been perfect, we should have seen an improvement of the human race to a pitch imagined by social dreamers. We should have seen developed, strong, healthy, beautiful bodies, and in harmony with them lofty intellects and pure and well-regulated emotions. But in practice the whole scheme has broken down, especially on the physical side. After centuries of careful diet regulations, ablutions, and choice in marriage, not by the parties themselves, but by "wiser people" from without, we see, in general, stunted men with low stamina and a sad lack of muscular power. It does not follow that there was nothing in the ideas with which the system started, but there have been many influences—notably climate—which made the breakdown inevitable. Perhaps, after all, "the best-laid schemes of mice and men" are inferior to the Stoic maxim: Follow Nature.

Speaking of the religious aspect of our social life, a consideration of the position of the Moslems in India is most instructive. As I have said before, practical Islam in India—the religion actually held and followed, as opposed to that professed—is very different indeed from the Islam of the books. The Moslems versed in the old learning are, of course, acquainted with the root ideas of Islam and preach them whenever they can—but do they, even they, carry them out? Not entirely. Else why should we see so much superstitious belief in amulets, so much labour wasted on the taking and interpretation of omens, so much of what Moslem satirists call "grave-worship" and "saint-worship"? If the Hindus offer cakes to the *manes* of deceased ancestors, the Moslems in India have developed the custom of *Shirni.* Why should poets like Háli fall into a mournful strain and sing a dirge, when they should and would be singing an epic of Islam? Why should the standard of education be so low, when it is laid down as one of the obligatory duties of the religion that every man and every woman should be educated? Why should Moslem appeals to Government be couched in terms, not of "fair field," but of "special favour"?[1] This being the case with the better-class Muhammadans, we can easily understand the extent of non-Moslem ideas in the life and religion of the lower-class Muhammadans. Their religion consists of paroxysms of *tazia* worship in the month of Muharram, and the aggressive slaughter of kine at one of their festivals, especially if it clashes with a Hindu festival, and religious

[1] This remark has no allusion whatever to the dignified address presented by the Moslem deputation to the Viceroy on the 1st of October 1906. I am referring to local appeals in which a wrong note is often struck.

animosities rule high. The Muhammadan Julaha or Teli in the remote villages will propitiate the Mata during an outbreak of small-pox with as much fervour and ceremony as his Hindu brother. He will march to the shrine of Ghazi Mian or sing the song of the Panchon Pir with as great a sense of duty as a Hindu pilgrim measuring his length along to Chitrakot, or a Sadhu devotee singing to the merry sound of the nimble *dafla* the loves of Radha and Krishna. No wonder that the cynical remark should be common among Moslems who bewail the decline of true Islam in India: "the bodies of Moslems are in their graves, and their religion is only in the books."

In the olden days the Hinduising tendencies among Muhammadans at least led to a certain amount of friendliness with the Hindus. It was difficult to say whether the Hindus or the Muhammadans were more numerous in the cult of the Tazia or of Ghazi Mian and the Heroes Five, or at the shrines of local godlings, such as the Bhumia Deo. At the country-side the fact of a man's professed religion made as little difference as his stature or the shade of his complexion. The religion would be a matter of private concern. Now, with the emphasis laid on the Shibboleths, the creation of party cries on all sides, and the severe strain of the modern competitive life, a note of bitterness is being imported which is calculated to do immense harm to the social advancement of the people. I do not assert that this bitterness did not formerly exist. But it was confined to the towns, and to camp and court life. The country-side was free from it. The rustic led his free and easy life, unruffled by storms from the larger world. Now there is a stream of immigration, on the one hand, from the country to the town, and on the other, from the town to the country. The rural immigrant into towns usually leaves his family behind in his native village, and returns as soon as he has earned a competence. But he returns a different man—less peaceful, less tolerant, more arrogant, more infected with the spirit of the low, grasping, anti-social tendencies of the competitive machine. He not only comes, feeling less of a brother to those around him, but he has brought a few glittering catch-words with him. With these he electrifies the atmosphere. If a crime takes place, and a police officer comes on the scene, our plausible egotist poses as more intelligent than the rest, and with his clever hints and whispers he manages to set so many parties by the ears, that a state of perpetual warfare is started, in which selfishness, greed, hate, and the worst human passions overcome the placid gentle nature of rural humanity.

In this way perhaps the fire may smoulder for years. But all hope of peace is gone when there comes on the scene a religious or political agitator. Perhaps he represents a sect, a newspaper, or an organisation. More probably he represents nobody but himself, though he has a mask which he puts on to deceive others. Let me not be misunderstood. I have the greatest respect for earnest agitation and careful organisation, even if they represent opinions that I do not agree with—provided they mean what they say, and their methods are free from all unscrupulous bigotry. Some of the ablest and best men of modern India have been "organisers" and "agitators" in the best sense of the terms. Indeed, organisation and public agitation are not only the best, but the only effective, means of advancing a cause in modern social conditions. The alternatives, viz. secrecy and violence, are not only bad ethics but bad tactics. By all means ventilate your opinions in public and discuss them, and if you can carry any honest enthusiasts with you on the merits of your plea band them together for collective effort. When I have said this, I hope I shall not be misunderstood when I express my strongest abhorrence of a certain type of agitation and organisation that violates the fundamental laws of social ethics, and is even more insidious in its poison than many more obvious diseases of the social structure. The exponents of this type aim not so much at advancing a cause as at aggrandising themselves. So far from sacrificing their own personal interests to an idea nobly held and nobly taught, they would have little hesitation in distorting it to minister to their own self-love and vanity. Their chief handmaidens are prejudice and ignorance. They have a marvellous genius for discovering the weakest lines of cleavage among an uneducated people, and for getting over the most explicit laws, sacred and profane. It is in the hands of such as these that religious animosities are aroused among His Majesty's loyal and law-abiding subjects—in one place between Shias and Sunnis, in another place between Aryas and Hindus, in a third place between Hindus and Muhammadans, and in a fourth place between Muhammadans and Christians. The beginnings of these quarrels are, if you trace them with sufficient care, generally personal. The people are sacrificed for the passions of their chiefs.

If this analysis of the bitterness and incoherence of our social life, and the nullifying effect of sectional antagonism on all our social aspirations, be accepted, it follows that the ground must be cleared for all social reform by eliminating the factors which blind our vision, and warp our judgment. The tendency towards accentuating each minute difference and magnifying every single grievance must be checked. It prevents the concentration of our energies on matters of vital importance, which are recognised by the collective conscience of mankind as the keys of human progress.

One of the most marked tendencies of Indian social life is that all forms of institutions making for order and joint action are getting disintegrated or undermined. Any unprejudiced observer of Hindu life must feel that the Joint Hindu Family—a phrase that supplies text-books and lawyers with abundant food for argument—is really breaking up through sheer top-heaviness. You may draw from the books a most beautiful picture of a united family that numbers a whole tribe, but you will find in practice that the artificial attempts to bolster up that hoary institution only drive the growing body of dissentients into an atmosphere of intrigue and chicanery that cuts at the roots of all human affections. The village organisation has suffered in the same way. We have examined in detail similar tendencies in the matter of caste and tribal organisations. In religion the Hindus never had an organised church or confederation of churches as the term would be understood in Europe. Islam had originally a strong idea of an organised social church, but it got inextricably mixed up with the State. Since the State in India is now absolutely neutral with respect to Indian religions, Indian Islam has become an abstract term with no visible organisation and no persons or bodies in whom authority is duly vested and recognised. The chaos, from a worldly point of view, exists equally in a Moslem state like Hyderabad, because the idea of a professional priesthood is foreign to Islam. The temple endowments among the Hindus and the Wakfs among the Muhammadans were meant in some way to maintain visible rallying centres; but in both cases the institutions have sadly degenerated in their aims and uses, and the judicial pronouncements are in many cases distinctly at variance with the needs of the times as interpreted by those most competent to judge from within.

The picture would be incomplete if it failed to indicate the healing tendencies—those which make for the building up of the structure in altered or developed forms. First, there is the *vis medicatrix naturæ*—the marvellous vitality and powers of recuperation shown by all Indian institutions, even those reputed most effete. Block them at the top, and they will put forth shoots laterally, and emerge triumphant through extraordinary obstacles. Then there are the conscious attempts by the best minds of the country to apply the best remedies—each in his own way—to the evils that strike them most. Men like Ram Mohan Roy, Ranade, Syed Ahmed, and Badruddin Tyebji did not live their strenuous and earnest lives without making a deep impression on the questions which they tackled. Then there are the societies, Sabhas, and other public bodies which attempt, according to their lights, to solve many of the vexed questions that confront the people. Lastly, there is the agency of Government, which by means of legislation and administration has, directly or indirectly, materially altered the current of the social life of the people.

And yet, without detracting from the value of these powerful influences, it can truthfully be said that there has been no co-ordinated effort at social reform. Sectional energies have been wasted in grappling with evils that are the symptoms rather than the causes of the abuses that reach the very core. Then the want of combination or even understanding among these different agencies sometimes leads to avoidable conflicts of opinion, which defeat the very purposes which all of them have at heart. It is only by a systematised effort in which Government receives the assistance of private associations and individuals of light and leading, that the paths of least resistance can be discovered and earnest action attempted on lines at once effective and statesmanlike. No hysterical propaganda can form or conciliate public opinion. No spasmodic spurts can win the race.

One of the suggestions made within recent times to deal with this subject has emanated from a distinguished High Court Judge in Southern India. Mr Justice Sankaran Nair advocates the establishment of a council of Indians for social legislation. To show the necessity for some such form of indigenous legislation he makes the following trenchant remarks[1]:—

"If he (the Hindu) makes up his mind to discard the outward forms of the creed, by the very act he cuts loose his moorings from Hindu Society, and can no longer take a wife or inherit

[1] *Contemporary Review*, May 1906.

property as a citizen of India. For, strange to say, there is no form of marriage or mode of inheritance for a citizen of India as such, but only forms appropriate for professed Hindus by religion, for professed Christians by religion, for professed Muhammadans by religion, and so forth: the so-called Hindu law which is administered to Hindus is indissolubly bound up with the Hindu religion, or rather with what somebody fancied somebody else had thought or written several hundred years ago about the Hindu religion. In the words of one of the best living authorities on the subject, 'The consequence was a state of arrested progress, in which no voices were heard unless they came from the tomb. It was as if the German were to administer English law from the resources of a library furnished with Fleta, Glanville and Bracton, and terminating with Lord Coke.'"

A similar attitude to the administration of Muhammadan law is taken up by Mr Ameer Ali, a distinguished jurist who filled for many years the position of a Judge of the Supreme Court at Calcutta. He is especially concerned with the interpretation of the law of Wakfs, or Muhammadan Trusts, and in this matter there is a strong body of influential Muhammadan opinion behind him. Other questions in Muhammadan law which give rise to many difficulties in practical life relate to dower, the registration of marriage and divorce, and the inheritance of real property to which local customs or incidents are attached.

It is difficult to see how a centralised popular Council for Social Legislation, even if one were established in each province of British India, would be able to meet the case. The matters on which more light and leading are required are precisely those on which the different sections of the people are widely divided, while those general ideas and tendencies in which they are united are of too wide and vague a scope to assist much in practical legislation. Would it not be wiser and more practical to try a scheme based on much smaller social units, whose internal coherence would give it a chance of success, and whose external isolation would not prevent it from attaining a comprehensive uniformity of plan which would allow the widest possible scope to local prejudices and sectional differences of opinion?

Such a plan in its barest outline would be easy to sketch; but to fill in the details would require much patient thought and long public discussion. In the first place, no one would wish to exclude from the scope of the existing legislative councils, either of the Viceroy or of the Provincial Governors, any of the subjects with which they deal at present. The tendency, as years go on, would be to enlarge their scope. But that vast body of personal law which governs the private life of an Indian would receive a vivifying influence by being brought into touch with the actual lives of men, and rescued from the obscurities and obsolete subtleties of voluminous text-books. It is quasi-religious, and therefore

Government is bound to refrain from itself interfering with it. But what if it recognised and registered the castes or communities, and allowed them to organise themselves for certain well-defined purposes, including legislation on a specified number of subjects? I have used the word "caste" for convenience. In fact, the group organisation would apply to Muhammadans as well as Hindus and men of other creeds. In the main the new Bodies would probably be based on Caste machinery and on the rough-and-ready procedure of Caste Panchayets.[1] But they would also partake of the character of the *Associations Cultuelles* as contemplated under the new French law for the disestablishment of the Church. In any case there would be a great deal of reconstitution of the castes. They would become very much localised, but their influence and responsibility would be strengthened. As long as the quasi-religious personal or caste law remains in India they would be valuable units in local administration, Government recognising the collective responsibility of each unit as it does in the case of a municipality or district board, but without their leading strings. The scheme would have to be worked separately for each district, the municipalities and district boards

[1] Forbes (*Oriental Memoirs*) gives an interesting account of the working of the Panchayet system as part of the administrative machinery one hundred years ago. Major Popham Young has revived the idea in Patiala State, and speaks enthusiastically, in his latest Report, of the success of the experiment.

themselves being organised on eclectic principles as applied to these units, and not to the artificial wards or electoral areas of the present day. Some of the castes or associations having too few individuals in a given district would no doubt register themselves in another district where their members are in greater numbers, or, so to speak, "at home."

The scheme would not be reactionary, but automatically progressive. A minimum number might be fixed: if the membership fell below that minimum, the members should find another group or association to affiliate themselves to, in order to enjoy the benefits of internal autonomy. No maximum number need be fixed, but the representation of each group in external matters of government, such as municipalities, district boards, and general legislative councils, should be roughly proportional to the literate population represented. A property or tax qualification might for certain purposes be deemed desirable, and could be introduced. Amalgamation by request should be freely permitted between hitherto separate associations, and, subject to the minimum limit, partition should also be allowed under a fixed procedure. This matter would be dealt with on the analogy of the union and partition of Mahals in land revenue administration, and, indeed, would not present as many difficulties as the revenue courts have to contend with in dealing with the countless number of Mahals. A large—and as time goes on, no doubt an increasing—number of individuals would not wish to belong to these caste associations, or to be governed by their personal law. They would be a sort of residuary group, who would be governed by the general law of India, not only in regard to crimes and penalties, excise and revenue, but in regard to matters touching the family, marriage, divorce, and succession. In these matters a general law does not now exist, but it would grow up in accordance with modern ideas, and develop independently of religious or ecclesiastical law. As the people who belong to this group would belong to it by their own choice, and not by the accident of birth or compulsion, there could be no legitimate ground of grievance. A great number of dissenters from the cast-iron usages of caste or personal law already exist, and they are among the most enlightened of the citizens of India. Their status would be defined, and their citizenship would be completed under some such scheme, and in the matter of representation in the municipal and other elective bodies, their rights would no doubt be co-ordinated to the rights of those who elect to remain under the caste associations. This body of men—free, loyal, and contented—would doubtless derive recruits from all classes, until a well-ordered system could be evolved suited to the ethnical needs of India, and capable of gradual expansion in response to the many ideals which would be evolved from India's readmission on terms of perfect equality among the family of nations.

The germs of a scheme like that are undoubtedly inherent in all living institutions built up under a wise and tolerant Oriental empire. Allowing for the difference in terms, and for the change in the conditions of life and travel, we may trace these germs in the great Eastern monarchies of ancient history, and in the large and splendid mediæval empires brought into being under the auspices of Muhammadan civilisation. The autonomy of *millats* in the Turkish empire has done much for the consolidation of Turkish rule among diverse subject populations. Failures there have been, and, at the present day, perhaps the very reference to the Turkish Empire would be construed in the West as carrying its own proof of weakness and failure. There is much prejudice in this attitude, as all who are intimately acquainted with the conditions of Eastern Europe and the Levant would easily realise. But apart from this prejudice, it should be borne in mind that there were two elements of failure in the otherwise admirable institutions granted by the Ottomans, which our scheme aims at avoiding. One was the weakness of machinery and the laxness of methods. The other was the omission of a supply of safety valves to facilitate automatic expansion and development, and to bring an ancient civilisation gradually into line with modern ideas. Our scheme, though comprehensive enough to affect all classes beneficently, and enlist their sentiment, their energies, and their talents to add strength to the fabric, would yet be cautious enough to safeguard the status, not only of those who choose to remain under the regime of the exclusive caste associations, but also the status, rights, and privileges of those who break away from them, and wish to be governed in their lives by the ideas of a free and progressive modern State. For class hatred it would substitute class co-operation: the bodies would be separate and yet not antagonistic. Within the bodies themselves there would be complete autonomy as regards the private affairs of life, with probably Elders of authority to consult with the people, to judge among them, to declare the law, and to carry out the penalties within well-defined limits. For external matters these bodies would form electoral colleges on which a whole fabric of representative institutions might be built up, quite original in its structure, but not to be put out of court merely because of the novelty of many of its features. For all social experiments must be founded on tendencies and aptitudes that already exist. Where these are utilised, even the faults may be easy of correction. Where these are resisted even the virtues may be twisted to undreamt-of uses, and made subservient to results the very opposite of those intended. At any rate, to present one's earnest convictions may be presumptuous, but can never be wrong.

INDEX